The New Woman in Fiction an

Also by Angelique Richardson

LOVE, EUGENICS AND THE NEW WOMAN: Science, Fiction, Feminism (*forthcoming*)

WOMEN WHO DID: Stories by Men and Women, 1890–1914

The New Woman in Fiction and in Fact

Fin-de-Siècle Feminisms

Edited by

Angelique Richardson

and

Chris Willis

Foreword by Lyn Pykett

in association with
Institute for English Studies,
School of Advanced Study,
University of London

First published in hardcover 2001
First published in paperback 2002 by
PALGRAVE MACMILLAN
Houndmills, Basingstoke, Hampshire RG21 6XS and
175 Fifth Avenue, New York, N.Y. 10010
Companies and representatives throughout the world

PALGRAVE MACMILLAN is the global academic imprint of the Palgrave Macmillan division of St. Martin's Press, LLC and of Palgrave Macmillan Ltd. Macmillan® is a registered trademark in the United States, United Kingdom and other countries. Palgrave is a registered trademark in the European Union and other countries.

ISBN 0–333–77665–8 hardback (*outside North America*)
ISBN 0–312–23490–2 hardback (*in North America*)
ISBN 978–0–333–99045–2 ISBN 0–333–99045–5 paperback (*worldwide*)

This book is printed on paper suitable for recycling and made from fully managed and sustained forest sources.

A catalogue record for this book is available from the British Library.

The Library of Congress has cataloged the hardcover edition as follows:
The new woman in fiction and in fact : fin de siècle feminisms / edited by Angelique Richardson and Chris Willis ; foreword by Lyn Pykett.
        p. cm.
    "Published in association with the Institute for English Studies, School of Advanced Study, University of London."
    Includes bibliographical references and index.
    ISBN 0–312–23490–2 (cloth)
    1. English fiction—19th century—History and criticism. 2. Feminism and literature—Great Britain—History—19th century. 3. Women and literature—Great Britain—History—19th century. 4. English fiction—Women authors—History and criticism. 5. Feminism—Great Britain—History—19th century. 6. Sex role—Great Britain—History—19th century. 7. Feminist fiction, English—History and criticism. 8. Women—Great Britain—History—19th century. 9. Feminism in literature. 10. Sex role in literature. 11. Women in literature. I. Richardson, Angelique, 1970– II. Willis, Chris, 1960– III. University of London. Institute for English Studies.

PR878.F45 N495 2000
823'.809352042—dc21
                                                            00–027246

10   9   8   7   6   5   4   3   2   1
11   10   09   08   07   06   05   04   03   02

Transferred to digital printing in 2008.

In memory of Angela Lodge

Contents

List of Figures

ix

Acknowledgements

Versions of a number of the essays in this collection were presented at The New Woman Conference, February 1998, at the Institute for English Studies, University of London. We would like to thank the conference speakers and audience. We are also grateful to the Institute for English Studies, and to our colleagues at the University of Exeter and at Birkbeck College, University of London. We would like to thank Eleanor Birne, Peter Faulkner, Regenia Gagnier, Charmian Hearne, Sally Ledger, J.P. Lodge, Rupert Mann, Laura Marcus, Claire Noble, Dorothy Porter, Anne Rafique and Ashley Tauchert for their advice and encouragement. With the exception of Figure 12, from the *Illustrated Police News*, the illustrations are all reproduced by kind permission of *Punch*. We would like to thank *Punch*, and Palgrave and Birkbeck College for financial assistance with copyright clearance.

Foreword

Lyn Pykett

The man and woman question, according to D.H. Lawrence the greatest of all questions, has had a habit of coming into prominence in the intellectual ferment that has marked the ends of centuries in recent times, and it has certainly been greatly amplified by the millenarian prognostications that have surrounded the end of the twentieth century. At the end of the nineteenth century this question (or, more accurately, complex of questionings) became focused on (among other things) the Protean figure of the New Woman, and on the social and psychological regeneration or degeneration that it promised or threatened.

But, ask the editors of this timely collection (echoing one of their contributors), 'Did the New Woman really exist?', or was she, as Mrs Morgan-Dockrell contended, 'a figment of the journalistic imagination'? The extent to which women in the 1890s self-identified as New Women is difficult to quantify. However, Elizabeth Tusan has recently given a new slant to the current debate by suggesting that women readers of *fin-de-siècle* feminist journals such as *The Woman's Herald* (1891–3, 'The only Paper Conducted, Written, Printed and Published by Women'), *Shafts* (1882–1900, 'A Paper for Women and the Working Classes'), *The Woman's Gazette* (1881–91) and *The Woman's Signal* (1894–9) did in fact identify themselves as New Women.[1] Indeed, they vigorously sought to reappropriate the term and establish their own definitions of it in opposition to the hostile or parodic representations of the New Woman in the mainstream press. As one of their number wrote in 1895:

> As 'New Woman' she is known.
> 'Tis her enemies have baptised her,
> But she gladly claims the name;
> Hers it is to make a glory,
> What was meant should be a shame.[2]

Who or what was the New Woman? Taken together, the essays in this collection demonstrate that *The* New Woman did not exist. 'New Woman', both in fiction and in fact, was (and remains) a shifting and contested term. It was a mobile and contradictory figure or signifier (the mobility is often quite literal, since as several of these essays testify, the New Woman, when she wasn't in a library or suffering from hysterical breakdown, was careering around on a bicycle). The New Woman was by turns: a mannish amazon and a Womanly woman; she was oversexed, undersexed, or same sex identified; she was anti-maternal, or a racial supermother; she was male-identified, or manhating and/or man-eating, or self-appointed saviour of benighted masculinity; she was anti-domestic, or she sought to make domestic values prevail; she was radical, socialist or revolutionary, or she was reactionary and conservative; she was the agent of social and/or racial regeneration, or symptom and agent of decline. *The New Woman in Fiction and in Fact* admirably resists any tendency (as its editors put it) to homogenize the category, by looking at the New Woman in relation (often a problematic and contradictory relation) to *fin-de-siècle* utopianism, socialism, imperialism, Aestheticism and Decadence, urbanism, mass culture, sex science, psychoanalysis, economics, eugenics, the discourses of evolution (and degeneration), and definitions of masculinity, as well as in relation to debates about modernity and modernism and early twentieth-century developments in feminism. One could go on, and no doubt this collection will encourage others to continue 'unpacking' the term 'New Woman', and exploring its various late nineteenth- and early twentieth-century contexts.

Notes

1. Elizabeth Tusan, 'Inventing the New Woman: Print Culture and Identity Politics During the *Fin-de-siècle*', *Victorian Periodicals Review* 31 (1998), 169–82.
2. 'The New Woman', *Shafts*, Jan/Feb 1895, 378. Quoted by Tusan, 174.

Notes on the Contributors

Ann Ardis is Director of the University Honors Program at the University of Delaware. She is the author of *New Women, New Novels: Feminism and Early Modernism* (Rutgers University Press, 1990) and co-editor, with Bonnie Kime Scott, of the conference proceedings from the Ninth Annual Virginia Woolf Conference, *Virginia Woolf Turning the Centuries* (Pace University Press, 2000); she has also published articles on feminist theory and criticism, turn-of-the-century British literature, and early modernism. She is currently editing a collection of essays on *Women and Modernity: Renegotiating the Public Sphere, 1880–1930*, and finishing a book-length study of modernism and the 'rise' of English studies.

Matthew Beaumont is Research Fellow and Tutor in English Literature at Keble College, Oxford, and is currently completing a thesis on late nineteenth-century utopias. He has published on Ernst Bloch and co-edits *Historical Materialism: Research in Critical Marxist Theory*.

Carolyn Burdett is Principal Lecturer in English at the School of Arts and Humanities, University of North London. She has published on gender and colonialism and is the author of *Olive Schreiner and the Progress of Feminism: Evolution, Gender, Nation* (Macmillan, 2000)

Gail Cunningham is Pro Vice-Chancellor and Dean of Human Sciences at Kingston University. She has published on various aspects of nineteenth- and twentieth-century fiction including, with Sarah Sceats, *Image and Power: Women in Fiction in the Twentieth Century* (Longman, 1996). She is currently writing a study on New Woman novelists of the 1890s, and working on representations of suburbia in Victorian fiction.

Regenia Gagnier is Professor of English at the University of Exeter, where she teaches Victorian Studies, especially the *fin de siècle*, social theory, feminist theory, and interdisciplinary studies. Her books include *Idylls of the Marketplace: Oscar Wilde and the Victorian Public* (Stanford University Press, 1986); *Subjectivities: A History of Self-Representation in Britain, 1832–1920* (Oxford University Press, 1991); an edited collection, *Critical Essays on Oscar Wilde* (Macmillan, 1992); and *The Insatiability of Human Wants: Economics and Aesthetics in Market Society* (Chicago University Press, 2000).

Lesley A. Hall is an archivist at the Wellcome Library for the History and Understanding of Medicine, and an Honorary Lecturer at University College London. She has published extensively on sex, gender and the history of sexuality and her books include *Hidden Anxieties: Male Sexuality 1900–1950* (Polity Press, 1991), *The Facts of Life: The Creation of Sexual Knowledge in Britain, 1650–1950* (with Roy Porter) (Yale University Press, 1995), and *Sex, Gender and Social Change in Britain since 1880* (Macmillan, 2000). She is currently working on a biography of F. W. Stella Browne.

Ann Heilmann is Lecturer in English at the University of Wales Swansea, where she teaches nineteenth-century literature and women's writing. She is the author of *New Woman Fiction* (Macmillan, 2000), editor of *The Late-Victorian Marriage Question: A Collection of Key New Woman Texts* (Routledge Thoemmes Press, 1998), general editor of a new Routledge series, 'History of Feminism', and co-editor, with Stephanie Forward, of *Sex, Social Purity and Sarah Grand* (Routledge). She is now working on a book on *New Woman Strategies: Sarah Grand, Olive Schreiner, Mona Caird* (Manchester University Press).

Sally Ledger is Senior Lecturer in English at Birkbeck College, University of London. Her books include *The New Woman: Fiction and Feminism at the Fin de Siècle* (Manchester University Press, 1997) and *Henrik Ibsen* (Northcote House, 1999).

Laura Marcus is Reader in English at the University of Sussex. Her publications include *Auto/biographical Discourses: Theory, Criticism, Practice* (Manchester University Press, 1994) and *Virginia Woolf* (Northcote House, 1997) and, as editor, *Close Up 1927–1933: Cinema and Modernism* (Cassell/Princeton University Press, 1998), *Culture, Modernity and 'the Jew'* (Polity/Stanford University Press, 1998), and *The Interpretation of Dreams: New Interdisciplinary Essays* (Manchester University Press, 1999). She is currently working on *The Tenth Muse: Cinema and Modernism* and on a collection of essays on *fin-de-siècle* topics entitled *The Psychopathologies of Modern Life*.

Lyn Pykett is Professor of English at the University of Wales Aberystwyth. She has written several books and articles on nineteenth-

and twentieth-century writing, including *Emily Brontë* (Macmillan, 1989), *The 'Improper' Feminine: The Women's Sensation Novel and the New Woman Writing* (Routledge, 1992), *The Sensation Novel from 'The Woman in White' to 'The Moonstone'* (Northcote House, 1994), and *Engendering Fictions* (Edward Arnold, 1995). She is also editor of two essay collections, *Reading Fin de Siècle Fictions* (Longman, 1996), and *Wilkie Collins* (St. Martin's Press New Casebooks, 1998). She recently edited Mary Elizabeth Braddon's *The Doctor's Wife* for Oxford World's Classics and is currently working on a study of Dickens.

Angelique Richardson is Lecturer in Victorian Literature and Culture at the University of Exeter. She has published widely on nineteenth-century literature and science, and is currently working on a study of Thomas Hardy and science. She is the author of *Love, Eugenics and the New Woman: Science, Fiction, Feminism* (Oxford University Press, forthcoming) and editor of *Women Who Did: Stories by Men and Women, 1890–1914* (Penguin, 2002).

Talia Schaffer is Assistant Professor of English at Queens College, City University of New York. She is the author of *The Forgotten Female Aesthetes: Literary Culture in Late-Victorian England* (University Press of Virginia, forthcoming) and co-editor, with Kathy A. Psomiades, of *Women and British Aestheticism* (University Press of Virginia, 1999). She has also published numerous articles on late-Victorian writers, including Lucas Malet, Alice Meynell, Thomas Hardy and Bram Stoker.

Rebecca Stott is Head of the English Department at APU, Cambridge, and Reader in English Literature. She is the author of *The Fabrication of the Late-Victorian Femme Fatale: The Kiss of Death* (Macmillan, 1992) and editor of *Tennyson* (Longman Critical Readers Series, 1996). She is currently working on Victorian science and literature for a book entitled *The Aqueous Age: Water, Science and the Victorian Imagination*, and writing a book on Elizabeth Barrett Browning.

Chris Willis is a member of the editorial staff of *Gender and History*. She has written widely on nineteenth- and twentieth-century popular fiction, and co-edited *Twelve Woman Detective Stories* (Oxford Popular Classics, 1997), a collection of early crime stories: she is also editor of a collection of Mary Elizabeth Braddon's short stories (Sensation Press, 2000).

Sarah Wintle is Senior Lecturer in English at University College London. She has published on a range of writers from Shakespeare through Rochester and Swift to Kipling and Eliot. She has edited Grant Allen's *The Woman Who Did* for Oxford Popular Classics, and is now writing a book on horses in literature.

Introduction

Angelique Richardson and Chris Willis

From Grant Allen's *The Woman Who Did* to Victoria Crosse's *The Woman Who Didn't*, the label 'New Woman' signalled new, or newly perceived, forms of femininity which were brought to public attention in the last two decades of the nineteenth century. According to the *Westminster Review* in 1895:

> it is not possible to ride by road or rail, to read a review, a magazine or a newspaper, without being continually reminded of the subject which lady-writers love to call the Woman Question. 'The Eternal Feminine', the 'Revolt of the Daughters,' the Woman's Volunteer Movement, Women's Clubs, are significant expressions a effective landmarks.[1]

New Woman novels soon became a vital and popular part of the late Victorian cultural landscape – between 1883 and 1900 over a hundred novels were written about the New Woman.[2] On the cusp, as she appeared to be, between fiction and fact, her status was fiercely debated in prose and parlours.

The New Woman did not appear from nowhere. During the course of the nineteenth century women had increasingly challenged their subordinate social and political position. They had a radical inheritance from the pioneering feminist Mary Wollstonecraft (1759–1797) whose *Vindication of the Rights of Woman* (1792), had condemned the sexual double standard and urged women's right to education, employment and full citizenship. Bearing the spiritual imprimatur of the radical socialist Thomas Paine (1737–1809), whose *Rights of Man* had just hit the streets, it had been banned from Walpole's library.[3] Writing in newly industrializing Britain when middle-class women who had

1

made a vital contribution to family economies were becoming increasingly leisured, Wollstonecraft saw the rise of the bourgeoisie as a major cause of women's enervation:

> From the respect paid to property flow, as from a poisoned fountain, most of the evils and vices which render this world such a dreary scene to the contemplative mind ... One class presses on another, for all are aiming to procure respect on account of their property; and property once gained will procure the respect due only to talents and virtue ...

She continued:

> It is a melancholy truth; yet such is the blessed effect of civilization! the most respectable women are the most oppressed and ... must, from being treated like contemptible beings, become contemptible. How many women thus waste life away the prey of discontent, who might have practised as physicians, regulated a farm, managed a shop, and stood erect, supported by their own industry, instead of hanging their heads surcharged with the dew of sensibility, that consumes the beauty to which it at first gave lustre; nay, I doubt whether pity and love are so near akin as poets feign, for I have seldom seen much compassion excited by the helplessness of females, unless they were fair; then, perhaps, pity was the soft handmaid of love, or the harbinger of lust.
>
> How much more respectable is the woman who earns her own bread by fulfilling any duty, than the most accomplished beauty! – beauty did I say? – so sensible am I of the beauty of moral loveliness, or the harmonious propriety that attunes the passions of a well-regulated mind, that I blush at making the comparison; yet I sigh to think how few women aim at attaining this respectability by withdrawing from the giddy whirl of pleasure, or the indolent calm that stupefies the good sort of women it sucks in.[4]

Versions of these ideas would recur in New Woman writing a century later. The South African New Woman writer Olive Schreiner (1855–1920) devotes the first three chapters of her political tract *Woman and Labour* (1911) to a malaise she terms 'parasitism': the condition of the unlabouring woman. While a discourse of health and nature was clearly present in Wollstonecraft, such arguments would intensify in the wake of Darwin, as New Women began to exploit the new biological discourses in their various demands for social change, giving not just a social and political but a *biological* rationale to their arguments against the reduction of women to a parasitic state. Early and mid-Victorian ideas on progress, passion, morality, femininity, domesticity, development and evolution are replayed and reworked by New Women in the last decades of the century.[5]

During the 1820s and 1830s Owenite socialists, inspired by Robert Owen (1771–1858) and informed by Wollstonecraft's radical egalitarianism, repeatedly voiced concern over women's status, arguing that the only way to end the theory and practice of women as property was to end private property itself. Owenites sought to extend the home and erase the boundary between the self-enclosing family unit and the wider community; they saw marriage and the nuclear family as impediments to the development of genuinely cooperative communities. In 1825 Anna Wheeler (b. 1755) and William Thompson (1775–1833), who were revolutionary democrats, Owenites and feminists, published their 'joint property' *Appeal of One-Half the Human Race, Women, against the Pretensions of the other Half, Men, to retain them in political, and thence in civil and domestic Slavery: in Reply to a Paragraph of Mr Mill's celebrated Article on Government.*[6] This collaborative work linked women's emancipation with general social emancipation, arguing that in all aspects of life 'men have invested themselves with despotic power' ... and concluding, 'all women, and particularly women living with men in marriage ... having been reduced to a state of helplessness, slavery, and of consequent unequal enjoyments, pains and privations ... are more in need of political rights than any other portion of human beings ...' (Thompson, Appeal, 107; Taylor, 23). A decade later Robert Owen's *Lectures on the Marriages of the Priesthood in the Old Immoral World* (1835) slammed the family as a source of competitive ideology, and a main vehicle for the transmission of private property (Taylor, 17, 39).

One factor in the early mobilization of feminism was the 1832 Reform Act, through which women's exclusion from the franchise was formalized. A petition was presented to parliament, demanding that the franchise should include women who met the property qualification. It was rejected, and a small but conspicuous group of women began to campaign for female enfranchisement and emancipation; this culminated in 1866 in the presentation to Parliament of a petition signed by 1499 women demanding that the suffrage reform then under consideration include votes for women. The organizers of the petition, which was presented in the House of Commons by John Stuart Mill and Henry

Fawcett, were drawn mainly from the moderate Society for the Employment of Women. The following year (1867), the National Society for Women's Suffrage was formed and private Bills for women's suffrage, seeking a limited suffrage (i.e. the extension of existing voting rights to woman) were presented every year from 1870 to 1878, and annually from 1884 (except 1899 and 1901). They were routinely defeated by the Conservatives, the aristocracy and the landed Interest. In 1918 the vote was given to women of 30 and over, and in 1928 to women of 21 and over. It had not been the easiest of victories.

In the development of early feminism pragmatic forces came into play no less than ideological ones. For example, in the census of 1851 it was revealed that there were 400 000 'surplus' women.[7] Without a husband women had no one to keep them or to enable them to reproduce legitimate children; unmarried women were thus surplus to social/reproductive requirements. They posed a considerable if inadvertent threat to separate-sphere ideology: uncontained by spouses they risked spilling out into the public sector, becoming public and visible. It was hard for a surplus woman to be an Angel in the House.

By the 1850s British feminism had gained an organized form and coherence, largely through the campaigns of middle-class female philanthropists.[8] Women's magazines proliferated by this time; several articulated women's dissatisfaction and desire for change, and novels were also a vehicle of feminist protest.[9] Equally, the women's rights campaigner was becoming a familiar if maligned figure, often satirized in cartoons and periodicals. In 1869 the leading British philosopher of the nineteenth century and left-liberal sex egalitarian, John Stuart Mill (1806–1873), published *On the Subjection of Women*. J. S. Mill was the eldest son of the middle-class Benthamite James Mill (1773–1836), author of *The History of British India* (1818), who, along with other middle-class reformers, had worked to ensure the exclusion of working men and all women from the expanded franchise of 1832. In 1859 J. S. Mill had written *On Liberty*, a compelling rebuttal of his father which aimed to provide an alternative view of humans and society, integrating 'intellectual culture' – reason and truth – with 'internal culture' – the individual's feelings, passions, personal impulses, inclinations and eccentricities.[10] *The Subjection of Women* was a natural extension of these enlightened ideas, and a landmark in British feminism, drawing parallels between slavery and the position of women under conditions of patriarchal law, and exposing female 'nature' – femininity – as culturally constructed. 'All women', wrote Mill, 'are brought up from the very earliest years in the belief that their ideal of character is the very opposite to that of men; not self-will, and government by self-control, but submission, and yielding to the control of others.' He continued:

> What is now called the nature of women is an eminently artificial thing – the result of forced repression in some directions, unnatural stimulation in others. It may be asserted without scruple, that no other class of dependents have had their character so entirely distorted from its natural proportions by their relation with their masters; for, if conquered and slave races have been, in some respects, more forcibly repressed, whatever in them has not been crushed down by an iron heel has generally been let alone and if left with any liberty of development, it has developed itself according to its own laws; but in the case of women, a hot-house and stove cultivation has always been carried on of some of the capabilities of their nature, for the benefit and pleasure of their masters.[11]

Mill was an ardent and loyal campaigner for women's rights, and his feminist contemporaries were not slow to acknowledge the crucial role he played in the emancipation of women.[12]

In the second half of the nineteenth century the social and economic position of women underwent accelerated change. For example, between 1851 and 1901 the total number of women in the workforce increased from 2 832 000 to 4 751 000 (see Patricia Hollis, *Women in Public*, 53). Hollis notes that the number employed in domestic service almost doubled during this time, and it is estimated that by the 1890s 175 000 women were employed in laundries; they worked long hours in hot, humid conditions and operated dangerous machinery: workplaces were not brought under state regulation until 1907. Those in the professional category (teachers, nurses, clerks) rose from 106 000 in 1861 to 429 000 in 1901. In 1861, of 110 000 teachers in the UK, 80 000 were women; by 1901 the figure had risen to 172 000 women out of a total of 230 000. Not all were fully trained and certificated, and women teachers earned about 75 per cent of the male rate. The Post Office was the first and largest government office to employ women: the census of 1881 recorded 6000 women clerks; in the 1901 census there were nearly 60 000 women employed by private firms and 25 000 in the public sector, mainly in the Post Office (Hollis, 45). However, the total number of unoccupied women also rose during this time, from 5 294 000 to 10 229 000, because of overall population growth (Hollis, 53).

Education was another area of advance for women (see Figure 1): reforms here were, often incidentally, to benefit unmarried women whose economic opportunities were being reduced by the increasing professionalization above all of teaching and medicine (see Evans, *The Feminists*, 64). In 1823, in the wake of Wollstonecraft's clarion call for equality, the political economist and feminist journalist Harriet Martineau began (aged 21), to campaign in the *Monthly Repository* (albeit under a male pseudonym) for equal educational opportunities for girls. During the 1850s informally organized groups of women began to campaign for educational reforms. This activity culminated in a Royal Commission Report in 1858 which recommended the establishment of a national system of girls' secondary schools, to educate middle-class girls in household management. Some girls' schools, like the Girls' Public Day School Company and the Church Schools Company, resulted from national organizations; others were financed through the Endowed Schools Act (1869), and some resulted from local pressure groups. However, the main changes in education were motivated by middle-class concerns and resulted in the provision of quality secondary education for middle- and upper-class girls; elementary schools, provided and controlled by the state, were intended for the working classes and attendance did not become compulsory until 1880.[13]

A degree of movement was occuring in higher education too; women were admitted to King's College, London in 1847 and the following year Queen's College, London began to offer lectures and examinations to improve the training of governesses and provide certificates of their proficiency; Bedford College for Women was established in 1849.

Figure 1   Girl Graduate: Single figure. *Punch*, 23 June 1894 Copyright © *Punch*

Owens College, Manchester, founded by the philanthropist and merchant John Owens (1790–1846), and the most distinguished of the university colleges, removed all obstacles for women in 1871 and, joining in the last years of the nineteenth century with university colleges in Liverpool, Leeds and Sheffield, created Victoria University, an institution with degree-granting status (when the institutions became independent early in the new century, the title Victoria University attached solely to Manchester). Leeds admitted women on the same basis as men from its inception in 1874, St Andrews removed all disabilities for women in 1877, and the University of London in 1878. By contrast Oxford and Cambridge failed to grant women fully accredited degrees until 1922 and 1947 respectively, though Girton College, Cambridge, opened its doors to women in 1869; Newnham in 1871, and Lady Margaret Hall, the first Oxford women's college, offered its first class in 1878; Somerville followed in 1879, St Hugh's in 1886 and St Hilda's in 1893.

Marriage law was another area of reform. In 1857 the Divorce and Matrimonial Causes Act transferred responsibility for matrimonial matters from the ecclesiastical courts to a newly created Probate and Divorce Court. The position of husband and wife was not equalized: while allowing a husband to divorce his wife on grounds of adultery, the Act required a wife to prove her husband guilty of rape, sodomy or bestiality, or of adultery in conjunction with incest, bigamy, cruelty or desertion. Nonetheless, the various measures of the 1850s clearly marked the beginnings of a new attitude towards women. The passage of the Married Women's Property Acts of 1870 and 1882 eventually gave all married women the right to their own property, extending the equitable concept of married women's 'separate estate', while dispensing with the need for settlements and trustees.[14] In 1884 the Matrimonial Causes Act decreed that refusal to comply with a decree for restitution of conjugal rights would simply render the refuser guilty of desertion: prior to this the Divorce Court had the power to imprison the refusing wife for contempt, and would release her only when she consented to return to cohabitation. The Act also provided that a husband who refused to return to his wife could be ordered by the court to make her a periodic allowance (if a disobedient wife deserted, and had separate earnings or happened to run her own business she too could be ordered to make a periodic allowance). Power was now given to the court to make orders regarding the custody of the couple's children. In 1891 the *R. v. Jackson* case established that a husband did not have the right to detain and imprison his wife. For women and men who sought the emancipation of women this was clearly a victorious decision; it was hailed as 'a charter of the personal liberty of married women' by *The Times* (3 April 1891). However, for Eliza Lynn Linton, media spokeswoman for patriarchy (female as well as male) it augured the beginnings of 'universal topsyturvydom'.[15] In any case, limited right of restraint was allowed by the Jackson case; a husband might seize and pull back a wife if he saw her in the act of going to meet a paramour,[16] and a husband could still force sexual intercourse upon his wife without being guilty of rape (this situation continued until the House of Lords decision in *R. v. R* in 1991) (see Doggett, 46).

Another area closely connected with developments in feminism in the second half of the nineteenth century was moral reform. In 1869 Josephine Butler (1828–1906) launched a campaign against the Contagious Diseases Acts. These Acts had been introduced in the 1860s in an attempt to control venereal disease among the military; they amounted to a state regulation of prostitution, allowing the compulsory examination, detention and treatment of any woman suspected of being a prostitute. Once these Acts were repealed in 1886 the abolitionists joined forces with (other) social purists who were campaigning, more broadly, against juvenile prostitution and what later became known as 'white slavery' – the abduction of women to brothels through deception or force.[17] The Abolitionists had been backed by the churches and unions but they were also riding on an increasingly repressive wave: the newly enfranchised petty bourgeoisie and labour aristocracy mimicked the moral postures of the established middle classes and, following the extension of the franchise from three million to a total of five million voters in 1884, fears were aroused in the electorate over political and social stability (see Evans, *The Feminists*, 64). All this contributed towards a moral climate in which notorious London night-spots were closed down, eminent politicians were condemned for moral failings, and a National Vigilance Association was formed to combat pornography, which it did through propaganda and parliamentary action. Under these conditions the social purity campaigns which had set out to challenge the idea of the male sexual urge as a biological fact now began to privilege nature over nurture, arguing that men were essentially sexually reckless while (unfallen) women were innately moral and the nation's best chance of 'race regeneration'. Social purity thus became transformed by the very discourses it set out to transform; it began to ground itself in biology, and to appeal to class-based hostilities and racism.[18] It was in this climate that the New Woman debates raged, and the enthusiasm for biological determinism which had informed social purity would also permeate these debates.

It is important not to impose late twentieth-century feminist agendas upon considerations of the nineteenth-century Woman Question. Victorian feminism is not a simple story of a radical break with tradition. For example, even by the *fin de siècle*, many New Women wanted to achieve social and political power by reinventing rather than rejecting their domestic role. Likewise, a markedly gendered difference in attitude towards sexuality and pleasure persisted from Wollstonecraft to the New Woman. Robert Owen, for one, had urged for 'marriages of Nature' in the New Moral World.[19] Owenites criticized not just the family wage and coverture (the legal non-existence of a married woman) but bourgeois sexuality itself, for its denial of pleasure. While socialist men tended to emphasize the 'naturalness' of sex and promoted sexual libertarianism, socialist women spoke more of rational relationships, based on equality and mutual respect, and argued that sex ought to be predicated on advanced *social* sentiment; they argued that while for men sex was a passion to be endured – or even enjoyed – women's sexuality had evolved to a higher stage of development than men's. Anna Wheeler argued as early as 1833 that passion would be the undoing of women: 'woman's love ... is a fearful thing, because it has fixed and perpetuated the degradation of her sex, and arrested the moral progress of man himself; why should he change his unjust, cruel, and insulting laws for woman, when he can ... through woman's power of loving, command worship and adoration ... ?'[20] All Owenites agreed that love – rational or erotic – could not flourish in a situation where women were economically dependent upon men (Taylor, 48). New Women would reinvent these arguments in the 1890s.[21] Similarly, the sexually repressive attitudes of social purists were not a million miles away from the earlier evangelical commitment to separate sphere ideology and the cult of domesticity which succeeded in the wide dissemination of ideas endorsing social hierarchy and sexual propriety. To Evangelicals, sexual liberation could only mean one thing: promiscuity. In the words of one early religious revitalist 'if our women lose their domestic virtues ... the men will be profligate, the public will be betrayed, and whatever has blessed or distinguished the English nation on the Continent will disappear'.[22] Enjoying an antagonisitc relationship with feminism and socialism, Evangelicalism was central to the development of middle-class cultural practices and institutions and the formation of a distinctive middle-class consciousness. Setting themselves up in opposition to Chartists and Owenites in the first half of the nineteenth century, Evangelicals chose to interpret political crises along moral and religious lines, privileging virtue and respectability and striving to find in the new economic power of the middle classes a moral and cultural authority.

The New Woman article from which this collection takes its name appeared in the *Humanitarian* in 1894 – the same year that a debate between Sarah Grand and Ouida in the *North American Review* introduced the term 'New Woman' into popular sexual and social politics. Mrs M. Eastwood, author of 'The New Woman in Fiction and in Fact', was keen to distinguish between the New Woman in fiction, whom she saw as a lamentable creation, joyfully confined to the (diseased) imaginary realm – 'like a riderless horse on the battle-field, it charges about with reckless abandon, unmindful of whom or what it may trample under foot' – and the New Woman who was 'a positive and tangible fact'.[23] The New Woman of fiction, she warned, was 'a creation of the hyperbolically emancipated woman's riotous imagination'. But it was not all bad, she assured her readers. Fiction was not fact. The real New Woman 'is altogether otherwise. Far from being unfitted for the world in which she lives, she is adapting herself with marvellous rapidity to its altered conditions. And why should she not? Why should the strong current of evolution which bears all else before it, leave woman alone behind?'

Borrowing heavily from, and seeming to take comfort in, the language of evolution, Eastwood urged:

> let not those wild and wayward suckers which have been thrown out from the superabundant vitality of the New Womanhood be mistaken for sound branches of the parent tree. They bear no closer relationship to the actual Evolving She, than the rag-tag and bobtail that careers at the heels of an advancing army bears to the army itself. (378)

The real New Woman – the 'abiding' new woman, Eastwood emphasized – would make not for social *disruption* but for social – and sexual – *reform*:

> her soaring ambition will be content with nothing less than the reformation of the entire male sex ... There are those who believe that the extreme remedy she is prepared to apply – that of refusing to unite herself in wedlock to the man whose morals are not as pure as her own – cannot fail in its salutary results. Her scheme of reform

extends also beyond the fathers of the coming race and includes the weak and foolish sisters who have obstinately remained behind in their crumbling preserves. (378–9)

Eastwood satirizes the endlessly self-analytical heroine of New Woman fiction who 'keeps on corking herself with a pin until she has laid bare every fibre of her being' (Eastwood, 376) and considers that Grand's and Egerton's sexually alluring, intellectual, discontented heroines have little relevance to the average woman. The heroine of New Woman fiction:

is 'Grand,' every 'Iota' of her! Quite too much so, however, for the usages of our grossly practical, work-a-day world; therefore, much as she entertains him, it is a relief to the ordinary mortal to discover that she has no existence in it, but is rather a creation of the hyperbolically emancipated woman's riotous imagination ... None the less is the New Woman a positive and tangible fact. (Eastwood, 376)

What is most striking about Eastwood's article is the extent to which she employs a reductive, binary logic, striving to present a clear-cut right and wrong New Woman; to draw a hard line between fiction and fact, and to go with 'fact' – with the New Woman who would make for social regeneration not only without sacrificing feminine charm and moral purity but by making these her very methods and goals. That Eastwood should have protested so much perhaps betrays a certain disbelief that the disruptive New Woman was really confined to fiction, or that the world in the hands of the New Woman would be a happy place after all, at least for those who desired moral reform but were terrified at the prospect of social revolution.

One of the central aims of this collection is to read between such lines of protest and pleasure which the *fin de siècle* offered, in evaluating late nineteenth-century forms of feminism, and to explore the polyphonic nature of the debates around femininity at this time. In doing so it has firm foundations on which to build. Over the last two decades, after more that half a century of neglect from publishers, literary critics and historians, the pages of New Woman novels, have been turned with growing fascination, and pioneering historiographical and literary works have established the centrality of the New Woman to late Victorian culture. Gail Cunningham's far-reaching *The New Woman and the Victorian Novel* (1978) was the first of these works; Penny Boumelha (1982) subsequently situated Thomas Hardy's novels among the gendered debates of the

1890s, showing important connections with the New Woman. In the last decade New Woman scholarship has burgeoned. In 1990 Ann Ardis established persuasive links between New Woman writing and early Modernism. More recent studies include Lyn Pykett's *The 'Improper' Feminine: the Women's Sensation Novel and the New Woman Writing* (1992) which focuses on 'gender anxiety' in these genres, making significant links between the New Woman and earlier writing by women, and Sally Ledger's *The New Woman: Fiction and Feminism at the Fin de Siècle* (1997), which explores the variety of literary and social forms adopted by New Woman writers, considering the relation of the New Woman to other social and cultural movements of the period. Teresa Mangum's *Married, Middle-Brow and Militant: Sarah Grand and the New Woman Novel* (1998), the first study to devote itself to Sarah Grand's novels as well as her life, brings to life Grand's social and sexual vision, gesturing also towards its limitations. Nonetheless, there is much still to be discovered and deciphered, and Ann Heilmann's five-volume collection of primary materials by and about the New Woman (1998) is a valuable resource for further research in this area.[24]

This collection of fourteen essays aims to explore both the commonalties and the tensions to be found in New Women writing, experience and social campaigns, and to offer a representative expression of the liveliness of current scholarly debate on the New Woman; a liveliness shared by its object of study. It is time to ask not who was the New Woman? but who *were* the New Women? – a question which was far from settled at the *fin de siècle*. For the anti-feminist Eliza Lynn Linton the New Woman was anti-social – a wild woman who would bring the nation into disrepute; for the publisher and essayist Arthur Waugh, she threatened to be the undoing of aesthetics (whether as author or subject); for Sarah Grand she was (or ought to be) a model of civic virtue who would stem and turn round Britain's tide of moral and biological degeneracy; for Mona Caird she was to resist the confusion of nature and history and recognize that social evolution was not biologically but historically determined. And New Women themselves did not always define their goals clearly: their fiction and prose-writing reveal contradictions and complexities which resist reductive, monolithic readings. Nonetheless, from the various competing definitions of the New Woman certain common features emerge: her perceived newness, her autonomous self-definition and her determination to set her own agenda in developing an alternative vision of the future.

Before we turn to the collection itself, we would like to consider the cultural pervasiveness of the New Woman, and her importance to literature and history alike. The New Woman was a cultural icon of the *fin de siècle*. In the guise of a bicycling, cigarette-smoking Amazon, she romped through the pages of *Punch* and popular fiction; as a neurasthenic victim of social oppression, she suffered in the pages of New Woman novels such as Sarah Grand's hugely successful *The Heavenly Twins* and Grant Allen's notorious *The Woman Who Did*. The New Woman was not one figure, but several (see Figures 2–7).

While these varied and conflicting popular images brought campaigns for women's rights firmly into public debate, they were often harmful and disparaging. In the words of Sarah Grand:

> Who is this New Woman, this epicene creature, this Gorgon set up by the snarly who impute to her the faults of both sexes while denying her the charm of either – where is she to be found if she exists at all? For my own part, until I make her acquaintance I shall believe her to be the finest work of the imagination which the newspapers have yet produced.[25]

But Grand herself was far from guiltless in the creation of this imaginary creature – as Talia Schaffer argues in the first essay of this collection. Grand's New Woman, though neither an epicene nor a Gorgon, was as much a fictional construct as those she cites in her article. *Punch* seized upon New Woman fiction as an easy target for parody, cashing in on the New Woman's diversity, while simultaneously seeking to reduce her to misandrous stereotypes that were either having too much or too little sex. Egerton's *Keynotes* was parodied as 'she-notes' by 'Borgia Smudgiton' and illustrated with oriental-style portraits of decadent, eroticized womanhood (17 March 1894) (see Figure 8).

Journalists and cartoonists played a significant part in establishing the cultural status of the New Woman. Smoking, rational dress[26] and bicycling provided cartoonists and satirists with easy targets and through such powerful visual iconography the New Woman became firmly established as a cultural stereotype. In Eastwood's words the New Woman had been 'flashed upon us in a rapid succession of startling and vivid pictures' (Eastwood, 375). As far as her opponents were concerned, the more startling and vivid the picture, the better. As Patricia Marks suggests, such caricatures of the New Woman embodied fears about the changing status of women.[27] They also embodied hopes and fears about racial development: the New Woman was seen either as a bespectacled, physically degenerate weakling or as a strapping Amazon who could outwalk, outcycle and outshoot any man.

A *Punch* cartoon of 1894 depicted the New Woman as 'Donna Quixote', a bespectacled intellectual (see Figure 9).[28] The caption explains that, like Don Quixote, she has been led astray by 'A world of disorderly notions *picked out of books*'. Books by Ibsen, Tolstoy and Mona Caird lie at

Figure 2   A 'New Woman'
The Vicar's Wife. 'And have you had good sport, Miss Goldenberg?'
Miss G. 'Oh, rippin'! I only shot one rabbit, but I managed to injure quite a dozen more!'
Punch, 8 September 1894

Figure 3 'I am afraid Mother doesn't much like the latter-day girl'
Punch, 19 May 1894
Copyright © *Punch*

Figure 4   Passionate female Literary Types
The *New* School
Mrs. Blyth (newly married). 'I wonder you never married, Miss Quilpson!'
Miss Quilpson (author of 'Caliban Dethroned,' &c., &c.). '*What? I* marry! I be a
man's plaything! No, thank you!'
Punch, 2 June 1894

Figure 5 Our Decadents (female)
'Tell me, Monsieur Dubosc. Of course you've read that shocking case of "Smith
v. Smith, Brown, Jones, Robinson, and Others"?'
'I confess I'ave, Miss Vilkes. I am a lawyer, you know.'
'Well, now, what do you think of it as a subject for dramatic treatment?'
'I–I–I do not know vat it may be as a subject for dramatic treatment,
Mademoiselle. I–I–I find it very–a–a *embarrassant* as a subject for conversation
viz a young lady!'
Punch, 23 June 1894

Figure 6   In Dorsetshire
Fair Cyclist. 'Is this the way to Wareham, please?'
Native. 'Yes, Miss, yew seem to me to ha' got 'em on all right!'
Punch, 6 September 1899
Copyright © *Punch*

Figure 7 What It Will Soon Come To
Miss Sampson. 'Pray let me carry your bag, Mr. Smithereen!'
Punch, 24 February 1894

Figure 8   She-Notes, by Borgia Smudgiton [Owen Seaman]
... *Japanese Fan de Siècle Illustration by Mortarthurio Whiskersly* [Edward Tennyson Reed]
Punch, 17 March 1894

her feet. She reads another book, whose title is not visible, and holds aloft a large key – a clear reference to Egerton's notorious *Keynotes*. In the background, a figure tilts at windmills, while another bears a banner saying 'Divided Skirt'. The cartoon's message is clear: the fictional New Woman is a bad influence on women readers. Similarly, Marie Corelli's 1895 best-seller *The Sorrows of Satan* features repeated attacks upon the apparently corrupting influence of New Woman fiction. New Woman novelists are described as 'self-degrading creatures who delineate their fictional heroines as wallowing in unchastity, and who write freely on subjects which men would hesitate to name';[29] they are instrumental in instigating the sexual sophistication and self-disgust which drive the main female character to suicide and, it is stated unequivocally, damnation. However, these arguments are implicitly undercut by the fact that the New Woman's most stringent critic in the novel is Satan himself, who is portrayed as a sadistic but persuasive misogynist. A lighter portrayal of the New Woman novelists' influence can be seen in Albert George Morrow's poster promoting Sidney Grundy's play, *The New Woman*, which opened at London's Comedy Theatre in September 1894. A pale young woman with dishevelled hair peers through pince-nez; books and papers litter the floor, flaunting titles such as 'Man the

Figure 9   Donna Quixote
'A world of disorderly notions *picked out of books,* crowded into his (her) imagination.'–*Don Quixote.*
Punch, 28 April 1894

Betrayer' and 'Naked But Not Ashamed'; a framed picture shows the key designed by Beardsley as a logo for the 'Keynotes' series, which began with George Egerton's notorious book of that title. In the foreground is a cigarette which appears to have been lit at both ends – a reference to an incident in the play when an inexpert New Woman smoker lights her cigarette at the wrong end. The poster thus incorporates the New Woman's literary and intellectual aspirations with her status as a sexual threat, but undercuts both by indicating her social ineptitude with another emblem of the New Woman – the cigarette.

Bicycling New Women abounded in fiction and in fact. A cartoon in *Punch* (13 October 1894) shows an elderly matron holding up her hands in horror at the sight of a muscular female cyclist in rational dress (see Figure 10). Sartorial oddities were a celebrated target for cartoonists: the eccentrically dressed minority were used to (mis)represent and undermine the various demands of *fin-de-siècle* feminisms. Two years on, a Du Maurier cartoon in *Punch* shows a horde of women cycling through a London park (see Figure 11).[30] While all bar one are

Figure 10   The Matron's Hiss
A lady-bicyslist the other day, riding in 'rational dress,' was roundly hissed by an elderly Mrs. Grundy, standing by. The wheel-woman is said to have retorted, 'Are you *women* who thus hiss me? When you bathe, you wear a special costume, which you deem suitable. When I ride, I do the same. Where's the difference?'
Punch, 13 October 1894

young and alluring, this portrayal of healthy, athletic womanhood is undercut by the caption, in which the two leading cyclists complain that they 'hate bicycling' but must do it because it is fashionable. The modern woman is thus portrayed as a featherheaded slave to fashion and, ironically, advertising rather than a woman of principle. A few pages on rational dress is the theme; a rhyme recounts the misadventures of a New Woman who advocates bicycling and rational dress – two of *Punch*'s favourite targets:

> There was a New Woman, as I've heard tell,
> And she rode a bike with a horrible bell,
> She rode a bike in a masculine way,
> And she had a spill on the Queen's highway.

Figure 11   Le Monde où l'on s'amuse
Toujours, Toujours,
La nuit comme le jour . . . .
Et youp, youp, youp, tra la la la là,
La la là!

Ethel. 'I hope bicycling will go out of fashion before next season, I *do* hate bicycling so!'
Maud. 'So do I! But one *must*, you know!'
Punch's Almanack for 1897

The unfortunate cyclist is knocked unconscious by her fall. A male doctor arrives on the scene and, alarmed by her rational dress, covers her split skirt with a petticoat – a more familiar and reassuring emblem of femininity. For *Punch*, cycling and rational dress provided visual emblems of the social, sexual and political disquiet caused by women's demands for equality.

A number of women took issue with journalistic versions of the New Woman, which undermined the causes that they advocated. Elizabeth Chapman, author of *Marriage Questions in Modern Fiction, and other essays on Kindred Subjects* (1897), condemned:

> the interminable flood of gaseous chatter to which the invention of a journalistic myth known as the 'New Woman' has given rise ... it has become necessary sharply to emphasize the distinction between this phantom and the real reformer and friend of her sex and of humanity, whom I would call the 'Best Woman'.[31]

The New Woman fictionalized by writers such as Sarah Grand was created as a means of advancing sexual and social change. The 'journalistic myth', on the other hand, simplified and satirized the New Woman's real concerns over social and moral issues.

Many New Woman novels were strongly and overtly didactic, bringing debates on femininity to a wider audience, and unwittingly underscoring the negative publicity which the periodical press lent to the figure of the New Woman. Elaine Showalter writes 'in the 1880s and 1890s, women writers played a central role in the formulation and popularization of feminist ideology'[32] and, likewise, Juliet Gardiner points out that New Woman novels 'testified to the power of fiction as an alternative means of exploration and a manifesto for change'.[33] However, like representations of the New Woman in the periodical press, sensational New Woman fiction proved a double-edged weapon. Widely popular, it was often criticized as sexually and socially irresponsible, portraying heroines who refused to consummate their marriages (Evadne in Grand's *The Heavenly Twins*); regarded marriage as merely an experiment (Gwen in Iota's *A Yellow Aster*); or had children outside wedlock (Herminia Barton in Allen's *The Woman Who Did*).

One of the most successful and controversial of the 'marriage question' novels, Allen's *The Woman Who Did*, ran to 19 editions in its first year of publication (Gardiner, 171), and, on account of Herminia's rejection of marriage, was condemned as an incitement to immorality. In his 1909 New Woman novel *Ann Veronica*, H. G. Wells has his heroine's father bemoan the influence of 'all this torrent of misleading, spurious stuff that pours from the press. These sham ideals and advanced notions, Women Who Dids, and all that kind of thing ... '.[34]

Allen's image of the New Woman as an advocate of free love became a popular talking-point, spawning a host of cartoons and parodies. Held to be typical of New Woman fiction, in fact this notorious novel made a striking contrast with the main thrust of New Woman fiction which was infused by social purity ideology. Various women involved in these debates, including Sarah Grand and Margaret Oliphant,[35] were outraged by Allen's purported representation of their case. Sarah Grand argued that Herminia's sufferings showed 'that women have nothing to gain and everything to lose by renouncing the protection which legal marriage gives'.[36] The leading suffragist and political economist Millicent Garrett Fawcett, president of the National Union of Women's Suffrage Societies (NUWSS) from 1897 to 1919, wrote in the *Contemporary Review* in 1895 that *The Woman Who Did* had damaged the feminist cause by linking 'the claim of women to citizenship and social and industrial independence with attacks upon marriage and the family'. She declared Allen 'purports to write in the interests of women, but there will be very few women who do not see that his little book belongs very much more to the unregenerate man than to women at all'.[37]

Contestations over, and constructions of, gender cannot be considered in isolation from issues of class or race. Essays by Burdett, Stott and Richardson here consider the complexities surrounding the New Woman's relation to the idea of race at a time when class was becoming an increasingly racialized discourse. While New Woman was essentially middle class, some of their social and political goals overlapped with working-class women's growing political activism at the *fin de siècle*. Although trade unionism had been a male preserve, the late 1880s saw a rise in women's trade union membership and militancy. In 1874 the suffragist Emma Paterson founded the Women's Provident and Protection League (WPPL) to encourage the formation of women's trade unions. The League got off to a slow start, being predominantly a middle-class organization rather than an initiative by the workers themselves. Paterson appealed to working women for their views and support, but the League's first conference was, in the words of Sally Alexander, a 'meeting of Christians, feminists and philanthropists'[38] rather than a trade union meeting. By the 1880s, however, working women had become more involved with the League and it was to play an important part in the Bryant & May match girls' strike of 1888 – probably the most famous example of working-class female militancy in this era. The living and working conditions of the match girls were a far cry from those of the wealthy educated, middle-class New Woman. It is estimated that in the 1890s 30 per cent of factory workers earned less than eight shillings a week (Hollis, 37). The media liked to present working-class women as more aggressive than their middle-class counterparts: for example, alongside its coverage of the Bryant & May match girls, the *Illustrated Police News* of 21 July 1888 carried an illustrated cover-page shocker 'Girls Attacking a Constable': the collapse of social order was nigh (see Figure 12).

Figure 12 Girls Attacking a Constable
The Illustrated Police News, 21 July 1888

While the majority of scholarly studies have focused on middle-class women it would be wrong to assume that it was these women who were the most politically active; the dramatic increase of women workers who were joining unions and campaigning for their rights tells another story. In 1876 female trade unionists numbered 19 500; by 1906 the number had risen to 166 425 (Hollis, 53). Various political pressure groups were to form over the next two decades; the Women's Cooperative Guild (1883); the Women's Industrial Council (1894), the National Union of Women Workers (1895), the Scottish Council for Women's Trades (1895), the Liverpool Women's Industrial Council (by 1896), the Hastings and St Leonards Women's Industrial Council (*c.* 1899–1900), the Women's Labour League (1906), and the Fabian Women's Group (1908). The socialist feminist Annie Besant joined the Marxist-based Social Democrat Federation (SDF) in the 1880s; the leadership she gave to the match girls' strike was as much a part of her political activism as were her advocacy of free contraception and her later involvement with the Suffragettes. Likewise Schreiner, arguably the first New Woman novelist, was a founding member of the SDF's Women's League. In the words of Doris Lessing, Schreiner's Marxist-inspired *Woman and Labour* (1911) was 'a classic of the Labour movement ... strong, large in scope, generous, bold'.[39] Schreiner's close friendship with the youngest and ardently socialist daughter of Karl Marx, Eleanor Marx (1855–98) and with Eleanor's socialist lover Edward B. Aveling (1849–98), the popular lecturer on atheism, drama critic and science teacher, testify further to her socialist credentials.

By attempting to confine late nineteenth-century feminism to the discursively produced New Woman, social commentators attempted to marginalize working-class women's increasing discontent with their lot.[40] This was a marginalization to which middle-class women were party, no less than middle- and working-class men, as socialist feminists were not slow to observe. Eleanor Marx attacked the narrow aims of the 'equal rights' women's movement with its almost exclusive focus on the suffrage, and subsequent neglect of economic issues, declaring that Mrs Fawcett and a laundress had no more in common that 'Rothschild and one of his employees'.[41] Likewise, responding to the Independent Labour Party's speech to the liberal feminist Pioneer Club in 1895, the feminist periodical *Shafts* stated emphatically that 'Tom Mann and the socialists were wrong in trying to drive women back into the home'.[42]

Equally, the late nineteenth-century media reduction of New Women to stereotypes might be considered a strategy of control, aimed at containing the threat they posed to the status quo. The bicycling Amazon and ugly bluestocking of caricature were more immediately accessible and memorable figures than women concerned with social and political change, and thus were often used as a way of obscuring the latter's goals. Campaigners agitated on diverse and sometimes mutually contradictory reforms: changes in the marriage laws, free love, pre-marital chastity for men as for women, free access to contraception, rational dress, an end to the 'White Slave Traffic', reform in the treatment of victims of sexual assault,[43] equal rights in education and employment, and – eventually – the vote. Journalistic exploitation of the more visual of these issues, such as rational dress, tended to downplay, or deny, the significance of more weighty issues. Nonetheless, the New Woman remained a central figure in late Victorian culture, and a notable force for social and political change.

*   *   *

The New Woman in Fiction and in Fact opens with Talia Schaffer's discussion of the term New Woman. Schaffer argues that the term was invoked in the 1890s by opposing camps, male and female, both to fictionalize the New Woman and to emphasize her status as a fact. She suggests that both Ouida and Grand were able to 'stretch, distort, and duplicate' the figure of the New Woman for a variety of rhetorical or psychological purposes which journalists were not slow to adopt, and that she became one of society's most exploited portents and scapegoats. Chris Willis takes the popular representation of the New Woman further in her discussion of mass consumption fiction, focusing on the beautiful bicycling Amazon. She notes that the New Woman of predominantly male-authored popular and detective fiction was physically and mentally healthy, but seldom able to find men that matched up. Largely depoliticized, the bicycling New Woman of popular fiction was presented as having to negotiate powerful maternal instincts, and was nearly always forced to reveal her womanly credentials at the story's end in order to salvage the romance plot. We meet more bicycling women in Sarah Wintle's essay, which takes a novel look at New Women's quest for physical freedom. Before turning to the novels of Mrs Edward Kennard, a rich source for her moving subject, Wintle provides an outline of the changing depiction of women riders in nineteenth-century fiction. While horses were symbolically articulate in the erotic realm, cars and bicycles also required skill and self-confidence and thus had an impact on the woman question.

Sally Ledger's essay considers not only Ibsen's challenging female character roles but also the ways in which he enabled the emergence of a particular species of New Woman in the shape of the modern actress, with the American Elizabeth Robins leading the field in the new, Ibsenite theatre of the *fin de siècle*. Whilst noting Ibsen's personal ambivalence towards the European feminist movement, Ledger at the same time explores his treatment of female desire and sexual freedom, which contrasts with the more repressive position adopted by some New Woman writers. Like a number of British New Woman novelists, though, Ibsen posits motherhood as a complex and tormented process and institution; he was immensely influential in the formation of 'New Womanly' identities in late-Victorian London.

Moving from male constructions of New Women, the next essay, by Gail Cunningham, explores New Woman constructions of masculinity, and male reactive discourses to the New Woman. Cunningham notes similarities between Hardy's defeatist New Woman narrative, *Jude the Obscure*, and New Woman fiction by women, and argues that these writers worked within a system of binaries which continued to privilege the male. Cunningham then focuses on Ménie Muriel Dowie's *Gallia*, which, she argues, inverts these terms and turns the male body into an object of female scrutiny, and on Egerton's male narrators whose voices prove inadequate to articulate the actions of the women in their stories.

Ann Ardis takes Oxford Hellenism as the frame of her analysis of the New Woman, gender and desire. Focusing on Olive Schreiner's 'The Buddhist Priest's Wife' and Ethel Arnold's *Platonics*, she asks whether the apparent legitimization of certain masculine codes of same-sex love enables or discredits female intellectuality, and whether it offers space for love between women. She demonstrates how Schreiner explores male resistance to female intellectual and sexual mentorship, and how the suspension of sexual difference customary in intellectual life has tragic potential from the woman's viewpoint. Likewise, *Platonics* critiques the Platonic ideal of disembodied intellectuality, and offers a portrait of New Women's responses to the New Hellenism before Wilde's trials crystallized its association with homosexual 'deviancy', leading Ardis to conclude that New Hellenism was ultimately disabling for New Women in late-Victorian Britain.

The 1890s witnessed the birth of psychoanalysis, and Ann Heilmann and Laura Marcus explore ways in which New Woman fictions play out a number of its contemporary concerns. Heilmann argues that in *The Heavenly Twins* Grand drew on contemporary medical discourse in order to explore the socio-sexual power relations between doctor and woman patient. She contends that, like Charlotte Perkins Gilman's narrator in 'The Yellow Wallpaper' (1892), and like 'Anna O' (Bertha Pappenheim), the first patient of psychoanalysis (in Breuer's and Freud's *Studies on Hysteria*, 1895), Grand's Evadne simultaneously resists and conforms to patriarchal strictures by suffering pathological withdrawal, the self-destructive impulses of which baffle, but fail to threaten, the existing order. Heilmann concludes that for Grand, Gilman and Pappenheim, it was the lack of intellectual and professional opportunities, compounded by forms of personal oppression, which impairs women's physical and mental health, rather than the repression of their sexual desire. Marcus examines further the withdrawal into 'private theatres' – fantasy, day-dreams and reveries in psychoanalysis and New Woman literature. Anna O used the phrase 'private theatre' to describe what Breuer called her 'systematic day-dreaming'. Considering Havelock Ellis's account of 'Auto-Erotism' – 'the spontaneous erotic impulse which arises from the organism apart from all definite external stimulation' – Marcus notes Ellis's contrasting images of auto-eroticism as external or, as in the production of daydreams, internal stimulation, which she formulates as the distinction between friction and fiction. This formulation can be mapped onto two contrasting images of the New Woman, one as seeking stimuli in the outer world (movement, experience, education), and the other as dreamer – the writer, for example. Marcus argues that the heroine of *The Beth Book* follows the path delineated by Bertha Pappenheim, passing from daydreaming to writing and from thence to political/social activism, but suggests also that fantasy may be a site of resistance and autonomy.

Stott, Burdett and Richardson's essays take us into the areas of race, colonization, and evolutionary discourse. Drawing on James Eli Adams's argument that 'when evolutionary speculation unsettles traditional conceptions of nature as a maternal being, it also disturbs Victorian typologies of the feminine',[44] Stott demonstrates ways in which Conrad, Haggard and Henry Morton Stanley cast their colonial landscapes as brooding or negligent, monstrous or man-eating mothers, embedded in the myth of the Dark Continent, and argues that in place of a nurturing landscape these mothers consume the life-blood of their victims. She contrasts this with the use of landscape in Schreiner's *Story of an African Farm*, where the landscape is figured as a negligent mother whose failings are understood as a symptom of the damaging effects of colonization. Burdett notes that although Schreiner emphasized that women can sometimes enter the public sphere of professions and politics, her last, and unfinished novel, *From Man to Man*, takes us firmly (back) into a traditional feminine wild, in which Rebekah suffers an unhappy, adulterous marriage, until Mr Drummond, an expression of New Manhood, enters the novel and it breaks off. Burdett notes that the New Womanhood of the heroine, Rebekah, is intimately linked to her position in South Africa as Schreiner explores interconnections between ideas of progress, nation, race and culture.

Richardson's essay considers Mona Caird's opposition to the forms of social and racial oppression examined by Stott and Burdett. Noting that Caird has suffered more than most from a homogenizing approach to the New Woman, from which this collection seeks to make a significant departure, Richardson contends that many New Women were adherents of Galtonian eugenics, and that their political and social commitments might accurately be termed eugenic feminism. Eugenics, founded by Francis Galton, Charles Darwin's cousin, was a class-based theory of society that aimed to improve on nature through the self-conscious control of human evolution through selective breeding,[45] and a number of New Women sought to apply these ideas in their development of the concept of 'civic motherhood', an expression of an emergent, moral and gendered citizenship which informed the mainstream New Woman rewriting of evolutionary narrative ('The Eugenization of Love'). Richardson argues that several New Women were thus party to 'the eugenization of love', a shift from romance to biology which demanded the excision of passion in favour of (women) choosing a sexual partner for his breeding credentials. By contrast, Caird exposed the various ways in which science was being used to justify barbaric social and sexual practices, and revealed the socially constructed nature of discourses on biological evolution. Rather than rejecting evolutionary theory, she strove to interpret it along lines which were much closer to Darwin's own thoughts on the importance of variation and change for biological progress, than the subsequent interpretations of many of his fundamentalist followers, past and present; she then translated her reading of Darwin into social terms. By emphasizing the differences between the civic maternalism of Grand and the humanitarian, anti-eugenic feminism of Caird, and underlining Caird's commitment to the historically-determined nature of social evolution, the plurality of beliefs and agendas which jostled under the umbrella New Woman is again brought home.

Matthew Beaumont argues for the importance of utopian ideas to late nineteenth-century feminist politics. He suggests that utopianism was informed by a politics of fellowship which was convinced that an egalitarian society could be birthed through individual choices and the interpersonal relations of its activists; in this climate of hope and apprehension, visions of an as yet non-existent new world proliferated. Focusing on Edward Bellamy's *Looking Backward* and Elizabeth Burgoyne Corbett's *New Amazonia*, Beaumont concludes that the political importance of utopian appeals should not be underestimated.

Continuing some of the themes of the collection into the twentieth century, Lesley Hall considers the work of Stella Browne (1880–1955) and her involvement with *The Freewoman*, founded in 1911. An uncompromising advocate of female sexual freedom and reproductive rights, Browne emphasized the range of sexual variation among women, and the physiological and emotional necessity for women to satisfy their sexual desires. Hall stresses continuities between women of Browne's generation and those of the late nineteenth century, most notably female Malthusians and members of the Legitimation League, and argues that the *Freewoman* group as a whole looked back to an older feminist tradition of the interrelation of the personal and the political.

Regenia Gagnier's afterword to the collection, 'Women in British Aestheticism and the Decadence', draws on her work in Victorian aesthetics and economics and provides us with new ways of understanding the role of women in the late nineteenth century. Drawing out the tensions between different forms of aesthetics in late nineteenth-century Britain, Gagnier emphasizes that while some aesthetics were concerned with productive bodies, whose work could be creative or alienated, others were concerned with pleasured bodies, whose tastes established their identities. Her essay here explores the relation of New Women to the Decadence in the light of these two aesthetic-economic models – productivist aesthetics and hedonics – and poses searching questions as to the motivations of New Women who rejected sex for pleasure in favour of sex for (re)production.

Notes

1. A. G. P. Sykes, 'The Evolution of the Sex', *Westminster Review* 143 (1895), 396–400.
2. Ann Ardis, *New Women, New Novels: Feminism and Early Modernism* (New Brunswick: Rutgers University Press, 1990), 4.

3. See Malmgreen, 'Women's Suffrage in England: Origins and Alternatives, 1792–1851' (MA diss., University of Hull, 1975), 25, and Barbara Taylor, *Eve and the New Jerusalem* (London: Virago, 1983), esp. chapter 1. See also Ashley Tauchert, *Mary Wollstonecraft: Athenic Writing and the Accent of the Feminine* (Palgrave, forthcoming) for an original study of Wollstonecraft; Tauchert offers an illuminating analysis of 'Pregnant-Embodiment and Writing' and a compelling argument for Wollstonecraft's understanding of same-sex desire.

4. Wollstonecraft, *A Vindication of the Rights of Woman* (published with John Stuart Mill, *The Subjection of Women*) (London: J. M. Dent, 1985), 154, 163, 168.

5. See Richardson, *The Eugenization of Love: Darwin, Galton, and Late Nineteenth-Century Fictions of Heredity and Eugenics* (Oxford: Oxford University Press, forthcoming). See also Gagnier, *The Insatiability of Human Wants: Economics and Aesthetics in Market Society* (Chicago University Press, 2000), esp. chapters 2 and 5; Gagnier notes that by the time of Olive Schreiner's *Woman and Labour* (1911) the idea of progress had become bio-logized, and hence narrower: progress for all was no longer considered an option.

6. The book was published under Thompson's name (republished London: Virago, 1983); for a discussion of its authorship see Taylor, *Eve and the New Jerusalem*, 22–3. See also Richard K. P. Pankhurst, *William Thompson, 1775–1833: Britain's Pioneer Socialist, Feminist and Co-Operator* (London: Watts, 1954). As Taylor notes, the book was written largely to refute James Mill's argument that female enfranchisement was unnecessary because the political interests of women were 'contained' in those of their fathers and husbands, and constituted a sustained critique of the bourgeois liberal assumptions on which James Mill's case had been based (Taylor, chapter 1).

7. *1851 Census of Great Britain: General Reports*, cited in Judith Worsnop, 'A re-evaluation of "the problem of surplus women" in 19th-century England: the case of the 1851 Census', *Women's Studies International Forum*, 13 (1990), 22. See also Philippa Levine, '"So Few Prizes and So Many Blanks": Marriage and Feminism in later Nineteenth-Century England', *Journal of British Studies* 28 (1992), and Mary Lyndon Shanley, *Feminism, Marriage and the Law in Victorian England, 1850–1895* (London: I. B. Tauris, 1989).

8. See, for example, Richard J. Evans, *The Feminists: Women's Emancipation Movements in Europe, America and Australasia, 1840–1920* (London: Croom Helm; New York: Barnes & Noble, 1977), 64. See also Patricia Hollis, *Women in Public: The Women's Movement, 1850–1900* (London: George Allen & Unwin, 1979, reprinted 1981); Philippa Levine, *Feminist Lives in Victorian England: Private Roles and Public Commitment* (Basil Blackwell: Oxford, 1990); Barbara Caine, *Victorian Feminists* (Oxford: Oxford University Press, 1992); and Martha Vicinus, *Independent Women: Work and Community for Single Women 1850–1920* (London: Virago, 1985).

9. For example, in 1846 the Association for Improving and Enforcing the Laws for the Protection of Women began a monthly journal, *The Female Friend*. In 1849 *Eliza Cook's Journal* was launched; in 1852 Samuel Beeton established *The English Woman's Domestic Magazine*. In 1858 the *Englishwoman's Journal* was founded. Funded by pioneering feminist Barbara Leigh Smith

(later Bodichon) and edited by Bessie Parkes and Matilda Hays, its main aim was to promote women's employment. After it ceased publication in 1864 the *Englishwoman's Review* took its place. For a pioneering study of feminism and the novel see Sander Gilbert and Susan Gubar, *The Madwoman in the Attic: the Woman Writer and the Nineteenth-Century Literary Imagination* (New Haven, Conn.: Yale University Press, 1979) and Elaine Showalter, *A Literature of Their Own, from Charlotte Brontë to Doris Lessing* (1977; London: Virago, 1982).

10. See Gertrude Himmelfarb, introduction to *On Liberty* (1859; Harmondsworth, Penguin, 1985), 16. In his *Autobiography* (ed. A. O. J. Cockshut) (written 1854–1870; first published in 1873; Halifax: Ryburn Publishing, 1992) J. S. Mill charts his recognition of the inadequacy of the Utilitarian formula 'the greatest happiness of the greatest number' which his father had espoused so tenaciously (77–8).

11. John Stuart Mill, *On the Subjection of Women* (1869; London: J. M. Dent, 1929), 232, 238.

12. For discussion of Mill's importance to feminism, see Millicent Fawcett's essay in Theodore Stanton (ed.) *The Woman Question in Europe* (New York and London: G.P. Putnam's Sons 1884); see also 'Mr Mill on the Subjection of Women', *Blackwood's Magazine* (1869); Amos Shanley, 'The Subjection of Women', *Westminster Review* (1870), 63; for discussion of Mill in relation to nineteenth- and twentieth-century feminists, see Richardson, 'Biology and Feminism', *Critical Quarterly 2000*.

13. See Carol Dyhouse, *Girls Growing Up in Late Victorian and Edwardian England* (London: Routledge & Kegan Paul; Boston, Mass., Broadway House, 1981); Felicity Hunt (ed.), *Lessons for Life, the Schooling of Girls and Women, 1850–1950* (Oxford: Basil Blackwell, 1987); Joan Burstyn, *Victorian Education and the Ideal of Womanhood* (London: Croom Helm, 1980); Jane McDermid, 'Women and Education', in Jane Purvis (ed.), *Women's History in Britain, 1850–1945* (London: UCL Press, 1995). For a thorough treatment of women in higher education, see Dyhouse, *No Distinction of Sex? Women in British Universities 1870–1939* (London: UCL Press, 1995).

14. See Doggett, chapter 4. See also Ann Sumner Holmes, '"Fallen Mothers", Maternal Adultery and Child Custody in England, 1886–1925', in Claudia Nelson and Ann Sumner Holmes (eds), *Maternal Instincts: Visions of Motherhood and Sexuality in Britain, 1875–1925* (New York, St. Martin's Press; London: Macmillan, 1997).Through an analysis of custody cases between 1886 and 1925 Holmes demonstrates that English judges began to recognize the significance of factors other than sexual purity in determining a woman's value as a mother.

15. Eliza Lynn Linton, 'The Judicial Shock to Marriage', *Nineteenth Century* 171 (1891), 700.

16. See [1891], 1 *Q. B.* 671. See also 'Husband and Wife – Right of Custody', *Justice of the Peace* 55 (18 April 1891), cited in Maeve E. Doggett, *Marriage, Wife-Beating and the Law in Victorian England* (Columbia, SC: South Carolina University Press, 1993), 3. For an excellent, detailed analysis of the *R. v. Jackson* case see Doggett, chapter 1; for further discussion of a husband's right of chastisement and confinement see in addition chapter 2.

See also William Blackstone, *Commentaries on the Law of England 4 vols*
(1765–9; London: Strahan, 1829); as a husband might be held legally
responsible for his wife's conduct, Blackstone held that he ought to have
the power to control that conduct; this was, as Doggett notes (35), the
essence of coverture. Doggett discusses the emergence of the fiction of
marital unity from the time of the Norman Conquest: it appears in the first
English law book, the twelfth-century *Dialgous de Scaccario*, and in the work
of every leading common-law writer since (70). See also L. I., *The Lavves
Resolution of Women's Rights* (London: Printed for John More, 1632). For
further, recent historical discussion of marriage and the social position of
women, see, for example, James C. Mohr, 'Feminism and the History of
Marital Law: Basch and Stetson on the Rights of Wives', *American Bar
Foundation Research Journal* (1984); Susan Staves, 'Where is History but in
Texts? Reading the History of Marriage', in John M. Wallace (ed.), *The
Golden and the Brazen World: Papers in History and Literature* (Berkeley:
University of California Press, 1985); and Carole Pateman, '"God Hath
Ordained to man a Helper": Hobbes, Patriarchy and Conjugal Right', in
Mary Lyndon Shanley and Carole Pateman (eds), *Feminist Interpretations and
Political Theory* (Cambridge: Polity Press, 1991). For a sense of the extent to
which marriage was exercising the nation in the nineteenth-century see, for
example, John Fraser MacQueen, *The Rights and Liabilities of Husband and
Wife* (1849; London: Sweet & Maxwell, 1905); Harriet Taylor Mill,
'Enfranchisement of Women', *Westminster Review* 55 (1851); 'The Laws
Relating to Women', *Law Review* (20–21) (1854–5); Margaret Oliphant, 'The
Laws Concerning Women', *Blackwood's Edinburgh Magazine* 79 (1856) and
'The Condition of Women', *Blackwood's Edinburgh Magazine* 83 (1858);
'The Laws of Marriage and Divorce', *Westminster Review* 82 (1864); Alfred
Dewes, 'The Injustice of the English Law as it Bears on the Relationship of
Husband and Wife', *Contemporary Review* (1868); Louisa Catherine Shore,
'The Emancipation of Women', *Westminster Review* (1874); Frances Cobbe,
'Wife-Torture in England', *Contemporary Review* 32 (1878); Courtney
Stanhope Jenny, *The History of the Law of England as to the Effects of
Marriage on Property and on the Wife's Legal Capacity* (London: Reeves &
Turner, 1879); John Williams Edwards and William Frederick Hamilton,
The Law of Husband and Wife (London: Butterworths, 1883); Montague
Lush, *The Law of Husband and Wife within the Jurisdiction of the Queen's
Bench and Chancery Divisions* (London: Stevens, 1884); William Pinder
Eversely, *The Law of Domestic Relations* (London: Stevens and Haynes,
1885); 'The Law in Relation to Women', *Westminster Review* 128 (1887);
'The Personal Liberty of Married Women', *Law Times* 90 (1890–1);
'Personal Relations of Husband and Wife', *Justice of the Peace* 55 (1891);
Matilda Blake, 'Are Women Protected?', *Westminster Review* 137 (1892) and
'The Lady and the Law', *Westminster Review* 137 (1892); Joseph Bridges
Matthews, *A Manual of the Law Relating to Married Women* (London: Sweet
& Maxwell, 1892); J. De Montmorency, 'The Changing Status of a Married
Woman', *Law Quarterly Review* 13 (1897); A. V. Dicey, *Lectures on the
Relation between Law and Public Opinion in England during the Nineteenth
Century* (1905; London: Macmillan, 1962). See the work of Mona Caird,
Sarah Grand and George Egerton, among other New Woman writers, for

widely divergent takes on marriage. For topical and controversial treatment of marriage and marriage laws by a male writer, see Thomas Hardy, *The Mayor of Casterbridge* (1886), *The Woodlanders* (1887) and *Jude the Obscure* (1895).

17. The term 'white slavery' was commonly used to describe sweated labour. Annie Besant's article 'White Slavery in London' appeared in the *Law and Liberty League*'s weekly newspaper, *The Link* (23 June 1888), and dealt with the working conditions of the Bryant & May match girls. Likewise, in an open letter to the shareholders of Bryant & May, published in *The Link*, Besant describes their exploitation of girls as 'the White Slavery on which you fatten' (*The Link*, 14 July 1888, 1, col. 2). However, W. T. Stead's *Maiden Tribute of Modern Babylon* had referred to pimps and procuresses as 'slave traders' (1885, reprinted as British Library transcript 1976, 75) and to the trade in female child prostitutes as a 'slave market' (Stead: *Maiden Tribute*, 11). By the early twentieth century the phrase 'white slave traffic' was commonly used to describe the traffic in prostitutes. For discussion of the social purity movement, see Jeffreys 6–26; Bland, *Banishing the Beast, English Feminism & Sexual Morality* (1885–1914) (Harmondsworth: Penguin, 1995); Ann Heilmann, *The Late Victorian Marriage Question: a Collection of Key New Woman Texts* I (London and New York: Routledge Thoemmes Press, 1998), vol. 1 (especially xix–xxii); Judith R. Walkowitz, *Prostitution and Victorian Society: Women, Class, and the State, and City of Dreadful Delight: Narratives of Sexual Danger in Late-Victorian London* (London: Virago, 1992), 87–93. See also Keith Thomas, 'The Double Standard', *Journal of the History of Ideas* (1959), 195–216 for a discussion of the Contagious Diseases Acts within a broader history of ideas relating to the double standard.

18. See Richardson, 'The Eugenization of Love: Sarah Grand and the Morality of Genealogy, *Victorian Studies* (Winter 1999/2000), 227–55

19. *Lectures on the Marriages of the Priesthood in the Old Immoral World* (1835), quoted in Taylor 184. See also Taylor, chapter 6.

20. *The Crisis* (31 August 1833); see Taylor, 47; see also Cora Kaplan, 'Wild Nights: Pleasure/Sexuality/Feminism', in *Sea Changes: Culture and Feminism* (London: Verso, 1986).

21. For the opposition of New Women to passion, see Richardson, 'The Eugenization of Love'.

22. Friend to Hannah More, after reading More's views on Female Duty, in More, *Life and Correspondence* (London: 1834), 4 vols; vol. 3, 453, quoted in Catherine Hall, 'The Early Formulation of Victorian Domestic Ideology', in Sandra Burman (ed.), *Fit Work for Women* (London: Croom Helm, in association with Oxford University Women's Studies Conference, 1979), 25. For the unhappy relationship of evangelicalism to feminism and socialism see Doggett, esp. 90–6, and Taylor, 14–15 and chapter 5, esp. 123–30. See also Leonore Davidoff and Catherine Hall, *Family Fortunes: Men and Women of the English Middle Class, 1780–1850* (London: Hutchinson, 1987), 18–19, 73–192, 450–4; Catherine Hall, 'The Early Formulation of Victorian Domestic Ideology', 17; Lawrence Stone, *The Family, Sex and Marriage in England, 1500–1800* (New York: Harper & Row, 1977), 666–80.

23. Mrs M. Eastwood, 'The New Woman in Fiction and in Fact', *Humanitarian* 5 (1894), 375–9.

24. Gail Cunningham, *The New Woman and the Victorian Novel* (London, Macmillan, 1978); Penny Boumelha, *Thomas Hardy and Women: Sexual Ideology and Narrative Form* (Brighton: Harvester Press, 1982); Ann L. Ardis, *New Women, New Novels: Feminism and Early Modernism* (New Brunswick: Rutgers University Press, 1990); Lyn Pykett, *The 'Improper' Feminine: the Women's Sensation Novel and the New Woman Writing* (London and New York: Routledge, 1992); Sally Ledger, *The New Woman: Fiction and Feminism at the Fin de Siècle* (Manchester: Manchester University Press, 1997); Teresa Mangum, *Married, Middlebrow, and Militant: Sarah Grand amid the New Woman Novel* (Michigan: University of Michigan Press, 1999); Ann Heilmann, *The Late-Victorian Marriage Question: a Collection of Key New Woman Texts* (London: Routledge Thoemmes Press, 1998). Forthcoming publications in this area include Carolyn Burdett, *Olive Schreiner and the Progress of Feminism: Evolution, Gender, Nation* (London: Macmillan, 2000), Ann Heilmann, *New Woman Fiction* (London: Macmillan, 2000) and *New Woman Strategies: Sarah Grand, Olive Schreiner, Mona Caird* (Manchester University Press, forthcoming).
25. Sarah Grand: 'The New Woman and the Old', *Lady's Realm* (1898), 466.
26. The Rational Dress Society was formed in 1881 under the presidency of Florence, Viscountess Harberton. 'Health, comfort and beauty' were its central goals, and it urged the adoption of the divided skirt. See, for example, Stella Mary Newton, *Health, Art and Reason: Dress Reformers of the Nineteenth Century* (1974).
27. Patricia Marks: *Bicycles, Bangs and Bloomers: the New Woman in the Popular Press* (Lexington, KY: University Press of Kentucky, 1990), 205.
28. *Punch*, 26 April 1894.
29. Corelli, *The Sorrows of Satan* (1895; Oxford: Oxford University Press, 1996), 178.
30. For an illuminating discussion of representations of a very different sort of woman at this time, The High Art Maiden, see Ann Anderson, 'Soul's Beauty: Burne-Jones and Girls on the Golden Stairs, *Nineteenth Century: Magazine of the Victorian Society in America* 18 (1998), 19–23. Anderson notes how the High Art Maiden's preoccupation with dress, and, by extension, interior decorating, was depicted as frivolous, even dangerous; her pursuit of Beauty and lassitude were likely to render her physically weak, while her self-centred contemplation took her attentions away from reproduction and housework (21). Du Maurier frequently stirred such fears through satirical cartoons in *Punch*.
31. Elizabeth Rachel Chapman, foreword to *Marriage Questions in Modern Fiction* (London, 1897), xiii.
32. Elaine Showalter, *A Literature of Their Own*, 182.
33. Juliet Gardiner, introduction to *The New Woman* (London: Collins & Brown, 1993), 3–4.
34. H. G. Wells, *Ann Veronica* (London: Ernest Benn, 1927), 27.
35. Margaret Oliphant, 'The Anti-Marriage League', *Blackwood's Edinburgh Magazine* (1896), 135–49.
36. Sarah Grand: 'The Woman's Question', *The Humanitarian*, March 1886, quoted in Elaine Showalter: *Sexual Anarchy: Gender and Culture at the Fin de Siècle* (Virago, 1992), 52.

37. M. G. Fawcett: 'The Woman Who Did', *Contemporary Review* (1895), 625–63, quoted in Elaine Showalter, *A Literature of Their Own* (Virago, 1979, reprinted 1988), 52 and Sarah Wintle, introduction to *The Woman Who Did* (1895; Oxford: Oxford University Press, 1995), 1.

38. Sally Alexander: *Becoming a Woman* (London: Virago, 1994), 63.

39. *The Guardian*, cited in Virago edn (1988).

40. For further discussion of working-class women see Meg Gomersall, *Working-Class Girls in C19th England: Life, Work and Schooling* (London: Macmillan, and New York: St. Martin's Press, 1997); Sally Alexander, 'Women's Work in Nineteenth-Century London: a study of the years 1820–1850', and D. Thompson, 'Women and Nineteenth-Century Radical Politics: a lost dimension', in J. Mitchell and A. Oakley (eds), *The Rights and Wrongs of Women* (Harmondsworth: Penguin, 1976), 59–111; J. Lown, *Women and Industrialization: Gender at Work in Nineteenth-Century England* (Cambridge, Polity, 1990); Angela V. John (ed.), *Unequal Opportunities: Women's Employment in England 1800–1918* (Oxford, Blackwell, 1986); Eddy Higgs, 'Women, Occupations and Work in Nineteenth-Century Censuses', *History Workshop Journal* 23 (1987), 59–79; June Purvis, 'Women's Life is essentially Domestic, Public Life being Confined to Men' (Comte): separate spheres and inequality in the education of working-class women, 1854–1900', *History of Education* 10 (1981), 227–43, and *Hard Lessons: the Lives and Education of Working-Class Women in Nineteenth-Century England* (Cambridge: Polity, 1989); Elizabeth Roberts, *A Woman's Place: an Oral History of Working-Class Women, 1890–1940* (Oxford: Basil Blackwell, 1984); Sonya O. Rose, 'Gender at Work: sex, class and industrial capitalism', *History Workshop Journal* 21 (1986), 113–31 and *Limited Livelihoods: Gender and Class in Nineteenth-Century England* (London: Routledge, 1992).

41. See Hal Draper and Anne G. Lipow, 'Marxist Women versus Bourgeois Feminism', *The Socialist Register* (1976), 224.

42. *Shafts*, 3 (June 1895), 35, cited in Ledger. For further, detailed discussion of the tensions between class and the emancipation of women, see Ledger, chapter 1, and Sally Alexander, *Becoming a Woman* (London: Virago, 1994), 129–31.

43. Sheila Jeffreys, *The Spinster and Her Enemies: Feminism and Sexuality 1880–1930* (London: Pandora Press, 1985), 60 and n. 19, National Vigilance Committee Minutes, 3 January 1889.

44. James Eli Adams, 'Nature Red in Tooth and Claw: Nature and the Feminine in Tennyson and Darwin', *Victorian Studies* 33:1(1989); reprinted in Rebecca Stott (ed.), *Tennyson* (Harlow: Longman, 1996), 87–111.

45. Galton coined the term 'eugenics' in *Inquiries into Human Faculty and its Development* (London: Macmillan, 1883), 24–25. 'Eugenics' – the process of artificial selection for reproduction in humans – was from the Greek *eugenes*, 'good in stock'.

1
'Nothing But Foolscap and Ink': Inventing the New Woman

Talia Schaffer

Did the New Woman really exist? The question is not quite as naive as it seems. Of course the *fin de siècle* saw real women who agitated for greater autonomy in everything from etiquette to employment. While there were some prominent leaders – women like Mona Caird, Lady Jeune, and Sarah Grand – most of the women associated with the new movement lived a much humbler life. Working as clerks, typists, teachers, college students, journalists, or perhaps even shopgirls, they often lived in painfully spartan flats, struggling to earn enough money for genteel gowns and living primarily on bread and tea. They walked without chaperones, carried their own latchkeys, bicycled, and the more daring ones smoked cigarettes, cut their hair, or wore divided skirts and plain costume in accordance with the principles of rational dress.[1] These women rarely described themselves as 'New Women'; that is a modern usage.

For when people wrote and spoke about the 'New Woman' in the 1890s, they were usually referring to a very different figure: the unsexed, terrifying, violent Amazon ready to overturn the world. The 'New Woman' was a comic fictional figure composed of *Punch* cartoons, much-vilified novels, and ominous warnings in popular articles. As Mrs Morgan-Dockrell declared, the 'New Woman' was 'a figment of the journalistic imagination'.[2] This grotesque buffoon, whether bicycling in bloomers, ogling men, or thrusting her fist in the assembled faces of Parliament, was a media construct, and, as such, we must ask why it appeared and who found it useful.

In *New Women, New Novels*, Ann Ardis perceptively points out that although there had been a 'plethora of highly charged rhetoric' over women's behaviour, when the New Woman was named, the debate's structure changed (11–12). 'Having been a social debate at its inception in the 1860s, what had once been termed the "Woman Question" became a more strictly literary affair following the naming of the New Woman,' she explains (12). Critics turned from excoriating real women to condemning characters in novels. Ardis cites a number of journalists on both sides of the New Women controversy who, by the late 1890s, were insisting that the New Woman was unreal (12–13). In her view, this shift was detrimental. 'To label something literary rather than "real" is to quarantine it, in effect: to isolate it in a special corner of life, to box it off as a special kind of phenomenon, not something one encounters in society at large' (12). The New Women could be marginalized and dismissed, she argues, once they were relegated to the ranks of the merely imaginary.

It is true that some of the New Woman's critics wanted to marginalize the movement, but this does not explain why the New Woman's supporters were equally concerned to assert the figure's fictionality. Why did so many 1890s writers, from all over the political spectrum, *want* the New Woman to be fictional? How might the emergence of such a parodic figure have enabled these writers to propound certain issues and raise particular questions? Our best clues can be found in the famous Ouida and Sarah Grand articles in the *North American Review* of 1894 which popularized the 'New Woman'. These articles' surprisingly complex rhetoric helps reveal how the New Woman emerged, what 'New Woman' actually meant to its inventors, and why subsequent writers adopted Ouida's and Grand's joint creation.

The term 'New Woman' was invented in the *fin-de-siècle* feminist press, according to Michelle Elizabeth Tusan, where it named a utopian feminist vision of the future. Several months later, when it migrated to the mainstream press, its meaning changed.[3] The term acquired its popular sense when it appeared in Sarah Grand's 'The New Aspect of the Woman Question', according to Ellen Jordan's lively account.[4] Grand argues that men's moral failures – especially their support for prostitution – makes them unworthy to marry the new breed of self-aware young women. Since Grand's article focuses on men, the New Woman is hardly even sketched out, and remains so idealized and so vague as to be nothing more than a standard of intellectual and ethical honesty against which men are measured and found wanting.

'The New Aspect of the Woman Question' uses what seem (at least to a modern reader) surprisingly conservative materials to build its case for a new woman, as Grand explicitly links herself with antifeminist critics and endorses a traditional view of women's work. Grand admits, 'we have our Shrieking Sisterhood, as the counterpart of the Bawling Brotherhood'.[5] Here she not only grants Eliza Lynn Linton's reactionary accusations about modern women, but even models her own discourse upon them.[6] If her invective comes from Linton, her idealism comes from an equally unexpected source, Ruskin's 'Of Queens' Gardens'. 'We have been reproached by Ruskin for shutting ourselves up behind park palings and garden walls, regardless of the waste world that moans in misery without, and that has been too much our attitude; but the day of our acquiescence is over,' she promises (274). Women's social activism is framed as a charitable activity undertaken from the middle-class home.

Grand emerges here as a 'difference feminist': one who believed that women and men were intrinsically different and that their public roles ought to reflect these innate character traits. She particularly wants women to assist helpless victims of men's sexual appetites. Grand justifies such rescue work according to women's natural housewifely and maternal instincts. 'True womanliness is not in danger,' Grand asserts, 'and the sacred duties of wife and mother will be all the more honorably performed' as sons' and husbands' characters improve (274). After all, 'it is the woman's place and pride and pleasure to teach the child, and man morally is in his infancy' (273). In line with difference feminism, then, Grand extrapolates a greater public role from women's duties: charity, child-rearing, and housekeeping. Women are attempting 'to make the world a pleasanter place to live in', Grand promises at the beginning of 'The New Aspect of the Woman Question', and this decorative dream reaches its climax by the end, when an extended metaphor promises a great ethical spring-cleaning for England (270):

> We shriek in horror at what we discover when [light] is turned on that which was hidden away in dark corners; but the first principle of good housekeeping is to have no dark corners, and as we recover ourselves we go to work with a will to sweep them out. It is for us to set the human household in order, to see to it that all is clean and sweet and comfortable for the men who are fit to help us make home in it. We are bound to raise the dust while we are at work, but only those who are in it will suffer any inconvenience from it, and the self-sufficing and self-supporting are not afraid. (276)

Here Grand writes in a particularly Ruskinian manner, as common experiences become metaphorically charged with great moral lessons. In 'The New Aspect of the Woman Question', housework fulfills the same function that gardening performs in 'Of Queens' Gardens'. Cleansing becomes the greatest womanly virtue, not just for families, nor even just for England, but for 'the human household', a semi-divine mission.

Grand has good reasons for turning her argument from potentially specific instructions for assisting fallen women into a general Ruskinian exhortation to purify the whole 'human household'. First, the vaguer Grand is, the harder it becomes to disagree with her. Given that her readers agree about the holiness of women's mission – a fairly safe assumption for 1894 – they will be swept along on a tide of good feeling. Second, Grand's utopianism continues the tradition of feminist writing on the New Woman, offering a reassuringly familiar argument for her more radical readers (Tusan, 171). Third, turning this article from reportage to myth gives Grand licence to create her own symbolic panoramas and sweeping mythic histories: 'Women were awaking from their long apathy, and, as they awoke, like healthy hungry children unable to articulate, they began to whimper for they knew not what. They might have been easily satisfied at that time had not society ... shaken them and beaten them and stormed at them until what was once a little wail became convulsive shrieks and roused up the whole human household' (271). Ouida caustically objects that 'we are not told either in what country or at what epoch this startling upheaval of volcanic womanhood took place', but that is precisely the point.[7] Had Grand been subject to ordinary rules of writing, she would have had to confess that the 'whole human household' was certainly not resounding to a few dozen Anglo-American magazine publications, or a few hundred young women with haircuts.[8] But by making the New Woman into a fiction, Grand enables herself to construct a meta-history which conveys her own psychological sense of the real enormity of the change, rather than the facts which produce a misleadingly minor sense of this movement. In that sense, Grand *wants* the New Woman to be a fiction; she's much more impressive that way.

Ouida responded to Grand's timelessly idealized figure by creating the grotesque creature who would become so familiar in the latter half of the 1890s. Ouida famously begins, 'It can scarcely be disputed, I think, that in the English language there are conspicuous at the present moment two words which designate two unmitigated bores: The Workingman and the Woman. The Workingman and the Woman, the New Woman, be it remembered, meet us at every page of literature written in the English tongue; and each is convinced that on its own especial W hangs the future of the world' (610). This passage is usually cited to demonstrate Ouida's antifeminism, but it also performs two other significant functions. First, Ouida clearly wants to convince us that the 'New Woman' already exists. This early usage of 'New Woman' already brackets it as something which all readers 'remember', something that 'meet[s] us' constantly, outside Ouida's own text. The article which popularizes the 'New Woman' begins with a lament that we are all tired of hearing about her. Second, she removes the New Woman from the lived world of women's experiences, the subject of Grand's article, and transfers it to a literary realm. The New Woman is omnipresent on 'every page of literature', not in life – she has already become a specifically fictional artefact.

Ouida turns the New Woman into a literary product not to contain her, but to expand her. Here is her description of the New Woman's appearance:

> Before me lies an engraving in an illustrated journal of a woman's meeting; whereat a woman is demanding in the name of her sovereign sex the right to vote at political elections. The speaker is middle-aged and plain of feature; she wears an inverted plate on her head tied on with strings under her double-chin; she has balloon-sleeves, a bodice tight to bursting, a waist of ludicrous dimensions in proportion to her portly person; she is gesticulating with one hand, of which all the fingers are stuck out in ungraceful defiance of all artistic law of gesture. Now, why cannot this orator learn to gesticulate and learn to dress, instead of clamoring for a franchise? (612–13)

This first description of the New Woman's body is particularly interesting because it apparently refers, not to a real person, but to a caricature which appeared in *Punch* ten years earlier.[9] She original drawing shows a woman addressing the House of Commons, wearing a limp and shapeless mid-calf-length dress over Turkish trousers. She glares at the Members through her glasses, her index finger extended, while a man's hat, a ball of yarn, and knitting sit on the bench beside her. Wholly 'unsexed', even her tightly curled hair resembles a lawyer's wig and her sole article of decoration is a ragged neckerchief which nods to a male cravat or tie.

Ouida reconfigures this image in different class terms. Whereas *Punch* depicts the orator in unattractively eccentric and male-inflected 'rational dress', Ouida gives her attire so fashionable as to be ludicrous. The small flat hat and the tightly cinched waist were popular 1890s styles. The balloon-sleeves which Ouida condemns were worn throughout the first half of the 1890s and got so large in the spring of 1894 as to become the object of *Punch*'s satire.[10] In Ouida's description, the male hat and the knitting, that emblem of middle-class thrifty productivity, have disappeared.[11] Ouida promotes the dowdy 1884 orator to the height of 1890s style. Furthermore, Ouida changes the audience from the House of Commons to the woman's club, thereby reducing the speaker's potential to effect suffrage reform, but also increasing the speaker's status by making her the leader of a group of supportive women, rather than a lone comic figure who disgusts her antagonistic listeners. Whereas Linley Sambourne's figure is labelled a 'dream of the future', Ouida addresses her subject as if she already exists. Ouida's New Woman is a modish, fairly wealthy club member who may be ungraceful but is certainly *au courant*. What she loses in political power, she gains in social networks. Ouida constructs the New Woman, not in the *Punch* tradition of a bizarre imaginary specimen, but rather as if she were a real, comfortably middle-class, vigorous participant in a well-settled community of like-minded women.

Fictionalizing the New Woman does not seem to relegate her to a safely marginal space, as Ardis suggests; on the contrary, when Ouida invents her New Woman, she constructs her as a more economically and socially powerful figure than her source indicated. In fact, it was precisely in Ouida's interest to emphasize the New Woman's reach, for, as we shall see, the more powerful, enormous, and significant this fictional caricature becomes, the more benign, sedate, and reassuring Ouida herself seems by comparison.

This description of the orator initiates a spectacular outpouring of misogynist hostility, which suffuses the remainder of the article. Ouida accuses the New Woman of corrupting men, destroying male geniuses' lives, stealing men's job and opportunities, and eventually hurling bombs at her enemies (616). David Rubinstein writes that this article 'express[es] virulent opposition to the emancipation of her own sex'. 'In terms of stereotype', he adds, 'she belonged to the Lilly-Nisbet school of misogynists.'[12] In an intriguing treatment of Ouida's complex gender politics, Pamela K. Gilbert explains that Ouida's antifeminist denunciation of the New Woman has contributed to her erasure from today's canon.[13]

Yet a close examination of 'The New Woman' reveals something unexpected: Ouida mainly objects to the New Woman's insufficient activism. Ouida calls for concerted action to end cruelty to animals, and is furious that woman 'wears dead birds and the skins of dead creatures; she hunts the hare and shoots the pheasant, she drives and rides with more brutal recklessness than men; she watches with delight the struggles of the dying salmon, of the gralloched deer; she keeps her horses standing in snow and fog for hours with the muscles of their heads and necks tied up in the torture of the bearing rein ...' (613). She excoriates (upper-class) women's insensibility to servants, exploitation of tradesmen, and cruelty to poor seamstresses. Although Ouida began by complaining about workmen, she ends up energetically supporting their cause. Until women take radical action to remedy their injustices to working-class people and animals, Ouida insists, 'so long as she orders her court-dress in a hurry; so long as she makes no attempt to interest herself in her servants, in her animals, in the poor slaves of her tradespeople ... she has no possible title or capacity to demand the place or the privilege of man' (619).

At this point we may wonder: if Ouida wants to produce radical political action, why critique the New Woman – including, in fact, those very earnest social activists who would be her natural allies in agitating for humane treatment of animals? Why, in fact, frame a call for activism as an attack on the New Woman?

In order to answer this question, we must first understand how Ouida's New Woman has shifted. The languid selfish aristocrat who hunts pheasant, 'orders her court-dress in a hurry', and 'courtesies before princes and emperors who reward the winners of distance-rides' is hardly the same bossy middle-aged woman with the plate on her head who gesticulated so gracelessly in the 'engraving' (618). Furthermore, neither of these figures resembles in the least Sarah Grand's New Woman, who, as we have seen, is an idealized nurturer. Nor do any of these mature, potent figures correlate to the real representatives of New Womanism: the young women who lived in London and worked in the new white-collar professions. Fictionalizing the New Woman allowed her to be defined in any way the author needed, at any time. It allowed Ouida and Grand to assimilate the New Woman to the powerful tradition of demonic/angelic women whose sway over the Victorian imagination Nina Auerbach has described.[14] As a mythic icon, the New Woman evokes an extraordinary range of emotional associations, a flood of feelings which can powerfully support whatever goal the writer has channelled it towards.

By inventing and then attacking a demonic New Woman, Ouida creates a straw (wo)man, and thereby constructs herself as its opposite. If Ouida can see that the New Woman is extremist and outrageous, why then, Ouida herself must be moderate and reasonable. In fact, the 'New Woman' functions as a demonic double of the writer. It serves the psychological and rhetorical function of evacuating unpleasant characteristics and thereby leaving behind a residually purified authorial self. This explains one of the most apparently illogical aspects of Ouida's article: her persistent tendency to ascribe her own traits to the New Woman. For instance, Ouida excoriates the New Woman generally (and Grand particularly) for bad manners and an inadequate grasp of grammatical and literary rules. To a casual reader, this seems exquisitely ironic – and oddly unselfconscious – since Ouida was famous for her appalling etiquette and many spelling, logical, and grammatical errors.[15] Similarly, the 'engraving' is eerily reminiscent of Ouida herself, who was a plain-featured middle-aged woman who insisted on wearing inappropriately fashionable attire. When Ouida condemns the New Woman's refusal to bear children, her insensate love of publicity, and her unfeminine passion for travelling, she is finding a way to distance herself from traits which had received a particularly negative press: her unmarried state, her relentlessly arrogant self-promotion, and her allegiance to France and Italy over England. When Ouida asserts that 'seclusion lends an infinite seduction to the girl, as the rude and bustling publicity of modern life robs woman of her grace', she hides how much she despised her secluded countrified upbringing (617). When she writes 'true modesty shrinks from the curious gaze of other women as from the coarser gaze of men', she occludes the fact that she presided over all-male smoking parties (617). The bold public-relations gambit of 'The New Woman' makes Ouida into the guardian of virtue instead of the dubiously free-living writer of dangerously immoral sensation novels.[16]

The New Woman, then, develops as a kind of split persona for Ouida, which fulfils two separate rhetorical roles. First, the New Woman's repulsiveness allows Ouida to construct herself decorously by contrast. Second, the New Woman, as the avatar of all extremism, leaves the field free for Ouida to propose her own political ideas without being branded a radical. Like a magnet, the New Woman draws all the shrapnel, so that other kinds of metal pass unnoticed. Thus Ouida can insist on increased activism for women, precisely because she has so publicly, quickly, and safely differentiated herself from activist women. Gilbert explains that in Ouida's novels, 'Ouida's conservatism is formulated through a radical rhetoric'. This article shows that it also works the other way: Ouida's radical calls for action get expressed via conservative language.

Although Ouida's article has been called 'misogynist' and 'anti-feminist', in many ways her notion of proper womanly behaviour resembles Grand's and the other New Women's.[17] 'Ouida is wholly opposed to Female Suffrage and the New Woman, but in part for reasons which are aligned with the reasoning of New Women like Egerton and Cross, who see in women's sexuality a power distinct from the power of men', Gilbert writes. Similarly, Ouida's fiction highlights her cynicism regarding the institution of marriage, her advocacy of women's sexual natures, her partisanship of animal rights, her revelations of marital abuse, her defence of the very poorest (and often racially hybrid) subjects, and her critique of the commodification of women (Gilbert). Certainly, Ouida's own life follows a New Woman pattern; as an unmarried woman who supported herself through writing, who initiated relationships with men outside of marriage, and who stubbornly followed her own rules for fashion and etiquette in spite of social norms, she might even have been a role model. These fairly radical positions and experiences, of course, account for the intensity with which she dissociates herself from the movement; it is precisely because she might be read as a participant that she needs to excoriate it.

Interestingly, Ouida, like Grand, locates herself in a conservative lineage by alluding approvingly to Eliza Lynn Linton and Ruskin.[18] Ouida adopts Ruskin's garden images, claiming that the New Woman covets her neighbour's land while she 'will not even look at the extent of ground indisputably her own, which she leaves unweeded and untilled' (618). In this respect, Grand and Ouida end their articles with the image of woman as nurturing improver, and ask readers to apply these domestic skills to national life. As the New Woman becomes a literary construct, Ouida and Grand appropriate the rhetorical lessons of their predecessors, placing Ruskinian metaphors and Lintonian invective in the service of their own notions of womanhood. Actual women disappear and the focus shifts to constructing an associative chain in which one text's characteristic emotional charge can reverberate down the line of its successors.

This persistent use of allusions, combined with both writers' tendency to fictionalize the New Woman, indicates that the real war may well have been a war of words – that the New Woman's literary status was the most challenging aspect of her identity, not a way of making it any 'safer'. By treating the New Woman as a purely imaginary caricature, Ouida and Grand were able to stretch, distort, and duplicate this figure for whatever rhetorical or psychological purpose they wanted. Grand uses the New Woman's fictionality to exaggerate her into a vast figure looming over an international human-scale revolt, while Ouida uses this caricature to frame her own injunctions for animal-rights activism in the most flattering way. Both are clearly doing something quite different from earlier writers, like B. A. Crackanthorpe, Alys Pearsall Smith, and Kathleen Cuffe, whose slightly earlier articles in *The Nineteenth Century* use autobiographical confessions to make pragmatic recommendations for reforming everyday etiquette. As Ardis notes, the 'naming of the New Woman' did indeed initiate a new discourse.

Ouida's and Grand's figure found immediate currency amongst other journalists. Jordan explains that Grand's second article, in May 1894, attracted attention in the *Observer*, the *Pall Mall Gazette*, and *Punch* (20–1). One of the earliest significant usages appeared in a long article by W. F. Barry in the *Quarterly Review*, July 1894.[19] Here, the New Woman becomes neither Grand's idealized mother, nor Ouida's wealthy lady, but takes on a third identity as the French Revolution Amazon, 'in her wide-spreading tumultuous battalions, many of them wearing the divided skirt, she advances, with drums beating and colours flying, to the sound also of the Phrygian flutes, a disordered array, but nowise daunted, resolute in her determination to end what she is pleased to define as the slavery of one-half the human race' (Barry, 290). She is an anarchist, a heathen, dangerously allied with decadents, a bad mother, hysterical, and doomed to sterility (Barry, 293, 298, 308, 311, 317). Barry has learned from Grand that a vast mythic sweep can endow his subject with a significance far beyond its real scope. The violence of Barry's article, moreover, derives from Ouida's and Grand's invective, itself indebted to Linton's style. Finally, Barry has also learned to position himself as the respondent in a preceding dialogue and the voice of reason in an extremist clamor. Like both Grand and Ouida, Barry emphasizes the literariness of the New Woman. Notice the slippage in this passage: 'Yet a change has come over society during the last fifteen or twenty years which the author of "Valentine" [George Sand] could scarcely have foreboded. Women are now graduates in half-a-dozen professions, and disciples in all. They practice medicine as well as novel-writing; the forceps is familiar to them no less than the bicycle; even dress-cutting advertises itself as "scientific" at six guineas the course. Instead of attending to deportment and "Mangnall's Questions", Miss Evadne, before she is nineteen, has studied, without a master, anatomy and physiology' (294). Barry begins with a sociological observation about new careers for women, describes an advertisement, and finally concludes with a fictional figure from *The Heavenly Twins*. The argument inevitably moves from a real observation to an imaginary example. The subsequent ten pages constitute a diatribe against *The Heavenly Twins*. Thus the New Woman has been transferred into the literary world. The entire trend towards female education gets embodied in Evadne; and this technique 'manages' the problem by reducing a nationwide trend into a single personality. Barry no longer has to analyse a demographic shift, but simply to explain where Evadne went wrong.

Today, 'New Woman' has a positive sense; in the 1890s, however, it generally referred to an exaggerated, parodic, grotesque version of feminism. Progressive women of the 1890s therefore used 'New Woman' with a different sort of resonance than we do today. The negative connotations the 'New Woman' rapidly accrued in the mainstream media must have annoyed many feminist thinkers; by 1895, feminists were trying to differentiate the 'real' New Woman to salvage her from the caricature (Tusan, 176). Suffragist Ella Hepworth Dixon was surprised and offended when a friend called her a 'new woman'.[20] Elizabeth R. Chapman, whose *Marriage Questions in Modern Fiction* demanded an end to dismissive jokes about 'the female sex', complained about 'the interminable flood of gaseous chatter to which the invention of a journalistic myth known as the "New Woman" has given rise'.[21] These women disavowed the term for the same reasons that today people who have risked career advancement by working to include writing by women or people of colour in the curriculum would be irritated at being dubbed 'politically correct'. By 1895, 'New Woman' – like 'politically correct' a century later – had become a wildly skewed, reductive media construct which did not represent the real lives and work of those people it purported to describe.

Although we can understand Dixon's and Chapman's annoyance, the invention of the 'New Woman' was not entirely a retrograde development. What Grand and Ouida loosed upon the world in May of 1894 became a hotly contested item, and in the process of rejecting, affirming, decrying, or defining the 'New Woman', writers were able to enunciate where they stood on various issues. In this respect, the 'New Woman' was a kind of oblique mirror whose distorted reflection forced people to deduce how they really looked. Indeed, as writers like Grand, Ouida, Emma Churchman Hewitt, Ellen Gosse, Janet E. Hogarth, and H. E. Harvey wrote about the 'New Woman' after 1895, we can see them defining themselves, selecting parties, forming alliances.[22] The 'New Woman' furore may have helped the multitudinous groupings of the *fin de siècle* settle down into the dominant 'feminist' and 'anti-feminist' camps which would dominate the twentieth century.

Punch may have summed it up best in the jingle which Ellen Jordan cites as the moment when the image of the New Woman cohered (21):

There is a New Woman, and what do you think?
She lives upon nothing but Foolscap and Ink!
But, though Foolscap and Ink form the whole of her diet,
This nagging New Woman can never be quiet![23]

Punch's main point is correct: it is quiet true that 'there [wa]s a New Woman', who 'live[d] upon nothing but Foolscap and Ink'. She existed only upon paper. She lived only in the written word. ('Foolscap', of course, conjures up not only paper but also a fool's cap, showing just what *Punch* thought of the New Woman.) *Punch* is also right that she could 'never be quiet'.[24] In her brief career, she was ascribed more opinions, positions, and beliefs than any real woman could have absorbed in a lifetime; she was used as a public relations technique; she was made to answer for every aspect of British life the writer feared or despised; she was held responsible for vast declines and mythic changes. For someone who never existed except in 'foolscap and ink', the New Woman was awfully prominent, and in her refusal to 'be quiet' – in the barrage of complaints, critiques, suggestions, and wishes which blasted her from all sides – she was instrumental in helping distinct parties coalesce out of the apparent chaos of 1890s gender politics. The 'ink' which constituted the New Woman was not just the stuff of journalism, but also resembled the magically hypnotic ink of another *fin-de-siècle* text: a mirror-like pool in which the gazer could see beyond her own face, into her past, and the future.[25]

Notes

I am grateful to Pamela Gilbert for kindly sending me a copy of her forthcoming article, Sally Mitchell for finding and sending me the *Punch* cartoon, and Chris Willis for alerting me to the Mary Braddon rhyme.

1. Evelyn March Phillips, 'The Working Lady in London', offers a fascinating account of working women's struggles to find adequate housing and food (*The Fortnightly Review* 58 (1892), 193–203). A series of articles on mothers and daughters in *The Nineteenth Century*, vol. 35 (1894), by B. A. Crackanthorpe, E. B. Harrison, M. E. Haweis, Kathleen Cuffe, and Alys W. Pearsall Smith, reveals some details of the chaperonage debate: see pp. 23–31, 313–22, 424–50. Many of the better-known New Women novels depict married middle-class subjects, but a subgenre of novels vividly depicting single women's hard-working and unglamorous lifestyle include Dorothy Richardson: *Pilgrimage 1* (Urbana and Chicago: University of Illinois Press, 1979, first edn 1915, 1916, 1917); Ella Hepworth Dixon: *The Story of a Modern Woman* (Leipzig: Bernhard Tauchnitz, 1895); Netta Syrett: *Rose Cottingham, or The Victorians* (Chicago: Academy Press, 1978, first edn 1915); George Gissing: *The Odd Women* (London: Sidgwick & Jackson, 1911); 'Lucas Malet' (Mary St Leger Kingsley Harrison): *Mrs. Lorimer: A Sketch in Black and White* (London: Macmillan, 1884).

2. Cited in Ann Ardis: *New Women, New Novels: Feminism and Early Modernism* (New Brunswick: Rutgers University Press, 1990), 13.
3. Michelle Elizabeth Tusan, 'Inventing the New Woman: Print Culture and Identity Politics During the Fin-de-Siecle' [*sic*], *Victorian Periodicals Review* 31:2 (Summer, 1998): 169–83.
4. Ellen Jordan, 'The Christening of the New Woman: May 1894', *Victorian Newsletter* 63 (Spring 1983): 19–21.
5. Sarah Grand, 'The New Aspect of the Woman Question', *North American Review* 158 (March 1894): 270.
6. Eliza Lynn Linton, 'The Shrieking Sisterhood', *Saturday Review*, 12 May 1870: 341–2.
7. Ouida, 'The New Woman', *North American Review* 158 (May 1894), 611.
8. It is hard to know how many New Women – or New Women novels – there actually were, since a few examples received disproportionate publicity, and since so much depends upon how strictly individual critics define 'New Women'.
9. Linley Sambourne, '"The Angel in the "House"; or, the Result of Female Suffrage. (A Troubled Dream of the Future)', *Punch*, 14 June 1884, 279. This is the most likely source, as it matches Ouida's description better than the other political cartoons I have found, but it is certainly possible that Ouida may have drawn on her memories of *Punch*'s other cartoons about female suffrage, including an image from 18 December 1875 of a women's meeting, Constance Rover, *The Punch Book of Women's Rights* (London: Hutchinson, 1967), 51.
10. See *Punch*, 24 March 1894: 133, and 8 July 1893: 3.
11. In the cartoon, she is predictably enough knitting a 'blue-stocking' (a derogatory term for intellectual women).
12. David Rubinstein, *Before the Suffragettes: Women's Emancipation in the 1890's*, (New York: St. Martin's Press, 1986), 15–16.
13. Pamela K. Gilbert, 'Ouida and the Other New Woman', *Victorian Women Novelists and the Woman Question*, ed. Nicola Thompson (Cambridge: Cambridge University Press, forthcoming).
14. Nina Auerbach: *Woman and the Demon: The Life of a Victorian Myth* (Cambridge: Harvard University Press, 1982).
15. A typically dismissive (though exceptionally long) example is Malcolm Elwin, 'Ouida', *Victorian Wallflowers*, rpt. in the *Chelsea House Library of Literary Criticism* vol. 10, ed. Harold Bloom (New York: Chelsea House Publishers, 1989), 6073–6.
16. All biographical information in this paragraph comes from Eileen Bigland: *The Passionate Victorian* (London: Jarrolds, 1950); Yvonne Ffrench: *Ouida: A Study in Ostentation*, (London: Cobden-Sanderson, 1938); Monica Stirling: *The Fine and the Wicked: The Life and Times of Ouida* (London: Victor Gollancz, 1957).
17. Rubinstein 15–16, and Jordan, 19.
18. Ouida cites Linton on p. 618.
19. W. F. Barry, 'The Strike of a Sex', *Quarterly Review* 179 (July and October 1894): 289–318.
20. Ella Hepworth Dixon: *As I Knew Them* (London: Hutchinson, n.d.), 41.
21. Quoted in Ardis 13. Elizabeth Rachel Chapman, *Marriage Questions in Modern Fiction* (London: John Lane, 1897).
22. Emma Churchman Hewitt, 'The "New Woman" in Her Relation to the "New Man"', *Westminster Review* 147 (1897): 335–7; Ellen Gosse, 'The

Tyranny of Woman', *New Review* 10 (1894): 615–25; Janet E. Hogarth, 'The Monstrous Regiment of Women', *Fortnightly Review* 68 (1897): 926–36; H. E. Harvey, 'The Voice of Woman', *Westminster Review* 145 (1896): 193–6.

23. *Punch*, 26 May 1894, 252.

24. Interestingly, *Punch* could 'never be quiet' either; it used almost exactly the same ditty thirty years earlier to make fun of Mary Braddon (11 April 1863, 154).

25. The hypnotic ink pool appears in Rudyard Kipling, '"The Finest Story in the World"', *Rudyard Kipling: Selected Stories*, ed. Sandra Kemp (London: J. M. Dent, 1987, first edn 1893): 54–82.

2
'Heaven defend me from political or highly-educated women!': Packaging the New Woman for Mass Consumption

Chris Willis

The New Woman of commercialized popular literature was a far cry from her sensitive, suffering sisters in the polemic fiction of the best-known New Woman novelists. Romances, comic novels and detective fiction portrayed attractive, independent, highly intelligent young women entering a range of professions before (almost invariably) falling in love. Some of the most striking examples of this type of fiction were written by men – perhaps attempting to defuse the threat of the New Woman by emphasizing her youth, sexual attractiveness, and the supposed folly of her desire for independence. Male fears of the New Woman's bid for sexual and social equality are expressed by the hero of Beatrice Harraden's *fin-de-siècle* bestseller *Ships that Pass in the Night*, who cries, 'Heaven defend me from political or highly educated women!'[1] In commercial New Woman fiction, a heroine who is 'political or highly educated' is almost sure to come to a bad end unless she abandons her socio-political and intellectual activities in favour of a conventional wifely role.

The typical New Woman heroine of commercial fiction is young, pretty and single. She is almost invariably a keen bicyclist. Popular fiction of the time often uses the figure of the female cyclist as a paradigm of the New Woman. If a character makes her first appearance on a bicycle, it is almost inevitable that she will turn out to be single and well-educated, with strong views on women's rights. Criticizing New Woman fiction in *Blackwood's* in 1895, Hugh Stutfield compared the New Woman novelist to a bicyclist:

The lady novelist of today resembles the 'literary bicyclists' so delightfully satirised by the late Lord Justice Bowen. She covers a vast extent of ground, and sometimes her machine takes her along some sadly muddy roads, where her petticoats – or her knickerbockers – are apt to get soiled.[2]

Though uncomplimentary, the comparison is apt: writing was as characteristic of the New Woman as was cycling. This 'literary bicyclist' was claiming a full right to participate in intellectual as well as physical life.

The New Woman was not always sympathetically portrayed in popular culture. Like her later counterpart the Suffragette, she was frequently caricatured as being ugly and unmarriageable. However, by the late 1890s, the image of the New Woman as a beautiful bicycling Amazon seems to have largely taken over from the image of her as an unattractive bluestocking. In this paper, I will look at ways in which this image was used in commercial fiction. The high-minded heroines of the New Woman novelists were scaled down and prettied up for popular consumption in a variety of novels and stories which possibly did as much for women's rights as did the more serious fiction produced by the campaigners. Much of this fiction was purely commercial: like the female detective or the sensation novel heroine, the New Woman was a novelty figure whose presence in a novel could virtually guarantee good sales. However, some authors used popular fiction as a polemic, using this popularized New Woman to draw attention to serious issues. Women's rights supporters such as L. T. Meade and Beatrice Harraden produced popular fiction featuring New Woman heroines in established genres such as romance or crime fiction. Such fiction reached a large audience, and could be used to convey a political message in a light-hearted way, without being overtly didactic. As John Sutherland puts it, 'Potentially, the bestseller is a powerful instrument for social change, instruction or enlightenment.'[3] Commercial fiction could be used to reinforce the points made by the more polemic New Woman novelists.

Having achieved success with *The Woman Who Did*, Grant Allen wrote detective adventures featuring heroines who shared Herminia Barton's courage and feminism but who were distinctly more light-hearted and considerably less eager to make martyrs of themselves. His New Woman detective heroines, Lois Cayley and Hilda Wade, enjoy a series of light-hearted adventures in which they effortlessly prove their intellectual and physical superiority to the men around them. However, both Lois and Hilda marry and give up detection in the final chapter. For the New Woman detective, a successful conclusion to a case is not the acceptable form of closure that it would be for a story with a male protagonist. The New Woman detective almost invariably moves within the romance plot as well as the detective plot, and the ending must fit the conventions of both genres, allowing the detective-heroine to 'get her man' in more ways than one. If there is a conflict between genre conventions, the romance plot predominates: evidently an escaped criminal posed less of a threat than an attractive young woman who was happy to be single.

The New Woman of popular fiction was physically and mentally healthy. There is no equivalent of the suffering of Allen's Herminia Barton or Hardy's Sue Bridehead, and no hint of the mental and physical collapse which many male critics supposed to be the inevitable fate of the celibate, educated New Woman. In her athletic activities she demonstrates her physical equality, or even superiority, to men. This is particularly noticeable in Grant Allen's *Miss Cayley's Adventures*, in which the heroine defeats all male competitors in a bicycle race, and rescues an injured (male) mountaineer who is a less skilled climber than herself. However, mental fitness was equally important. A Girton education became the stock attribute of the intellectual New Woman of popular fiction. As the first women's college, Girton was subject to considerable public interest. The 'Girton Girl' became a cultural stereo-type, being the subject of many news stories, articles, cartoons and novels. She was invariably referred to as a 'girl' rather than a woman, although university educated men of her age were referred to as 'Varsity *men*'. As well as providing a convenient alliteration, the term 'Girton girl' implicitly denigrated the achievements of university women by suggesting that they were not fully adult. The 'Girton girl' setting out to earn her own living was a popular character in fiction of the time. That archetypal New Woman Herminia Barton, the *Woman Who Did*, has just left Girton at the start of the novel. She doubts the value of the education she received there because 'the life was one-sided – the girls thought and talked of nothing else on earth except Herodotus, trigonometry and the higher culture'. However, she sees women's education as a means to a worthy end: 'if you begin by edu-cating women you must end by emancipating them.'[4]

Popular novelist Beatrice Harraden portrayed a 'Girton girl' heroine who offered an answer to these criticisms. First published in 1893, Harraden's sentimental romance *Ships that Pass in the Night* was one of the best-sellers of its day. Its heroine, Bernardine Holme, is a serious-minded intellectual who contracts tuberculosis and falls in love with a fellow patient in a sanatorium. Before her illness, Bernardine was a typical New Woman:

> she was in the full swing of her many engrossing occupations: teaching, writing articles for newspapers, attending socialist meetings, and taking part in political discussions – she was essentially a modern product. (Harraden: *SPN*, 8)

Girton-educated Bernardine objects violently to press portrayals of the ugly bluestocking:

> The writers who rail against the women of this date are really describing the women of ten years ago. Why, the Girton girl of ten years ago seems a different creation from the Girton girl of today. Yet the latter has been the steady outgrowth of the former ...
>
> The Girton girl of ten years ago ... was a sombre, spectacled person, carelessly and dowdily dressed, who gave herself up to wisdom, and despised every one who did not know the *Agamemnon* by heart. She was probably not lovable; but she deserves to be honoured and thankfully remembered. She fought for woman's right to be well educated, and I cannot bear to hear her slighted. The fresh-hearted young girl who nowadays plays a good game of tennis, and takes a high place in the Classical or Mathematical Tripos, and is book learned without being bookish, and ... who does not scorn to take a pride in her looks because she happens to take a pride in her books ... she is what she is by reason of that grave and loveless woman who won the battle for her. (Harraden: *SPN*, 159–60)

defending bluestockings

The tennis-playing mathematician or classical scholar described by Bernardine is very much the positive version of popular images of the New Woman. However, having created a heroine in the Amazonian 'Girton girl' mould, writers of popular fiction were left with the problem of what to do with her. She could romp cheerfully through a series of serio-comic adventures, proving her mental and physical superiority at every point, but some form of closure had to be provided at the end of the story or novel, and for the nineteenth-century heroine, closure almost inevitably meant marriage. But how could the New Woman be found a suitable mate? Female submission to a dominant man would be unconvincing for such a heroine. Authors were left with the problem of finding a man to match the New Woman. *Punch* joked about the New Man of the future as the anxious, downtrodden house-husband[5] of an emancipated wife. The male love-interest of popular New Woman fiction is often little better. The heroine spends most of the novel proving her superiority to him, only to capitulate unconvincingly in the final chapter and give up her career aspirations for the dubious delights of marriage to a man who is her physical and mental inferior. If she does not marry she is almost invariably left disconsolate and unsatisfied, having lost her lover to a conventionally 'womanly' woman.

Harraden's heroine is unusual in that she wins the heart of a man who is her intellectual equal and who decides that he prefers her to conventional 'womanly' women, despite his earlier comment of 'heaven defend me from political or highly educated women!' (Harraden: *SPN*, 158). Bernardine's successful wooing of him represents the victory of feminism over chauvinism. However, they are not allowed to enjoy happiness: in the best tradition of New Woman fiction, Bernardine meets with a fatal accident before they can marry. It would seem that the New Woman cannot be allowed to attain the conventional romantic happy ending and still keep her principles intact.

Grant Allen's 1897 comedy-romance *The Type-writer Girl* portrays a 'Girton girl' heroine who is a far cry from his martyred Herminia Barton, but whose intelligence and principles similarly prevent her from attaining the happy ending of the romance plot. Juliet Appleton is a lively, good-looking young woman who lives alone and earns her living by typewriting. Juliet embodies all the popular paradigms of the New Woman: she is physically fit, a keen cyclist and a Girton girl. In the first chapter she explains that circumstances have forced her to earn her own living, discusses the theory that a woman wrote the *Odyssey*, then resolves to set out on a modern odyssey of her own, concluding, 'From all of which you may guess that I am a Girton girl'.[6] Allen wrote this novel under a female pseudonym, possibly hoping that readers would assume it was in fact written by a 'Girton girl'. Juliet's comic adventures include a spell of living in a commune, which at first appears to present an alternate closure to the 'happy ending' of marriage and maternity which was the standard end for fictional heroines. However, Juliet returns to normal life and her typing, and proves her true 'womanly' credentials by falling in love with her handsome employer. Unfortunately he is already engaged to an insipid and unassertive woman, and Juliet's principles prevent her from betraying another woman by stealing her fiancé. The New Woman is thus portrayed as attractive, intelligent and honourable, but she ultimately loses out to the 'womanly' woman. The message recurs throughout popular New Woman fiction: if the New Woman is to find a mate she must become as 'womanly' as her less politicized sisters.

A more complex New Woman is the heroine of L. T. Meade's 1898 novel *The Cleverest Woman in England*. Meade, who had a strong belief in women's intellectual equality with men, creates a strong, independent and somewhat intimidating heroine, Dagmar Olloffson, who is a dedicated campaigner for women's rights. Unfortunately Dagmar tries to combine her beliefs with marriage to a man who is best described by the 1960s term 'male chauvinist pig'. Meade sets the conflict out clearly in the opening chapter: announcing the engagement, Dagmar tells her friends that, 'He disapproves at every single thing that I love best in the world, and we are to be married in less than a month.'[7] Dagmar is 'one of the most popular lecturers on the Woman movement of the present day' (Meade: *CWE*, 55) and 'mean(s) to devote her whole life to women' (Meade: *CWE*, 50). In the best tradition of popular New Woman heroines, she is young, rich and exceptionally beautiful. Meade overloads her heroine with feminine attractions in order to gain the reader's sympathy and counteract the stereotype of the ugly women's rights campaigner which occasionally still surfaced in the pages of *Punch* and the popular press. The novel's villain, Geoffrey Hamlyn, 'loathe[s] the new woman' (Meade: *CWE*, 43) but attends Dagmar's meetings because he has fallen in love with her. He proposes to her after rescuing her from a group of men who attack her after she has spoken at a women's rights meeting. However, he turns out to be a more dangerous opponent that the men he has rescued her from. He finds the cause of female suffrage 'the most mistaken in all the world' (Meade: *CWE*, 70), asks her to give up her campaigning work after marriage, and tells her, 'you fulfil your highest mission when you help a man' (Meade: *CWE*, 89). The resulting conflict threatens to wreck the marriage, until Dagmar conveniently dies from smallpox, leaving her husband free to marry 'a girl who was truly domestic in her tendencies' (Meade: *CWE*, 340). Once again, the New Woman loses her man to the 'womanly' woman. However, Dagmar's influence lives on: 'noble and courageous women got their first impetus from her, who but for her would not have dared to break through the thraldom of the narrow walls of old prejudice' (Meade: *CWE*, 341).

Meade, who was herself strongly feminist, gives a sympathetic portrait of the New Woman, offering a positive picture of her attributes. She makes great use of the concept of 'womanliness', usually seen as the antithesis of the New Woman. Dagmar is given the traditionally womanly attributes of beauty, maternal instinct and heterosexuality, none of which need necessarily conflict with her belief in women's rights. One of her fellow campaigners, Imogen Pryce, asks Geoffrey, 'Have you discovered that a new woman can possess both brains and womanliness?' (Meade: *CWE*, 24) but Geoffrey finds the very question offensive. Significantly, Geoffrey is the literary editor of a popular newspaper: Meade uses him to gently satirize prejudice against the New Woman in the popular press of the day. Like some of the more polemic New Woman novelists, Meade attacks sexual double standards. Dagmar gives a home to a woman who has been seduced, abandoned and left pregnant by a man who promised to marry her. Geoffrey and his ultra-conventional sister, Rose, are scandalized. Geoffrey refuses to allow the woman to stay in the house, despite the fact that she is severely ill. He comments that 'The man is a scoundrel, but we will say nothing of that; the fact remains that the girl is ruined and disgraced. Dagmar, she is not to stay here' (Meade: *CWE*, 230). His statement summarizes the double standard which feminist campaigners of the time fought to change, and is as telling as several pages of polemic.

Detective fiction offered a particularly effective field for portrayal of the popularized New Woman heroine. McDonnell Bodkin's detective-heroine, Dora Myrl, is 'a Cambridge wrangler and a Doctor of Medicine'.[8] Although she has qualified as a doctor, Dora has taken up detection because she has been unable to attract any patients. Dora is almost an identikit New Woman. She is a keen cyclist and plays tennis and croquet as well as a man (Bodkin: *DM*, 4). Her chequered career provides a virtual roll-call of the professions regarded as typical of the New Woman: before taking up detection, she says that she has been 'a telephone-girl, a telegraph-girl' and 'a lady journalist' (Bodkin: *DM*, 6). Dora remains single at the end of the first book of her adventures, but in the sequel she shows an uncharacteristic wish to be 'a real womanly woman'[9] with a husband and children. Bodkin marries her off in this second volume, *The Capture of Paul Beck*. The title refers not to Dora's capture of a criminal, but to her capture of a husband. Paul Beck is a male detective who is one of Dora's professional rivals until they marry. Like the New Woman, the professional female detective represents a threat to the convention that women should be financially dependent on men. Her threat had to be negated by offering proof of her compulsion towards marriage and maternity, demonstrating that she was 'womanly' enough to be incomplete without a husband and children.

By marrying Dora off, Bodkin puts her firmly in her place as a sub-missive wife rather than a threat to her male rival. It is Dora who solves the case: Paul is misled by the criminal throughout most of the book. However, the happy ending comes from her sexual submission rather than his professional submission. The result is incongruous within the already established conventions of the detective genre. From the start of the novel, Dora plays the role of Holmes, while Paul plays the role usually assigned to Holmes's dimmer rivals such as Lestrade or Hopkins. It is as if Holmes were to suddenly retire from public life, leaving the field to his less efficient rivals.

Grant Allen's detective-heroine Lois Cayley is very much the posi-tive image of the New Woman. She took honours in maths, rowed for Girton, and, despite being a Socialist, she is 'a first-class business woman',[10] as well as being what Allen coyly describes as 'a lady of considerable personal attractions' (Allen, *MCA, Strand 15*, 515). After completing her time at Girton, Lois is left in poverty as the result of male intransigence: her stepfather gambled away her mother's fortune. Throughout the stories, she demonstrates her own financial acumen, working her way around the world in a variety of jobs. Confident and capable, she is determined not to be dependent on a man. She is independent and unconventional, but it is financial necessity, not abstract principle, which leads her to transgress the accepted social norms of 'ladylike' behaviour. However, Allen emphasizes his heroine's physical attractions: like Meade's Dagmar Oloffson she is both a New Woman and 'womanly'. She proves her 'womanliness' by falling in love with the handsome and wealthy (but rather insipid) Harold Tillington. They meet as equals: Harold (like Allen, a Merton graduate) notes that he and Lois are 'two 'Varsity men' (Allen, *MCA, Strand* 15, 429), recognizing her as his intellectual equal rather than using the dismissive term 'Girton girl'. It is as if her university education has made her an honorary man: she is part of 'a queer sort of freemasonry to which even women are now admitted' (Allen, *MCA, Strand* 15, 429). (Allen conveniently ignores the fact that, unlike Oxford men, Oxford women could not take degrees.)

Allen uses his characters' romance to expound his own theories on equality in marriage. Harold tells Lois:

'A man ought to wish the woman he loves to be a free agent, his equal in point of action, even as she is nobler and better than he in all spiritual matters. I think he ought to desire for her a life as high as she is capable of leading, with full scope for every faculty of her intellect or her emotional nature.' (Allen, *MCA, Strand*, 15, 432)

Allen cannot let his New Woman heroine be emotionally independent from men, or she might pose a threat to the future of the race. After refusing to marry Harold, Lois tells the reader:

> I dashed into my own room, locked the door behind me, flung myself wildly on the bed, and, burying my face in my hands, had a good, long, obdurate cry – exactly like any other mediaeval woman. It's all very well being modern; but my experience is that, when it comes to the man one loves – well; the Middle Ages are still horribly strong within us. (Allen, *MCA, Strand* 16, 74)

Once again, the New Woman must prove her 'womanly' credentials at every opportunity in order to be an acceptable heroine for popular fiction.

Allen's work frequently plays on the suppressed sexual and maternal instincts which he feels lie at the heart of the New Woman's personality. His detective fiction offers two mutually contradictory pictures of the New Woman. His detective-heroines are strong, independent women who use their superior physical and mental attributes to defeat male criminals. However, this positive portrait of the New Woman is undercut by repeated references to the heroines' rejection of their stereotypically 'womanly' instincts. Allen's self-styled 'mediaeval' woman with strong sexual and maternal urges becomes the *doppelganger* of the egalitarian 'modern' woman. In this Jekyll-and-Hyde scenario, suppressed reproductive urges threaten to overwhelm the conscious personality of the rational, logical New Woman, and thus undermine her claims to sexual equality. This conflict is played out on a literal level in two of Allen's earliest crime novels. *What's Bred in the Bone* and *Recalled to Life* both feature heroines who have dual personalities. To provide a satisfactory narrative closure, the solution of the crime must also involve the merging of the heroine's conflicting personalities into a single consciousness. His two later detective serials, *Miss Cayley's Adventures* and *Hilda Wade* portray this conflict in a less psychologically complex way. Both heroines fall in love but suppress their sexual and maternal urges, refusing to marry their suitors until their detective work is completed.

In *Miss Cayley's Adventures*, Allen inverts the gender politics of the traditional romance plot by giving Lois the dominant role. She rescues the hapless Harold from a mountaineering accident, then does some efficient detective work to prevent his being wrongly convicted of forgery. Lois appears in court, where she is accused of being Harold's accomplice, and her assertiveness and adventurous spirit tell against her. The all-male legal establishment is unable to accept that she has worked her way around the world by any means other than trading her sexual favours, although she explains that she has been employed as a lady's-maid, a journalist, a bicycle saleswoman and the proprietor of a typing bureau. The legal establishment seem to find it easier to believe that a 'lady' would sell her virtue than that she would earn her own living by honest means. Lois has transgressed against the behaviour expected of her gender and class just as much as if she had indeed become a courtesan. At best, the prosecutor interprets her adventures as 'rather an odd thing for an officer's daughter to do' (Allen, *MCA*, *Strand* 16, 688): at worst he concludes that she is 'an adventuress' in a context which makes it clear that he means a high-class prostitute (Allen, *MCA, Strand*, 16, 695). The scene can be seen as the trial of the 'New Woman' at the hands of the male establishment. Lois despairingly concludes that a woman 'can't justify originality to a British jury. Why, they would send you to prison at once for that alone, if they made the laws as well as dispensing them' (Allen, *MCA, Strand*, 16, 694). The jury is, of course, entirely male. At this time, women were campaigning for women to be allowed to become jurors and magistrates. A speaker at an 1890 meeting of the strongly feminist Moral Reform Union commented that:

> Every case in the *Police News*, as reported in the press, told the same story, – men making and executing the laws and women tried without one woman to represent them.[11]

The situation was made worse by the practice of clearing the court of women when sexual abuse cases were being tried. The Moral Reform Union felt that in such cases the victim should have 'one or two of her own sex in court to give her moral support' (MRU, 62). The point was evidently lost on the male-dominated machinery of the law. Allen's novel echoes the point made by such campaigners: as the Moral Reform Union put it, 'a woman was not tried by her peers – that is, she was only tried by a jury of men' (MRU, 62).

Allen followed the success of *Miss Cayley's Adventures* with *Hilda Wade*, featuring another independent, determined heroine. Hilda Wade can be seen as a toned-down version of Lois Cayley. Hilda is a 'pretty girl' who has the traditional feminine attributes of being 'gentle and lovable',[12] but her main antagonist, Professor Sebastian, sees her as being unsexed by her detective abilities, feeling that she 'stands intermediate between the sexes' because she combines 'feminine sensitivity with the 'masculine' ability to reason from facts (Allen, *HW, Strand* 17, 328). Sebastian echoes the concerns of commentators who felt that the New Woman was in danger of becoming unsexed by her distraction from marriage and maternity. The story is told in the first person by Hilda's devoted admirer, Dr Hubert Cumberledge. Hubert is a more lively figure than Harold Tillington: in the later adventures he takes an active part as Hilda's equal rather than simply being a victim to be rescued. Hilda is a nurse, which was a highly acceptable middle-class profession by this time, thanks to the work of Florence Nightingale and Mary Seacole. Socially acceptable though it was for an unmarried 'lady' to be a nurse, nineteenth-century convention still saw any career for a middle-class New Woman as a substitute for marriage. (Working-class women, of course, usually had little option: economic necessity forced them to work.) One of her friends remarks that Hilda 'didn't intend to marry, she said, so she would like to have some work to do in life. In her case, the malady took the form of nursing' (Allen, *HW, Strand*, 17, 329).

The campaign for women's rights is thus pathologized as a 'malady'. This inverts the dialogue in which social problems were seen as a sickness within society which must be cured. It is not the social problem but the campaign against it which is seen as unhealthy: feminism is seen as an illness for which marriage and maternity are the cure. Discussing New Woman fiction in *Blackwood's*, Hugh Stutfield saw the neurotic New Woman heroine as part of 'the pathological novel (which) is beyond question a symptom of the mental disease from which civilized mankind is suffering'.[13] By claiming that the New Woman's discontent was the result of mental illness rather than social injustice, the threat which she presented could be conveniently defused and the true social causes of her discontent could be ignored.

Commercial New Woman fiction offered a vehicle for feminism without being as overtly didactic as the polemic New Woman fiction written by New Woman novelists such as Sarah Grand and George Egerton. Polemic New Woman fiction sold extremely well, but it was largely preaching to the converted. Readers knew what was in these notorious novels before they bought them, and presumably would not spend money on them only to disagree with their message. Commercial New Woman fiction reached a wider and more varied audience. People who would not normally buy New Woman fiction bought detective and romantic novels which featured New Woman protagonists. These novels were not necessarily written by supporters of the women's movement: the New Woman had become a marketable novelty figure whose presence in a story increased its chance of good sales. The New Woman of popular fiction is a commercialized version of the heroine of didactic New Woman fiction. By taking her positive attributes of physical and mental health, and allying these with the romantic heroine's traditional attributes of youth and beauty, authors were able to create an attractive heroine who was thoroughly modern and topical. She was largely depoliticized in the process: her 'New Woman' activities are social (bicycling, smoking, playing tennis) rather than political, and any threat she presents is almost invariably defused by her submission to marriage in the last chapter. The unconventional, anti-romantic heroine is thus firmly integrated into the conventional romance plot. Meade's Dagmar Oloffson is a welcome exception to this general rule, possibly because Meade was writing to make a political point as well as to make money. In 1895 Hugh Stutfield said of the polemic New Woman novelist:

> With her head full of all the 'ologies and 'isms, with sex-problems and heredity, and other gleanings from the surgery and the lecture-room, there is no space left for humour, and her novels are for the most part merely pamphlets, sermons or treatises in disguise.[14]

The same could not be said of popular New Woman fiction. By marketing the New Woman for mass consumption, the writers of commercial fiction ensured her a prominent and lasting place in popular culture.

Notes

1. Beatrice Harraden, *Ships that Pass in the Night* (henceforward *SPN*) (1893; repr. London: Lawrence & Bullen, 1900), 158.
2. Hugh E. M. Stutfield, 'Tommyrotics' in *Blackwood's Edinburgh Magazine*, 157, 1895, 837.
3. John Sutherland: *Bestsellers: Popular Fiction of the 1970s* (London: Routledge & Kegan Paul, 1981), 246.
4. Grant Allen, *The Woman Who Did* (1895; repr. Oxford: Oxford University Press, 1995), 28–29.
5. *Punch*, 16 May 1894, 249, and 6 October 1894, 167.
6. Grant Allen (writing as Olive Pratt Rayner), *The Type-writer Girl* (London: C. Arthur Pearson, 1897), 17.
7. L. T. Meade, *The Cleverest Woman in England* (henceforward *CWE*) (1898; London: Ballantyne, Hanson, undated) 3.

8. McDonnell Bodkin, *Dora Myrl, the Lady Detective,* (henceforward *DM*) (London: Chatto & Windus, 1900), 1.
9. Bodkin, *The Capture of Paul Beck,* (London: Fisher Unwin, 1909) 77.
10. Grant Allen: *Miss Cayley's Adventures* (henceforward *MCA*) *Strand Magazine,* vols 15–17, 1898–9; vol. 16, 66.
11. Moral Reform Union, Annual Report 1890, 13, (henceforward MRU) quoted Sheila Jeffreys: *The Spinster and Her Enemies* (Pandora, 1985), 62.
12. Grant Allen: *Hilda Wade* (henceforward *HW*) *Strand Magazine,* vols 17–19, 1899-1900; vol. 17, 328.
13. Hugh E. M. Stutfield: 'Tommyrotics', in *Blackwood's Edinburgh Magazine,* 157, 1895, 837.
14. Hugh E. M. Stutfield: 'Tommyrotics', in *Blackwood's Edinburgh Magazine,* 157, 1895, 837.

3
Horses, Bikes and Automobiles: New Woman on the Move

Sarah Wintle

In the foreword to the 1923 edition of *The Heavenly Twins*, first published in 1893, Sarah Grand wrote:

> A man might keep a baby-linen shop if it paid – anything that paid was 'masculine' – but a woman could not drive a pair of horses for profit, however good a whip she was, without the odium of being 'unsexed'.[1]

The choice of occupations here is of course rhetorically and symbolically loaded, and not simply about economics. Driving horses, it is implied, is as absolutely masculine as anything to do with babies is absolutely feminine. Mastery of horses was from the very beginning almost always associated with power, status and masculinity and so, as the quotation suggests, might be something New Women had their eye on. However, although women and horses, as we shall see, figured significantly in pre-New-Woman nineteenth-century fiction, New Women themselves were much more likely to ride bicycles as an individualized mode of transport. Sarah Grand herself learned to ride one in the 1890s and even featured in 'A Chat with Sarah Grand – Women of Note in the Cycling World' in *The Hub* in 1896.[2] The automobile, the invention of which was almost exactly contemporary with both New Women and bicycles, was less readily available for female use; unlike the bicycle and like the horse it was fast, powerful and expensive to run and keep; it also required specialized mechanical knowledge. Nonetheless, in different ways the freedom, physical independence and sense of personal control offered literally and symbolically by all three kinds of transport was, when seized by women, a kind of trespass on traditionally masculine territory, as, among other things, the obvious anxiety about suitable female dress for all three activities bears witness. In this essay I start to explore and compare the ⟵ responses in some New-Woman and New-Woman-influenced fiction to all three modes of locomotion, a task made easier by the fact that between the 1880s and the first decade of the twentieth century one popular novelist, Mrs Edward Kennard, wrote novels in which the horse, the bicycle and even the car play a major role. But first a little literary history.

By the early nineteenth century writing about women riding horses for pleasure, if not for profit, already offered a fruitful way of registering female physical energies and of exploring the subtleties of female sexual feeling and the relation of both to social and psychological patterns of domination and subservience.[3] Fanny Price in *Mansfield Park* for example displaces her sexual jealousy of Mary Crawford onto feeling sorry for the horse that, unlike Fanny herself, Mary rides with dangerously suggestive ease. In Walter Scott's *Rob Roy* Diana Vernon leaps her horse over a five-bar gate straight into the narrator's heart; she thus originates a stock romance topic about an independent young woman whose attractive physical energy manifests itself in equestrian accomplishment. Aurora Floyd, the eponymous heroine of Mary Elizabeth Braddon's second bigamy novel of 1863, is a spirited but wilful horsewoman whose first, impulsively contracted union is in part a consequence of her passion for all things horsey. In 1856, the hunting novelist Whyte Melville wrote *Kate Coventry*, a novel devoted to a wholesome horsey young woman, a type who can also be found in the later novels of Braddon, such as *Vixen* (1879). In this novel the lovers, prevented from marrying for conventional dynastic and financial reasons, take illicit and lovingly described midnight rides together, before true love and good-hearted horsiness win the day.

There are many reasons, historical, social and material, for this female encroachment on, and transformation of, a traditionally male topic. Horses after all belonged primarily in the worlds of work, military action and ceremonial, and in the masculine sports of racing and hunting. However one consequence of romanticism was an increasing use of animal imagery in the exploration of the psychology of the instincts and emotions.[4] As riding became a more popular and socially widespread leisure pursuit, it also became more customary for women to ride for display or pleasure and even to hunt. Riding manuals written specifically for aspiring female 'amazons', a sure sign of widening middle-class approval, started to appear in the 1890s.[5] The development of the modern side-saddle with its extra pommel giving a firmer and more secure seat allowed women to achieve a much greater mastery of horsemanship than before, while retaining an elegant feminine appearance. Riding astride in breeches was mostly unacceptable well into the twentieth century, and long carried a certain ambivalent meaning.

At the very end of the nineteenth century, both the actual uses of the horse itself and its symbolic literary history encounter first the bicycle and then the automobile as rival modes of locomotion. The modern bicycle, as opposed to the fixed-wheel penny-farthing type, quickly became associated with new female freedoms. The first model with a sprocket-chain drive powering an equal-sized rear wheel was produced in 1885, the pneumatic tyre dates from 1888. This new machine was relatively cheap to buy, easy to ride and required little maintenance. Frances Willard in her little book *A Wheel within a Wheel* or 'How I learned to ride a bicycle with some reflections by the way', a sort of *fin-de-siècle Zen and the Art of Motor-cycle Maintenance*, points out that cycling may be seen as a democratized version of riding, and she knowingly demonstrates the appropriation of the metaphorical resonances of horse language:

> Already I know well enough that tens of thousands who could never afford to own, feed and stable a horse had by this bright invention enjoyed the swiftness of motion which is perhaps the most fascinating feature of material life, the charm of a wide outlook upon the natural world, and that sense of mastery which is probably the greatest attraction in horse-back riding ... she who succeeds in gaining mastery of such an animal as Gladys will gain the mastery of life.[6]

Gladys was, I am afraid, the name of her bicycle. Although Sarah Grand praised the opportunities cycling gave for physical 'refreshment', she also expressed some anxiety about the effects on the complexion, and about 'rational dress'. This she felt took years off one's age but, despite its convenience for cycling, was 'so unsightly'.[7]

The Daimler-Benz internal combustion engine dates from 1885/6 and cars were soon widely manufactured in Europe and the United States. It was not however until the Model T Ford of 1908 that motoring became in any way other than a pursuit for the rich. It was, however, the internal combustion engine, not the bicycle, which finally to replace the horse. Sarah Grand's woman driving her pair for hire would then, in order to preserve the full force of her symbolic antithesis, have to become a female truck driver. Cars were to become both economically significant and symbolically resonant, of status, class and masculinity. Gail Cunningham maintains, in her discussion of literary equine sexual symbolism, that 'cars were annexed at the outset by men as requiring mechanical expertise and carrying phallic associations, and there is nothing remotely erotic about a bicycle'.[8] However, the point here is that even if cars and bicycles are less symbolically articulate in the erotic realm than horses, they still operate as real objects with gendered social and literary meanings which have interesting similarities to and differences from the complex vocabulary of equine symbolism. All three demand a reasonable level of skill and physical self-confidence if they are to be ridden or driven, and all three bring with their mastery a promise of some kind of freedom or independence. What then did New Woman writers make of horses, bikes and automobiles?

The books of Mrs Edward Kennard – for so, as the wife of a country gentleman and JP, she called herself – are not at first sight overtly exploratory or programmatic, and she is neither well-known nor ostensibly a serious writer. She was originally, in the 1880s, a writer of popular yellow-back fiction almost entirely concerned with horses and hunting. These are romantic novels about upright, healthy, horsy girls in the tradition of Whyte Melville and the later less adventurous fictions of Braddon. However, New Woman caught up with Mrs Kennard in the early years of this century, just as she turned her novelist's attention from hoofs to wheels, so providing an exemplary case study. Her literary career thus provides an example of what one might call, after neo-liberal socio-economic theory, the trickle-down effect of New Woman thinking. Nonetheless her turning from romance and horses to bicycles and marital difficulties is not wholly surprising, given both earlier metaphoric treatments of women and horses, and the development of the topic in some New Woman writing proper.

Mrs Kennard's *A Crack County* (1889) may be compared to *Anne Mauleverer* (1899), a novel by the fully paid-up New Woman novelist Iota, or Kathleen Caffyn. The heroine of Mrs Kennard's romance of the hunting field is the wholesome daughter of a country doctor who wins the heart of the handsome and eligible Bob, not through riches and social distinction, but through her exemplary but definitely daring horsemanship, and all that it implies in the way of energy and competence. Intrepid girl riders demand both courageous young men and rather sexy horses:

> She set Kingfisher resolutely at the stile, and just touched him with her hunting crop.

Bob uttered an exclamation of alarm, which immediately changed to one of admiration, for the noble hunter, getting his legs well under him, bounded with the lightness and springiness of a fawn over the stiff unyielding timber, giving a playful grunt of satisfaction as he landed. Dot patted his swelling neck enthusiastically. He was a king among hunters.

'Oh you beauty! you are a real ripper!' she exclaimed.[9]

Bob of course turns out a 'real ripper' too: Mrs Kennard's horsy narratives are absolutely conventional, and there is no sense that Dot's obvious abilities, her 'mastery of life', in Frances Willard's words, might not be wholly satisfied by her inevitable marriage.

Iota's *Anne Mauleverer* uses its heroine's horsemanship in a rather more complex fashion. Anne, an Anglo-Irish artist living in Italy, is also a fine horsewoman. Indeed she is so expert on horseflesh that the King of Naples employs her to buy some Irish hunters for him, for she has fearlessly pointed out to him that his own stud is much too finely bred and needs a touch of coarse Irish hunter blood to give it a bit of substance. Nonetheless her horsemanship turns out to be something of a double-edged weapon, as might be expected from this rather startling female takeover of the traditionally male role of horse-dealer and stud-manager. Anne is not, though, quite like Sarah Grand's imagined 'whip', because there is no question of payment involved here. Like most horsy stories, this is a tale of upper-class landed people.

Anne's horsemanship is in the first place a manifestation of her extraordinary management abilities, and this word management deserves a brief etymological digression. Rather appropriately, it was first adopted into English from the Italian *maneggiare* by writers of Renaissance riding manuals, and indicated 'to handle with skill'; the riding arena was for a long time known as the *manège*. The word was contaminated in the seventeenth century by the French *mènager*, 'to use carefully, to husband, to spare'; compare *mènage*, meaning household. Anne is good at both aspects; she ends up not only improving the genetic management of the King of Naples' stud but overseeing the agricultural modernization of her own rundown ancestral estates. As a New Woman she is a better business manager than many men – certainly than her hopelessly laid-back brother who conforms charmingly but ineffectually to the neglectful old ways of Anglo-Irish landlords.

However, Ann literally kills her brother when she dares him to jump his horse over a large and awkward fence and ditch. She of course, like Mrs Kennard's Dot, jumps them with magnificent ease; he has a fatal fall. Her horsemanship here is both a sign of her life-affirming bodily energies and her equestrian mastery, and of how such qualities threaten the old masculine order. Unlike Mrs Kennard, Iota sees that there is a problem in matching such energies and competences with normative gender roles. Although many men court Anne, only one is fit, sexually and intellectually, to be her mate – the radically modernizing owner of the neighbouring estate, and he is already married, unhappily of course. The matching of people, even on the hunting field, is altogether a trickier business than improving a breed of horses. The characteristic New Woman interest in eugenics is here implicitly given an odd angle.

The novel is thus a story of sexual and emotional renunciation as well as of achievement in the masculine world of work. It is yet another variation on the purity idea. The story ends with its surviving major characters returning from a day with the hounds. The goddess of hunting is of course Diana 'Queen and huntress chaste and fair'. To celebrate riding is often to celebrate freedom and independence from all human social ties. But because horses also obviously enough figure sexual energies, there is a strong element of unresolved tension in Iota's tale. The novel is supposed, I think, to reduce the reader to tears at the physical waste as well as to elicit admiration of the spiritual and managerial triumph. Anne is a tragic heroine, and her *fin-de-siècle* tragedy speaks of the 'not yet' – of radical modernization not yet achieved.

Now horses of course lend themselves to such symbolic manipulations or operate as tools for thinking about bodily energies and their social repercussions and uses precisely because they themselves are charismatic living creatures with a long literary and symbolic pedigree. Bicycles and cars are intrinsically less suggestive because constructed objects in a literal as well as a literary sense. However in the 1890s they had time on their side – like New Women themselves they were heralds of a new age.

I have already quoted from Frances Willard's book on bicycling. She herself was an American temperance campaigner living in England, and she was prompted to take up bicycling in order to recover from the breakdown she suffered when her mother died. Significantly Willard starts her narrative not with her first effort to master her machine or even with her mother's death, but with her adolescence and the loss of freedom that growing up female entailed:

> I 'ran wild' until my 16th birthday when the hampering long skirts were brought, with their accompanying corset and high heels; my

hair was clubbed up with pins, and I remember writing in my journal, in the first heartbreak of a young human colt taken from its pleasant pasture, 'altogether I recognize that my occupation is gone'.[10]

Because the horse, and later the bicycle and car, are associated with ideas of physical freedom as well as accomplishment they seem to be particularly associated with certain rites of passage or times of life crisis, when for women in particular the tensions between the physical and free and the social and bound are particularly acute. In Braddon's *Vixen*, for example, the heroine feels she must give up hunting on the death of her father, and in the later desert romance E. M. Hull's *The Sheik* (1919), the heroine, an accomplished horse-woman, is literally pulled off her horse and onto her lover's. She exchanges breeches for frocks, riding for sex.[11] The relation between womanhood and physical activity, between adult female sexuality and physical freedom is thought to be problematic. Thus riding or cycling may promise physical independence and freedom, but at the cost either of regression to a kind of pre-sexual state or of difficult male–female relations. Or to put it the other way round, writing about riding, cycling and driving may be used to explore such difficulties.

Mrs Kennard herself wrote a *Guide for Lady Cyclists* in 1895 (the British Library copy was destroyed by a bomb in the war) but didn't address the topic in her fiction until 1902 when she published *The Golf Lunatic and his Cycling Wife*. This novel is not a romance, but a story about an unsatisfactory marriage narrated by the disaffected wife:

> We *are* a funny couple – funny in the sense of being totally dissimi-
> lar in thought, taste and temperament ... the theory is magnificent.
> Two brains, two wills, two temperaments completely fused. But in
> practice, the soldering of the matrimonial rivet is not so complete.[12]

Here Mrs Kennard breezily and directly tackles New Woman topics; not only unhappy marriage, but gender reversal, women at work, female friendship and so on. The narrator Cynthia Jenningham, a woman with the temperament and ambitions of a man, is married to the weak philanderer Adolphus, commonly known as Dolly; 'a nice little girl' as his wife comments; no hint, in the work of this engagingly enthusias-tic writer, can be left unelaborated. However, despite the narrator's play with ideas of gender reversal, other aspects of sexual radicalism are raised only to be refused. Cynthia reads a disapproving review of what is obviously a New Woman novel. The novelist is taken to task for suggesting that 'if a man failed his wife after matrimony in any respect, she had a perfect right to seek happiness elsewhere'. Remember what happened to Anna Karenina is the male reviewer's stern injunction, which Cynthia takes to heart.

However, her marriage really is shown as unhappy. Dolly chases hopelessly unsuitable women, and then becomes obsessed with golf. Cynthia, remembering Anna Karenina, refuses a possible affair with an attractive admirer, and takes up cycling instead:

> I often went forty or fifty miles on my wheel before returning home ... what a field of new experiences the cycle opened out to modern womanhood! It freed her from a multitude of conventional shackles [remember those 'matrimonial rivets'. SW]. She could wander at her will, go where she listed, stay where she elected; dependent on no man, no horse, no carriage, but solely on the clever bit of mechanism constructed by the ingenuity of human brains and hands. She owed them a debt of thanks, for nowadays she could fancy herself a beggar or a queen according to her proclivities. (63)

Cycling literally gets her out of the house into which marriage might be thought to have shut her, and away from the domestic social niceties and cares of motherhood. Cynthia has a small daughter of whom she takes very little notice. We may assume that servants look after the child, so that the mother may ride alone. No lady at the time would be likely to have ridden a horse out unaccompanied by at least a groom, and horses, unlike bicycles, entail grooms and stableboys. Thus, through the simple agency of the bicycle this novel celebrates female solitary and autonomous enjoyment of the open road, even gesturing towards fantasies of the tramping life more usually connected with male authors like W. H. Davies: 'To me it was an unmixed pleasure to throw off the bonds of society and travel the roads like a tramp' (63).

Her bicycle also significantly provides Cynthia with paid work and the status of expertise: she starts to write a cycling column and ends up as a regular contributor to three cycling magazines. Indeed she quickly and competently learns to repair and mend bicycles, and 'test-drives' new models as part of her journalistic endeavours. There is a surprising amount of loving detail in this woman's novel about gears and cranks, oil and spanners, grease and mud.

Two long cycling expeditions explore further how the bicycle potentially enables or even necessitates the breach of conventional gender expectations. Cynthia persuades the reluctant Dolly to go on a cycling tour of Belgium with her. She is much fitter and more competent than he is, and also does all the engineering, as it were; she can mend a puncture in a trice, oil and repair a broken chain while her husband stands hopelessly by, a parody of *fin-de-siècle* lassitude.

> I was Cynthia Jenningham, the new and peculiar woman, who chafed at the yoke of convention and considered herself born to direct; and Dolly became converted into the modern man, who does not care to do anything for himself that others can do for him, and who evades all the responsibility of life in a truly wondrous manner. (98)

Although Dolly disapproves of his wife's cycling clothes, which show too much of her gaitered legs, both halves of this odd but very English couple are shocked when they meet a Belgian lady cyclist in a 'very short full skirt – so short that it worked past her knees at every upward movement of the pedal'. After encountering this figure who seems to have stepped out of one of those French bicycling posters inspired by Toulouse-Lautrec, Dolly can no longer object to Cynthia's skirt. Indeed, shortly after this encounter, in an act of renewed marital solidarity, they are mutually disgusted at the Belgian habit of eating steak *au bleu* or at least *saignante*. Cycling may be the making of a New Woman, but its transgressiveness for the fox-hunting patriot Kennard may only go so far.

Cynthia's second cycling tour is made with Dora, a young girl who tellingly is recovering from a love affair. Cynthia expresses her delight in liberty: 'Don't you feel curiously enterprising and independent, Dora?' Who, the reader is prompted to ask, needs husband or lovers? These women's independence is manifested not only in the genuinely impressive physical achievement of cycling from one end of England to the other, but in the exciting social freedoms that come with it. The two upper-class women stay at humble pubs and at CTC (Cycling Touring Club) hotels. Often there are no baths, and they eat a high tea of ham and eggs instead of the formal dinners they are used to. 'After that', as Cynthia points out in words reminiscent of Miss Willard,

> who will dare affirm that women can't get on together, and are helpless without a man to look after them ... Oh little wheel, I am grateful to you. You are a deliverer of the female sex. (210–11)

Finally, however, this is a popular novel, and its rather touchingly suggestive radicalism is in the end limited by formulaic narrative demands. After her adventure Cynthia returns home, not only refreshed, but also 'with renewed powers of resignation to sink back into the old, dull, monotonous, *golfy* groove'. She is now prepared for middle age, a time not of 'passion but duty and right'. There is little sense of the 'not yet' here.

Mrs Kennard herself did not resign herself to bicycles, but pushed on into the technological future. In the same year she published another novel *The Motor Maniac*. As the approving reviewers remarked of her earlier hunting novels, she had 'lots of go', and was herself a pioneering female motorist, driving in 1900 a 40 hp Napier car, a De Dion voiturette, and a 15 hp Darracq; she also rode a motor tricycle.[13] Another early motoring novel, by a husband and wife couple Charles and Alice Williamson, *The Lightning Conductor: the Strange Adventures of a Motor Car* was also published in 1902, which may be compared with Mrs Kennard's work. The Williamsons' novel is at bottom a conventional romance involving a lovesick gentleman disguising himself as a chauffeur and getting employed to drive the girl he has fallen for from England right down to Sicily. Endless travelogue and some conventional intrigue are only enlivened by description of the heroine and her flightly rival learning to drive. Of course the heroine is a natural and her rival a disaster, but the thematic focus is on their attractiveness and worthiness to make a good marriage, rather than on their independence.

In contrast Mrs Jenks, the heroine of *The Motor Maniac*, is already married, like Cynthia Jenningham, to an unsuitably lazy golfing husband, and Mrs Kennard again proclaims her New Woman heritage:

> Like the heroine of Olive Schreiner's celebrated 'Story of an African Farm' she could not conceive of a mental attitude which did not aspire to probe into everything. She too had an intense desire to try and experience.[14]

As a prosperous New Woman then Mrs Jenks wants every modern thing, so she resolves to give up her 'Victoria and pair', and goes out to buy copies of *Autocar* and the *Motor-Car Journal*. After several encounters with shifty car-dealers, each offering a valuable lesson in the tricky ways of the world outside the drawing-room, and some driving lessons with an engaging character who lives alarmingly far from Kensington in the Mile End Road, she acquires 'a blue engineers' jacket', a rather unreliable second-hand Daimler-Benz, and a cheerfully disrespectful young man called Snooks to look after it. One of the anxieties expressed in the books on riding for women written in the 1890s was precisely the unavoidably attentive relationship between female rider and the necessary male escorts, whether they be inappropriately forward young gentlemen or uncomfortably closely involved grooms. Mounting and dismounting were moments of considerable risk, given most women's need for a leg-up. Mrs Jenks and Snooks, however, become intimate accomplices not only when they mend the inevitable punctures together, but when Mrs Jenks decides to buy a motor tricycle, first a second-hand one and then a 23/4 hp De Dion. This is obviously something special: Mrs Kennard herself of course drove a De Dion voiturette.

The man who sells her first machine is disapproving: 'they may be well enough for men, but they are not suited for ladies.' She finds the machine heavy and difficult, and has problems with what to wear, even a divided skirt being faintly unsatisfactory. Snooks finds the machine easier to handle and although he admits 'she is a born engineer' – there is more really serious oil and grease in this book than in *The Golf Lunatic and His Cycling Wife* – cruelly reminds her she 'is only a woman'.

> This was scant consolation for Mrs Jenks, although kindly meant. She reflected on the cruel fortune which had ordained she should belong to the despised and inferior sex, whilst possessing all the energy and ambition of the stronger vessel. Talk of nature indeed! She made the most ghastly mistakes. (177)

Nonetheless working on her old tricycle with Snooks's help and encouragement, she learns much about cleaning and grinding valves. There is a curious episode where the two of them are 'discovered' by Mr Jenks in a scene which displays a confused mix of an artlessly displaced intimacy with almost infantile regression, as well as a more overt undoing of categories of gender and class:

> Mrs Jenks surprised the fellow-workers late in the afternoon, squatted side-by-side on the square of cocoanut matting, with a bowl of dirty petrol between them, engaged in the congenial task of washing the balls of the main axle bearing. Mrs Jenks was arrayed in an engineer's jacket similar to that of her companion. She wore a

short skirt reaching to her ankles, covered by a long blue apron, and a cap of the same hue, adorned by sundry oil-stains. Mr Jenks could not help laughing at his wife's total disregard for appearances: 'Why' he exclaimed jocularly. 'What have we here? A female mechanic? Upon my word, Janet, this is scarcely a lady's job.'
    Perhaps he was right, but then there was no classifying Mrs Jenks as an ordinary lady of the accepted type. She was either a lunatic or a pioneer, according to the way people looked at things. (190)

It is after this that she buys her De Dion tricycle and adventurously drives it to her Bedfordshire home from London on her own. To her husband's disgust clothes are still a problem:

She was clad in an old covert coat, a sailor hat while the redoubtable divided skirt was pinned closely round either leg with a large safety-pin, so that the engine should obtain as much air as possible ...
    'You have made a fool of yourself Janet. Upon my soul, in the distance I could hardly tell if you were a man or a woman.' (242)

Later, she and Snooks get a 'whippet trailer' for the machine so that so they can have fun riding it together. Mrs Jenks' exciting adventures are summed up by the author in a sentence that makes her sound like a juvenile delinquent, or a female version of Toad in *The Wind in the Willows*:

Mrs Jenks had gone to London, bought her tricycle, ridden it home, smashed it up, been summoned for furious driving [she has frightened a horse in the Daimler-Benz] and paid her fine – all within a fortnight. (239)

Paying her own fine for frightening a horse in her local high street is the nearest she comes to the independence displayed by Cynthia Jenningham in finding some economic profit in her passion for bicycles. There is something both exhilaratingly anarchic and curiously infantile about this book, as if Mrs Kennard did not quite know what to do with her spirited heroine's pioneering enthusiasm for these new machines. Mrs Jenks uses her mania for motoring rather less constructively than Cynthia Jenningham does her bicycle. The last chapters give some clue as to why this might be the case.
    The novel ends with Mr Jenks, finally infected with his wife's motoring bug, buying a powerful Napier. Snooks, oil, axle bearings and blue

engineer's jackets are forgotten as the couple get involved in organized motoring. First there is an 'automobile gymkhana' at the Crystal Palace when the ladies race is the last item in a very long programme. Then Mr Jenks, at the wheel of his Napier, wins an important durability trial, so proving to the author's patriotic satisfaction the superiority of British cars. The reader however may feel that he also re-appropriates the machines for masculinity, and money as well as nation. The automobile had rather less to offer 'the woman question', it would seem, than did in their different ways either the horse or the bicycle.

Notes

1. Quoted by Gillian Kersley, *Darling Madame* (London: Virago, 1983), 67.
2. Ibid., 80.
3. See Gail Cunningham, 'Seizing the Reins: Women Girls and Horses' in Sarah Sceats and Gail Cunningham, eds, *Image and Power: Women in Fiction in the Twentieth Century* (Harlow: Longman, 1996).
4. See Alex Potts, 'Natural Order and the Call of the Wild: the Politics of Animal Painting', *Oxford Art Journal*, 13, 1990, 13–33.
5. See Anne Grimshaw, *The Horse: a Bibliography of British Books 1851–1976* (London: Library Association, 1982), 72–4.
6. Francis Willard, *A Wheel within a Wheel* (London: Hutchinson, 1895), 11.
7. *Darling Madame*, 88.
8. Gail Cunningham, *op. cit.*, 69.
9. Mrs Edward Kennard, *A Crack County* (London: F. V. White, 1889), 220.
10. Willard, *op. cit.*, 10.
11. See Sarah Wintle, 'The Sheikh: What can be made of a Daydream', *Women: a Cultural Review* 7, 1996.
12. Mrs Edward Kennard, *The Golf Lunatic and his Cycling Wife* (London: Hutchinson, 1902), 1.
13. See John Sutherland *The Longman Companion to Victorian Fiction* (London: Longman, 1988), 348–9.
14. Mrs Edward Kennard, *The Motor Maniac* (London: Hutchinson, 1902) 9.

4
Ibsen, the New Woman and the Actress

Sally Ledger

Ibsen's knowledge of humanity is nowhere more obvious than in his portrayal of women. He amazes me by his painful introspection; he seems to know them better than they know themselves.[1]

More than any other modern writer he has proved himself a prophet and an apostle of the cause of woman; no other modern writer has shown more sympathetic comprehension of her nature and its latent powers.[2]

It would be an exaggeration – but only a small one – to claim that Ibsen invented the 'New Woman' in England. From the moment that his plays began to be translated and performed in Western Europe in the late nineteenth and early twentieth century, he began to receive remarkable accolades for his dramatic representation of women and womanhood. Numerous feminists of the time acknowledged a debt to the Norwegian's radical intervention in the gender debates of the *fin de siècle*; his impact on Victorian cultural modernity in the 1880s and 1890s was immense. On 7 June 1889, the first unbowdlerized production of *A Doll's House* was performed at London's Novelty Theatre. It was attended by a dazzling array of bohemians and intellectuals, including George Bernard Shaw, who was subsequently to become one of the Norwegian's most significant publicists in England. Eleanor Marx, one of the first to translate Ibsen's plays into English, and other metropolitan feminists and novelists such as Olive Schreiner, Edith Lees Ellis and Emma Frances Brooke, were also there. This was not the usual London theatre audience that would have attended the mainstream productions of comedies, romances and melodramas throughout the Victorian period. Writing thirty years after the London premier of *A Doll's House*, the writer Edith Lees Ellis wrote how:

> A few of us collected outside the theatre breathless with excitement. Olive Schreiner was there and Dolly Radford the poetess ... Emma Brooke ... and Eleanor Marx. We were restive and almost savage in our arguments. What did it mean? ... Was it life or death for women? ... Was it joy or sorrow for men? That a woman should demand her own emancipation and leave her husband and children in order to get it, savoured less of sacrifice than sorcery.[3]

Eleanor Marx, who was to become one of London's leading 'Ibsenites', had written to her friend Havelock Ellis in 1885: 'I feel I must do something to make people understand our Ibsen a little more than they do.'[4] Accordingly, Marx sent out invitations to a 'few people worth reading *Nora* to', and on 15 January 1886, in their flat in Great Russell Street, Marx and her common-law husband, Edward Aveling, hosted a reading of *A Doll's House* in the reliable Henrietta Frances Lord translation. George Bernard Shaw took the role of the blackmailing bank clerk Krogstad, and William Morris's daughter May played the long-suffering Christine Linde; Eleanor Marx took the lead with Nora Helmer, whilst Edward Aveling played the chauvinistic and hypocritical husband, Torvald Helmer. This private performance of *A Doll's House* proved to be an auspicious occasion for what emerged in the 1880s and 1890s as 'Ibsenism', a political and cultural formation consisting of Marxists, socialists, Fabians and feminists, who jointly hailed Ibsen as spokesman for their various causes. Eleanor Marx regarded Ibsen as a herald of change, both recording and contributing to what she hoped would be a catastrophic implosion of the bourgeois social fabric. For Marx, Nora's domestic oppression was analogous to the exploitation of labour. In her 1886 tract, *The Woman Question* (co-authored with Edward Aveling), she had argued that 'women are the creatures of an organized tyranny of labour, as the workers are the creatures of an organized tyranny of idlers'.[5] Ibsen's status as a radical icon endured well into the twentieth century, with a writer for the *Bookman* in 1913 acclaiming Nora Helmer as an early New Woman – '[a] woman "new" enough to do the *Freewoman* criticisms of H. G. Wells's latest novels!'[6]

Not everyone responded to Ibsen's work so enthusiastically, though. The same London premier of *A Doll's House* which so enthused the English capital's early socialists and feminists outraged more conservative commentators. Clement Scott, the Theatre Critic for the reactionary *Daily Telegraph*, signalled his future role as Ibsen's bitterest critical enemy in England when he reviewed the Novelty Theatre's first night production of *A Doll's House*. Scott was outraged by Nora Helmer's desertion of her children, reflecting on this 'unnatural ... creature' that: 'A cat or dog would tear any one who separated it from its offspring, but the socialistic Nora, the apostle of the new creed of humanity, leaves her children almost without a pang. She has determined to leave her home. ... It is all self, self, self! This is the ideal woman of the new creed.'[7] The 'new creed' was 'Ibsenism', and Ibsenism sounded the death knell for those 'Victorian Values' which had been so pervasive in Britain throughout the second half of the nineteenth century, values which had ensconced 'woman' firmly in the domestic sphere.

Ibsen's challenging and subversive female character roles were, then, immensely influential in the formation of the identity of the New Woman in 1890s London. The extent of the Norwegian's personal sympathies for late-nineteenth-century feminism is, though, somewhat ambivalent. Whilst in the notes he made for *A Doll's House*, for example, Ibsen reflected that 'A woman cannot be herself in contemporary society, it is an exclusively male society with laws drafted by men, and with counsel and judges who judge feminine conduct from a male point of view',[8] in a speech he made at a banquet given in his honour by the Norwegian Women's Rights League on 26 May 1898 he notoriously disavowed the apparent feminism of his dramas:

> I am not a member of the Women's Rights League. Whatever I have written has been without any conscious thought of making propaganda. I have been more poet and less social philosopher than people generally seem inclined to believe. I thank you for the toast, but must disclaim the honour of having consciously worked for the women's rights movement. I am not even quite clear as to just what this women's rights movement really is. To me it has seemed a problem of humanity in general.

The 'problem of humanity is general' to which Ibsen refers is his preoccupation with the obstacles put in the way of individual liberty and freedom by bourgeois society in the late nineteenth century. It was his commitment to individual freedom which appealed to nineteenth-century liberal feminism in Scandinavia and Western Europe, for it was on this that the Women's Movement based its claims for women's independence. So that although Ibsen tended to believe in a relatively abstract concept of the freedom of the individual, his dramatic quest for such freedom happened to coincide with the demands of a radical counter-culture in late-Victorian Britain as well as comparable radical movements in Norway and Sweden.

Ibsen does appear to have a number of feminist credentials in biographical terms. In 1884 he supported a petition in favour of separate property rights for married women, and was on confidential terms with Camilla Collett, Norway's best-known feminist in the nineteenth century. He and Collett had intensively debated marriage and women's place in society in the 1870s, and he acknowledged without reserve the considerable influence she had on his writing.[9] Ibsen chose as his lifelong partner Suzannah Thoresen, who, widely read in literature and drama and with 'advanced' social views, was a distinctly 'modern' woman: what we would now call a feminist. She married Ibsen in 1858.[10] Ibsen also sympathetically represents distinctly 'emancipated' women in his plays: Lona Hessel in *The Pillars of Society*, Petra Stockmann in *An Enemy of the People*, and Hilde Wangel in *The Master Builder*, for example. Both Lona Hessel and Hilde Wangel dress in a decidedly unladylike fashion, with Hessel cutting her hair short and wearing men's boots, and Wangel marching on stage with her skirt hitched up and carrying a rucksack. Such 'masculine' attire would have struck a chord with the feminist rational dress campaign in late-Victorian Britain, which rejected the physically confining clothes deemed suitable for 'respectable' women. A number of Ibsen's women are well-educated, too (Rebecca West, in *Rosmersholm*, and Petra Stockmann, for example), or at least have a strong desire to be educated (Nora Helmer in *A Doll's House* and Bolette Wangel in *The Lady From the Sea*). One of the major projects of the nineteenth-century women's movement was to improve educational opportunity for women, and Ibsen clearly demonstrates sympathy for women's educational ambition in his plays.

It would be wrong, though, to try to claim Ibsen for a polemical canon of propagandist feminist literature, for his plays characteristically diagnose women's ills rather than propose cures, and there are few feminist victories in his drama. The interest of his plays in relation to nineteenth-century womanhood is their painful dissection of the constrictive nature of women's experience in contemporary society, and the psychological and emotional damage such experience has on them. Arguably the most interesting roles for female actresses, and the most searching interrogations of what it was like to be a woman in the bourgeois backwaters of nineteenth-century Norway, are to be found in plays where women are defeated, despairing or resigned to the disappointments and imperfections of a nineteenth-century woman's life. In this respect Ibsen's late-nineteenth-century articulation of the 'woman question' strikes a chord with the proliferating New Woman fiction of the 1880s and 1890s, which rarely provided reassuring denouements for readers.[11]

Ibsen's interest in individual liberty and freedom, which guaranteed his appeal to Victorian feminism, also affiliates him with political liberalism, and the focus of his plays is very much on middle-class lives. The class-specific nature of Ibsen's interest in 'freedom' was, again, something his work had in common with British New Woman fiction, the heroines of which are almost invariably of the middle and upper classes. This does not mean, though, that the Norwegian's plays lack an analysis of the economic basis of the bourgeois domesticity he so savagely satirizes. Nowhere is his attack on the bourgeois social economy more powerfully displayed than in his dramatic account of the cash-nexus upon which late-nineteenth-century bourgeois marriage is built. In the dramatic final Act of *A Doll's House*, Nora Helmer bitterly characterizes herself as an object of exchange between her father and her husband,[12] and Ellida Wangel, in *The Lady From the Sea*, regards her marriage contract in much the same light. As she and her husband, Dr Wangel, contemplate their now sexless marriage, she reflects bitterly that when Wangel had proposed to her:

'... I – I stood there, helpless, so completely alone. So when you came and offered to – support me for life, I – agreed. ... But I shouldn't have accepted. I shouldn't have sold myself, not at any price. ... I didn't come to your home of my own free will'.[13]

In a comparable way, Hedda Gabler, at twenty-nine, is driven by her own complicity with bourgeois social conventions to marry the well-meaning but idiotic George Tesman, to whom she is brutally open about the economic basis of her choice of marriage partner: 'You agreed that we should enter society. And keep open house. That was the bargain.' It is when she realizes that they will not be able to afford 'to have a liveried footman' nor 'the bay mare you promised me' that Hedda begins to despair of her marriage.[14] In *Little Eyolf* the situation is reversed. Alfred Allmers, we learn, married his wife Rita mainly for her wealth – for 'your "gold and your green forests"' as he so delicately puts it.[15] In his desire to take care of his half-sister, Asta (to whom, it later transpires, he is unrelated), Allmers is willing to sell himself into a marriage with a woman he fears. Allmers's fear of Rita is explicit:

> *Allmers*: My first feeling for you was not love, Rita.
> *Rita*: What was it, then?
> *Allmers*: Fear.
>
> (*Eyolf*, Act Two, p. 267)

It is Rita's passionate sexuality that frightens Allmers, and it is interesting that Ibsen's most openly sexual and sensuous female protagonist is one who can afford to marry for love rather than for the accoutrements of bourgeois domesticity. Rita's sexuality is pronounced. Her husband hesitantly acknowledges this in his recognition of the particular quality of her beauty – 'You were so – so consumingly beautiful, Rita' (*Eyolf*, Act Two, p. 267), and she herself makes no secret of her sexual needs throughout the play:

> *Rita*: ... I only want you! Nothing else, in the whole world! (throws herself again around his neck) I want you, you, you!
> *Allmers*: Let me go! You're strangling me!
>
> (*Eyolf*, Act One, p. 24)

Ibsen's dramatic expression of female sexuality goes far beyond what most writers of the period would have dared to represent. Although in the Decadent literature of the period women are frequently figured as *femmes fatales* or sexual vamps, such representations only offer negative accounts of women's sexuality. Women's sexual desire in Ibsen's plays is treated with far more insight than is the case in most other textual productions of the period.[16] Ellida Wangel's sexuality, in *The Lady From the Sea*, is expressed symbolically through the myth of the mermaid who, now married to the land, pines away, longing for the sea. The sea in the play is associated with freedom and sexuality, a sexuality with a dangerous edge to it given its association with the murderous sailor who tries to lure Ellida away from her marriage to Dr Wangel. Ellida describes the 'Stranger' (the sailor) as 'demonic', as 'something that appals – and attracts' (*The Lady*, Act Four, p. 189), and his hold over her is clearly sexual.

An early reviewer scoffingly described Ellida's attraction to the Stranger as a symptom of her crazily disordered mind: 'We have the crazy woman all over again, only crazier than ever'.[17] Women's sexuality has – when recognized at all – often been regarded in Western cultures as a symptom of madness or, to used Freud's clinical terminology, hysteria. Hedda Gabler's 'crazy' preoccupation with her dead father's pistols – she twice threatens sexually predatory men with them, lends one to a spurned lover, urging him to commit suicide, and finally shoots herself in the head – dramatically represents both her own frustrated sexuality, stifled as it is in a conventional marriage to a man with the sex-appeal of an overweight puppy-dog, and a desire to escape her femininity altogether; the Freudian symbolism of the pistols too obvious to require commentary. Hedda's sexuality is complex. Described in the stage directions as having 'steel-grey' eyes 'with an expression of cold, calm serenity' (*Hedda Gabler*, Act One, p. 252), she is shown clearly to be repressing her real feelings for most of the play's length, and this greatly increases the dramatic tension. We learn that as a young woman she used to wring from Loevborg details of his erotic, licentious life, because as a young girl she wanted 'to be allowed a glimpse into a forbidden world of whose existence she is supposed to be ignorant' (*Hedda Gabler*, Act Two, p. 292). And yet, we are informed, as soon as Loevborg proposed a sexual relationship with her, on the night of these erotic revelations, she reacted violently against him, threatening him with her father's pistol, refusing her lover's advances on the basis that 'I was afraid. Of the scandal' (*Hedda Gabler*, Act Two, p. 292). Hedda, finally, is a victim of her own conventionality, preferring to die than openly to flout social codes. But her denial of her sexuality leads to violence and trauma. The most telling outbreaks of violence are triggered by any reference to the pregnancy which Hedda denies, even to herself, for much of the play's length. The well-meaning maiden Aunt Juliana, who wants nothing better than a nest of babies to attend to, fails to spot the great irritation she produces in Hedda every time she refers to a possible pregnancy, and when George Tesman himself ponders the possibility – 'Hasn't she filled out?' as he oafishly puts it to Judge Brack – Hedda tersely silences him: 'Oh, do stop it' (*Hedda Gabler*, Act One, p. 267). With Judge Brack she is more explicit:

> *Brack*: ... suppose you were to find yourself faced with what people call – to use the conventional phrase – the most solemn of human responsibilities? (Smiles) A new responsibility, little Mrs Hedda.
> *Hedda (angrily)*: Be quiet! Nothing like that's going to happen. ... I've no leanings in that direction, Judge. I don't want any – responsibilities.
> (*Hedda Gabler*, Act Two, p. 282)

It is his dramatic presentation of women's complex and often tormented negotiation of motherhood that singles out Ibsen as one of the greatest delineators of women's lives in the late nineteenth century. Ibsen's mothers either abandon their children (Nora Helmer), farm them out for others to look after (Mrs Alving), wish them dead (Rita Allmers) or kill them pre-natally through an act of suicide (Hedda Gabler). Such unhappy experiences of motherhood had loud echoes in British novels of the period, with New Womanish heroines such as Sue Bridehead (in Hardy's *Jude the Obscure*, 1895), Evadne Frayling (in Sarah Grand's *The Heavenly Twins*, 1893), Lyndall (in Olive Schreiner's *The Story of an African Farm*, 1883), Hadria Fullerton (in Mona Caird's *The Daughters of Danaus*, 1894) and Herminia Barton (in Grant Allen's *The Woman Who Did*, 1895) all experiencing motherhood as a fraught and finally unrewarding phase of their lives. In Ibsen's preliminary notes for *Hedda Gabler* he wrote of women that 'They aren't all created to be mothers',[18] a non-judgemental insight that cut right across contemporary expectations of middle-class women in particular. And Ibsen's plays are littered with illegitimate children, the unwelcome by-products of illicit sexual relationships: Regina in *Ghosts*, Gina's daughter Hedvig in *The Wild Duck*, and Asta Allmers in *Little Eyolf*. There is also large-scale infant mortality: Ellida's dead baby in *The Lady From the Sea*, the sacrificial suicide of Hedvig in *The Wild Duck*, the baby Hedda Gabler takes with her into oblivion, and the Solnesses' dead infant twins in *The Master Builder*. Motherhood, for the nineteenth-century bourgeoisie, was meant to be the acme of a woman's experience; in Ibsen's plays it is the defining experience of women's lives, but rarely fulfilling.

Hedda Gabler's horror of maternity – and of the domestic paraphernalia that would go with it in the bourgeois fjordlands – plays a complex role in her violent death. Rita Allmers's resentment of a maternal role is just as pronounced in *Little Eyolf*. That the guilt-inducing presence of their crippled child has been a major factor in her husband's sexual paralysis quickly becomes clear. Equally, Rita's sexual needs are given full dramatic expression: her inability emotionally to fulfil herself through maternity distinguishes her sharply from traditional models of femininity in the nineteenth century, when motherhood was regarded as the emotional goal of all women, their sexuality awakened only in the interests of procreation. By contrast, Rita finds Little Eyolf's disruptive presence in their marital relationship a 'hateful' thing:

Allmers: You call our child hateful?
Rita (violently): I do! For what he has done to us! ... this child is a living wall between us. ... I wish to God I had never borne him.

Allmers: Sometimes you almost frighten me, Rita.

...

Rita: ... I can't be just a mother. ... I won't, I tell you – I can't. I want to be everything to you. To you, Alfred.

Allmers: But you are, Rita. Through our child –

(*Eyolf*, Act One, pp. 245-6)

Many literary texts in the late nineteenth century began to explore the burdens rather than the joys of motherhood, and in *Little Eyolf* the staring eyes of the dead child, drowned in the fjord, return to haunt Rita Allmers, wracked as she is by guilt at her failure to love him:

Rita: They say he lay on his back. With his eyes wide open.

Allmers: With his eyes open? And quite still?

Rita: Yes, quite still. ... Day and night I shall see him lying there.

Allmers: With his eyes wide open.

(*Eyolf*, Act Two, p. 261)

Rita comes to regard Eyolf's death as retribution for the love that she was unable to give him.

Ellida Wangel's response to motherhood in *The Lady From the Sea* anticipates, but is more ambivalent than, Rita Allmers's tragic negotiation of the maternal role. Early in the play we learn that she and Wangel had a child who died in infancy, and that it was during her pregnancy that Ellida withdrew from a sexual relationship with her husband. Ellida also confides in Wangel that the dead child's eyes seemed to change colour whenever storms blew up in the fjord, and that – although clearly fathered by Wangel – he had the eyes of the Stranger, the sailor to whom Ellida had once promised herself. Ellida's psychological disorder dates from her pregnancy, and it gradually emerges that the pregnancy and the subsequent death of her child have become linked in her mind to the infidelity she has shown towards the sailor, the man who first claimed her as his own. The child was not his, but should have been. In this play as in *Little Eyolf* maternity becomes associated with sexual guilt. In modern terms Ellida might be diagnosed as suffering from postnatal depression, a depression compounded by her unacknowledged grief (Wangel cannot even remember how old the infant was when it died).

The loss of her child is exacerbated by the rejection Ellida feels she suffers at the hands of her stepdaughters, Bolette and Hilde Wangel. Ellida feels that she lacks a role in the Wangel family. Deprived of her own child, she has nothing left but the erotic attraction to the Stranger, who wants her to be his alone:

> *Ellida*: Don't you see? In this house I have nothing to keep me. I have no roots here, Wangel. The children are not mine. They don't love me. ... I have been – outside – outside everything. From the first day I came here.
>
> (The Lady, Act Five, pp. 194–5)

Interestingly in this regard, we never actually see Ellida *inside*, in the domestic sphere, throughout the whole play, which is mostly set in the garden, on the edge of domestic space, from which Ellida looks out longingly to the fjords, to the sea and to freedom. Wangel's initial response as doctor and husband to Ellida's nervous depression is to protect and incarcerate her in much the same way that the doctor-husband does in Charlotte Perkins Gilman's short story, *The Yellow Wallpaper*, another 'New-Womanish' text from the *fin de siècle*, published four years after *The Lady From the Sea*. But unlike the husband in Gilman's tale, Wangel does not insist on the notorious 'rest cure' for his wife, but instead gives her freedom; the freedom to choose where she wants to live and with whom. That she freely decides to stay with him is anticipated in the play by Bolette's revelation that Hilde, the younger of the two girls, needs a mother:

> *Ellida (half aloud to Bolette)*: What's the matter with Hilde? She looks quite upset.
> *Bolette*: Haven't you noticed what Hilde has been yearning for day after day?
> *Ellida*: Yearning for?
> *Bolette*: Ever since you entered this house.
> *Ellida*: No, no. What!
> *Bolette*: One single loving word from you.
> *Ellida*: Ah! Could there be a place for me in this house?
> *(She clasps her hand to her head and stares ahead of her, motionless, as though torn by conflicting thoughts and emotions)*.
>
> (The Lady, Act Four, p. 192)

Both Ellida, at the end of this play, and Rita, at the end of *Little Eyolf*, take on the role of foster parent to children to whom biologically they are unrelated. It is only as foster parents that mothers are shown to have any chance of maternal fulfilment in Ibsen's plays. It is as if only when there is no biological or cultural coercion that 'motherhood' can bring emotional satisfaction to women. Aunt Juliana performs a comparable role in relation to George Tesman, in *Hedda Gabler*, as does Ella Rentheim in relation to Erhart Borkman in *John Gabriel Borkman*. And arguably Dr Stockmann, in *An Enemy of the People*, altruistically 'fosters' the street urchins whom he hopes to transform into a revolutionary force. A socialized view of parenting, divorced from the usual confines of the bourgeois nuclear family, seems to be more firmly endorsed in Ibsen's plays than traditional parental roles.

For Ellida Wangel and Rita Allmers the fostering of others' children is an arguably weak alternative to the passionate sexual fulfilment that both women have desired and been denied. Whilst Ellida chooses this course of action of her 'own free will' (and it is for this reason that *The Lady From the Sea* is Ibsen's most optimistic play as far as the marriage relation is concerned), Rita's adoption of the village boys is a desperate act of expiation, an attempt to 'placate the eyes that stare at me', the accusing eyes of her dead child (*Eyolf*, Act Three, p. 285). For both women, motherhood has brought more in the way of sorrow than of joy. Hedda Gabler's plight is much worse. For her, maternity becomes implicated with a shabby, sexually dishonest life with a husband she despises. So grotesque a prospect does it become that she chooses to end her life rather than play the role of wife and mother to which she feels herself desperately unfitted.

The dramatically central and emotionally demanding roles for women in Ibsen's plays made a significant impact on the career of the actress in late-nineteenth-century London. Elizabeth Robins, the great *fin-de-siècle* American actress, remarked that 'no dramatist has ever meant so much to the women of the stage as Henrik Ibsen',[19] and she and other radically inclined actresses of the 1890s memorably recreated his female character roles. Robins's role in promoting an Ibsenite feminism in London provides us with concrete evidence of the extent to which the British New Woman was indebted to her American counterpart.[20] Robins was to become a significant figure in the political campaigns for women's suffrage, and from the moment that she arrived in Britain in 1888 she presented herself as belonging to an exceptional, 'new' order of womanhood. She had already completed 300 roles with the Boston Museum and other US tour companies, and her husband – also an actor – had committed suicide in a fit of anger when Robins refused to give up acting to be a full-time wife.[21] The actress was, herself, a species of New Woman. Making inroads into the masculine public sphere of the city and breaking out of the domestic and suburban confines of ideal Victorian womanhood, nineteenth-century actresses tended to be isolated from 'respectable' society. Nonetheless, 'first-wave' feminism in the second half of the century initiated women's gradual emancipation from exclusively domestic roles, and the women's movement almost certainly played an indirect role in the increase in the number of actresses in England and Wales from 891 in 1861 to 3696 in 1891.[22] The most ambitious of this growing army of actresses wanted more than the decorative roles offered by London's famous actor managers, such as Henry Irving and Beerbohm Tree, to whom feminine beauty was deemed more important than acting ability.

The first uncut performance of *A Doll's House* in London in 1889 was co-produced (with her husband) by Janet Achurch, who took the lead as Nora Helmer. Like Elizabeth Robins, Achurch was to make a name for herself as a great player of Ibsen's female roles. Robins's first Ibsen part was in *The Pillars of Society* where she played Martha Bernick. Initially she was disturbed by Ibsen's plays: on first reading *Ghosts* she 'turned from [it] with horror'. But she later radically adjusted her view, and it was in *The Pillars of Society* that she first discerned that the Norwegian was making available to actresses 'a new kind of play', one with real women in it.[23] Ibsen's theatre increasingly became associated with women, and this was one reason why Max Nordau amongst others diagnosed the Norwegian's 'feminization' of the drama as a neurotic, 'degenerative' symptom of a decaying society. Ibsen's female audiences he feared as a bunch of degenerate, crazy women, applauding 'their own portrait'.[24]

The fact was that at the *fin de siècle* a growing number of women produced plays either written by women or, like Ibsen's drama, centrally concerned with women. Ibsen's plays were increasingly produced, in *fin-de-siècle* London, by women in matinee performances, with mainly women in the audience.[25] Elizabeth Robins and another North American actress working in London, Marion Lea, having sought in vain for a theatre manager who would put on *The Lady From the Sea*, decided to stage *Hedda Gabler* themselves, at Robins's own expense. Robins considerably rewrote the English translation of the play for their production, and experienced the mounting of the play, which was finally put on at the Vaudeville in April 1881, as 'a very inspiring kind of freedom'.[26] The production was a great success with London's bohemian intelligentsia, with Eleanor Marx writing glowingly of Robins's performance in the title role of *Hedda Gabler* as 'simply magnificent'.[27] Encouraged by the success of this production. Robins went on to organize a production of *The Master Builder* at the Trafalgar Square Theatre in 1893, being the first to create the role of the feisty Hilde Wangel in English.

The success of Elizabeth Robins's productions of Ibsen's women-centred plays did not enhance her career in the fashionable West End theatres, which remained dominated by the male-centred culture of the actor-managers. It remained almost impossible to persuade these men to stage plays with strong roles for women. Eventually, Robins tired of the attempt to transform London's theatre land, and increasingly turned to the writing of fiction as a more amenable and fulfilling medium for feminist artistic endeavour. As for the other New Women – actual and fictional – of *fin-de-siècle* London, there was no triumphant denouement to Elizabeth Robins's attempts to challenge a male-centred metropolitan culture. But the plays of Henrik Ibsen, having been a potent vehicle for feminist endeavour in London's theatreland, triumphantly survived the initial moral censorship they provoked. And his drama still offers, in the twenty-first century, a powerful critique of the 'Doll's House' prison in which so many middle-class Victorian women were confined.

Notes

1. James Joyce, 'Ibsen's New Drama', *Fortnightly Review* n. s., 67 (1 April 1900), 575–90. Quoted in Michael Egan, *Ibsen: the Critical Heritage* (London: Routledge & Kegan Paul, 1972), 388.
2. Louie Bennett, 'Ibsen as a Pioneer of the Woman Movement', *Westminster Review* 173 (1910), 278–85, 278. Other feminist accounts of Ibsen's plays include Inga-Stina Ewbank, 'Ibsen and the Language of Women', in Mary Jacobus (ed.): *Women Writing and Writing About Women*. (London: Croom Helm, 1979), 114–32; Gail Finney, 'Ibsen and Feminism', in James McFarlane (ed.), *Cambridge Companion to Ibsen* (Cambridge: Cambridge University Press, 1994); Joan Templeton, 'The Doll's House Backlash: Criticism, Feminism, and Ibsen', *PMLA* (Publications of the Modern Language Association of America) 104, 1 (1989), 28–40; and A. Velissarious, 'Mental Illness and the Problem of Female Identity in Ibsen', in James Redmond (ed.), *Madness in Drama* (Cambridge: Cambridge University Press, 1993).
3. Edith Ellis, *Stories and Essays* (Berkeley Heights: Free Spirit Press, 1924), 128.
4. Yvonne Kapp, *Eleanor Marx*, vol. 2 (London: Virago Press, 1976), 103.
5. Edward and Eleanor Marx-Aveling, *The Woman Question* (London: Swan, Sonnenschein, Le Bas and Lowrey, 1886), 6.
6. David Rubinstein, *Before the Suffragettes* (Brighton: Harvester Press, 1986), 24.
7. Clement Scott, 'A Doll's House', *Theatre* 14 (July 1889), 19–22.
8. Quoted in Finney: 'Ibsen and Feminism', 89–105, 90.
9. See Mary Morison: *The Correspondence of Henrik Ibsen* (London: Hodder & Stoughton, 1970), 128.

10. Michael Meyer: *Henrik Ibsen: The Making of a Dramatist, 1828–1864* (London: Rupert Hart-Davis, 1967), 146.

11. All of the following popular New Woman novels of the period close with either the death, suicide or mental illness of the feminist heroine: Grant Allen, *The Woman Who Did* (1895); Emma Frances Brooke, *A Superfluous Woman* (1894); Mona Caird, *The Wing of Azrael* (1889); Sarah Grand, *The Heavenly Twins* (1893); Olive Schreiner, *The Story of an African Farm* (1883).

12. Nora: '... When I lived with papa, he used to tell me what he thought about everything, so that I never had any opinion but his. ... Then I came here to live in your house – ... I mean, I passed from papa's hand into yours. You arranged everything the way you wanted it, so that I simply took over your taste in everything – ... You and papa have done me a great wrong.' Henrik Ibsen, *A Doll's House*, in *Ibsen, Plays: Two*, transl. Michael Meyer (London: Methuen, 1982), Act Three, 98.

13. Henrik Ibsen, *The Lady From the Sea*, in *Ibsen, Plays: Three*, transl. Michael Meyer (London: Methuen, 1988), Act Four, 187. All subsequent references to this play will be given in parentheses in the main body of the essay.

14. Henrik Ibsen, *Hedda Gabler*, in *Ibsen, Plays: Two*, transl. Michael Meyer (London: Methuen, 1990), Act One, 271–2. All subsequent references to this play will be given in parentheses in the main body of the essay.

15. Henrik Ibsen, *Little Eyolf*, in *Ibsen, Plays: Three*, transl. Michael Meyer (London: Methuen, 1988), Act One, 239. All subsequent references to this play will be given in parentheses in the main body of the essay.

16. Of the so-called English-language 'New Woman' writers of the period, only George Egerton, in her *Keynotes* and *Discords* (1893 and 1894), matches Ibsen's sympathetic treatment of female sexuality.

17. Unsigned Notice of *A Lady From the Sea*, *Referee* (17 May 1891), 2. Quoted in Michael Egan: *Ibsen: The Critical Heritage* (London: Routledge & Kegan Paul, 1972), 250.

18. Quoted in Michael Meyer: Introduction to *Hedda Gabler* in *Ibsen, Plays: Two* (London: Methuen 1990), 233.

19. Elizabeth Robins: *Ibsen and the Actress* (London: Hogarth, 1928), 3.

20. See Kate Flint: 'The American Girl and the New Woman', *Women's Writing* 3, 3 (1996), 217–30 for further discussion of the American influence on the formation of the New Woman's identity in Britain.

21. Kerry Powell: *Women and Victorian Theatre* (Cambridge: Cambridge University Press, 1997), 150–1. Two other important books which more centrally concern themselves with the Victorian actress are Tracy C. Davis: *Actresses as Working Women: Their Social Identity in Victorian Culture* (London: Routledge, 1991) and Sandra Richards: *The Rise of the English Actress* (London: Macmillan, 1993).

22. Richards, *Rise of the English Actress*, 90.

23. Elizabeth Robins: *Both Sides of the Curtain* (London: Heinemann, 1940), 208–9. Quoted by Powell: *Women and Victorian Theatre*, 156. Powell has an excellent chapter on 'Elizabeth Robins, Oscar Wilde and the "Theatre of the Future"', to which I am indebted here. There are two recent biographies of the heretofore neglected figure of Elizabeth Robins: Angela John, *Elizabeth Robins: Staging a Life* (London: Routledge, 1995) and Joanne Gates, *Elizabeth Robins, 1862–1952: Actress, Novelist, Feminist* (Tuscaloosa: University of Alabama Press, 1994).

24. Max Nordau: *Degeneration* (1892; New York: Appleton, 1895, first English translation), 413.
25. Powell: *Women and Victorian Theatre*, 71.
26. Ibid., 161.
27. Quoted in Yvonne Kapp: *Eleanor Marx: the Crowded Years, 1884–1898* (1976; London: Virago, 1979), 476.

5

'He-Notes': Reconstructing Masculinity

Gail Cunningham

But this is Masculinity as it existed, Not reconstructed.

What was the New Woman's construction of masculinity? The question may provoke some seemingly obvious answers: 'masculinity', as the concept embracing the social, political and sexual behaviour of men, was what upheld the patriarchal hegemony against which the New Woman was rebelling. Her attack – in the 1890s at least – on the social and domestic constructs of marriage, the family, sexuality, constituted a subversion of the male power-base so fundamental as to produce, in the words of Gilbert and Gubar, a 'crisis of masculinity'.[1] It is this crisis, they argue, which is responsible for such *fin-de-siècle* texts of demonized or marginalized female figures as Haggard's *She*, Stoker's *Dracula*, Wilde's *Salome* or MacDonald's *Lilith*.

It certainly appears that the rise of the New Woman in the last two decades of the nineteenth century did provoke some male writers into various forms of reactive discourse. Gissing's *In the Year of Jubilee*, for example, is a disturbingly direct, often vicious, counterblast to emerging female independence. Haggard and Stoker, working with romance or neo-Gothic genres 'intended to reclaim ... the English novel ... for male readers',[2] produce texts of multi-layered complexity in their figurings of power relations between women and men which are frequently interpreted by feminist critics as masculinist revenge on the New Woman. The landscape of *She*, indeed, featured prominently in one of the dreams Freud used for his self-analysis, a dream which Sandra Gilbert interprets as 'not only enacting crucial male anxieties but also offering ... a paradigmatically patriarchal hope, the hope of renewal through a reiteration of the Law of the Father'.[3]

Yet if we were to judge the New Woman's capacity to induce such powerful masculine fears solely from her fictional representations we should surely have to ask what exactly was so profoundly disturbing to men. Writing, in his 1912 Preface to *Jude the Obscure*, on the initial impact of his New Woman heroine Sue Bridehead, Hardy cites a German critic who regretted that 'the portrait of the newcomer had been left to be drawn by a man, and was not done by one of her own sex, who would never have allowed her to break down at the end'.[4] The interest of this observation lies not merely in the fact that Hardy was endorsing a claim – that he was the first novelist to portray a New Woman – which he knew perfectly well to be false, but more significantly that in ultimately consigning his New Woman to defeat of all her principles he was following a near-universal pattern in the New Woman fiction. Not only did the female New Woman novelists allow their protagonists to break down at the end, they almost invariably created fictional closures which either killed or re-conventionalized their New Woman figures. The incidence of death or despair amongst fictional New Women is extraordinarily high: Edith Beale in *The Heavenly Twins* (dead of syphilis); Jessamine Halliday in *A Superfluous Woman* (self-induced death in childbirth); Hadria in *The Daughters of Danaus* (enduring a lived and hopeless despair); Lyndall in *The Story of an African Farm* (a protracted and painful death); Herminia in *The Woman Who Did* (suicide). And of those New Women who survive in some serenity, a positive ending is purchased at the expense of principle: Angelica and Evadne in *The Heavenly Twins* enter conventional marriages; the heroine of George Egerton's 'A Cross Line' accepts pregnancy as a substitute for passion.

It is tempting to attribute the relentless despair-and-death fixation of so much New Woman fiction to the general morbidity which, as much as radicalism and revolt, suffused the *fin-de-siècle* spirit. This was certainly a common reaction of contemporary critics, who frequently claimed to find symptoms of decadence and degeneration in these texts. An alternative explanation could be sought in the social realities on which the New Woman writers grounded their critique of the female position; whatever the justice of their fictional heroines' theoretical positions, late-nineteenth-century society continued to be so arranged as to make a lived experience of their principles necessarily self-destructive. There is some truth in both, though neither is fully persuasive. More significant, I think, is the fact that the New Woman writers of the early 1890s continued on the whole subliminally to work within a theoretical framework which accepted the subordination of female to male terms. The New Woman's attempts to claim parity were also attempts to annex space for women within a system of binaries which continued unquestioningly to privilege the male. Demands for

lived theories = self-destructive

Not Male = female but a space for the female within the male-dominated extant system independence focused on male professions and education; anti-marriage sentiments claimed autonomy for women equivalent to men's; the desire for female sexual fulfilment was based on envious observation of masculine behaviour. Even the George Egerton of *Keynotes* and *Discords*, who more than any New Woman writer continually insisted on the 'otherness' of women, constructed a tantalizing female figure which teased and fascinated male taste.

In this essay I want to examine some New Woman texts which invert the oppositional terms and, in different ways, attempt to valorize the female. Interestingly, these are found in the latter part of the 1890s, after the period of the New Woman fiction's prime flourish. As Edmund Gosse observed in February 1896, 'it is now the better part of a year ago since the collapse of the "New Woman" fiction began'[5] a collapse attributable in part at least to the publication in March 1895 of *The Woman Who Did*. My chosen authors are Ménie Muriel Dowie, whose *Gallia* appeared in the same month as *The Woman Who Did*, and George Egerton, focusing not on the early works which formed her reputation but on two stories from the 1897 collection *Symphonies*.

The *Saturday Review*'s first notice of *Gallia* praised the novel for its 'coolness and daring' but remarked also that this was something 'for which the ordinary male reader finds himself unprepared'.[6] This is a revealing comment, suggesting something beyond the normal rhetorical nod to the New Woman fiction's shock value. In singling out the 'ordinary male reader' as prime recipient of the novel's attack, the anonymous reviewer was instinctively, though critically naively, recognizing its most subversive quality. *Gallia* is a novel which, uniquely amongst the 1890s New Woman fiction, systematically and satirically inverts the binary terms of male/female oppositions and constructs a New Woman's masculinity in which the male body becomes the object of female scrutiny and evaluation, and manliness is comically reduced to the functional ability to breed.

Early reviewers of *Gallia*, and some contemporary critics, have puzzled over the novel's apparent 'false start'. Its opening words – 'A little thought will usually show where a story begins. Gurdon considered ... that his began with a visit'[7] – appear, for readers taking the title to indicate a work grounded in the life of its eponymous heroine, misleadingly to identify the locus with Mark Gurdon rather than with Gallia. This view, I think, seriously misunderstands the novel's transgressive point. On the contrary, it is essential to Dowie's enterprise that the reader is lured first into a comfortable sense of the male as prime subject in order for his subsequent deflation into sexual object to achieve maximum satiric impact. To a significant extent, *Gallia* really does consist of his rather than her story – a story in which the New Woman features not as a female subject exemplifying proto-feminist entries into male worlds, but as an ironic foil for the deconstruction of masculine values.

Dowie constructs through Gurdon a model of the unexceptionable manly male, a model which, as the *Saturday Review*'s critic noticed, is designed for the discomfiture of its ordinary male prototype readers. Embodying all the values of the upright Englishman – hard work, clean living, honest ambition – Gurdon's masculinity is set up by Dowie for a rigorous course of deconstruction. Thrust at the beginning of the novel into the bohemian world of Paris *ateliers*, sexual licence and gender ambiguity, Gurdon's manly qualities acquire instant ambivalence: 'There was about him that suggestion of baths and shaves and tailors and general precision, of which one is ashamed to feel a little tired, because it is in itself so admirable.'[8] Within the world of the impoverished artist's vibrant squalor, this well-groomed embodiment of English masculinity encounters an alternative male model (quite literally a model, since he makes a living by exhibiting his well-defined musculature and classical features to life-drawing classes), 'old Lemuel'. A professional 'character' of the artistic scene, Lemuel displays features which hint at parallels with Gurdon which will be disturbingly deployed as the novel develops: like Gurdon, he began his career as a minor government official; and like Gurdon his sexuality – 'I wanted to marry'[9] – diverts him into a course where his value resides solely in his body.

These opening chapters of the novel, then, begin delicately to lay the foundations of its subsequent, more comically brutal, eugenic theme. Gurdon's unease at encountering in Paris an Englishman who lives by his body sits alongside a complacent view of himself as a highly satisfactory product of his own mother's breeding credentials:

> Mark always did his mother justice when he thought of her. He was far too keen and fair-minded not to see that she had done very well by him; she had given him a splendid constitution, a very nice nose, which was not too suggestive of talent to be handsome and even aristocratic, and a very useful kind of name.
>
> (*Gallia*, 18)

He is, clearly, ripe for an ironic hoisting with his own petard.

Gurdon is set up as a conventional type of masculinity, one whose 'belief ... was concretely rooted in himself' (20) but whose apprehension of self is to be progressively deconstructed through Dowie's anatomisation of male sexuality. Rejecting the extremes of earlier New Woman fiction, which tended to signal male sexuality through syphilitic or promiscuous husbands, Dowie instead takes two tropes of fictionally acceptable indicators of male sexual behaviour – the proposal and the mistress – and entirely inverts their significance.

Proposal scenes provided a useful device for Victorian novelists through the expectation that a man should make some sort of declaration to his prospective bride about his sexual past. Casaubon's fusty reassurance to Dorothea that 'I can at least offer you an affection hitherto unwasted'[10] confirms sophisticated readers in their suspicion that he is a sexual inadequate; Angel Clare's failure to confess his sexual peccadillo at the appropriate pre-marital point alerts us to his hypocrisy. Similarly, a man's possession of a mistress, whether within or prior to marriage, is a direct reification of his sexuality. Dowie sequences Gurdon's progress through both devices. His proposal to the English rose Margaret Essex brilliantly exposes the ambivalence of the man's attitude to his sexual self, as he simultaneously lays claim to virility and avoids moral censure:

> He knew she was particular about some things, Mark said to her ... Well, he shouldn't like to brag about it, but – and then he made the well-known speech without which no proposal is really complete. He wore that air of humility and seriousness, combined with a rigid sense of right and wrong. He wouldn't like to call himself a *good* man ... but he would say that most men would call him a very decent specimen. He had 'lived' to a certain extent (he was very careful to put in this ambiguous qualification, and tradition justified him; no man with any respect for himself ever leaves it out) – to a certain extent he had lived the life of an ordinary man of the world, but he had had his limitations, and there were lengths to which he had never gone.
>
> (*Gallia*, 79)

As the reader, unlike Margaret, has previously been told that Gurdon's sexual experience consists solely of 'moments of almost wholly forced abandonment' (86) his confessions reveal themselves as indulgent self-aggrandizement rather than honest humility. Towards the end of the novel, Dowie permits herself a biting parody of this sort of masculine position:

> Men are like children who have come home from the seashore ... They have to tell about how they paddled, and just how deep they

went in, and all about the queer things they fished out ... And all
the time you see how awfully frightened at the crabs they have
been. 'But our little shoes were hanging round our necks, Nursey
dear ... and see how clean we've kept our overalls!'

(*Gallia*, 198–9)

When Gurdon is politely refused by Margaret Essex, he discovers to
his surprise that an unfamiliar degree of urgency has entered his sexual
being. Accidentally meeting old Lemuel's daughter Carla in the street,
he accompanies her to her lodgings, seduces her, and subsequently sets
her up as his mistress. And it is in her treatment of this conventional
device for signalling male sexuality that Dowie's transgressive project
becomes most apparent.

Gallia, following her New Woman principles of plain speaking and
rigorous self-analysis, declares herself to be in love with Margaret's
brother 'Dark' Essex, a cool, sardonic academic accustomed to the
quasi-monastic life of an Oxford college. Put firmly in her place by
Essex – 'don't you think the world is still a little too raw for your very
advanced treatment of it?' (59) – Gallia shifts her evaluation of men
from the romantic to the reproductive. Dowie reconstructs her as a
eugenicist, scrutinizing men for their breeding potential; thus when
she learns not only that Gurdon keeps a mistress, but crucially also
that his mistress is ill following a self-induced abortion, her attention
turns to him as possible partner. This is the heart of the novel's radicalism, since it brilliantly and satirically inverts the conventions of gendered response to sexuality. Where Victorian custom expected women
practically to connive at though in principle to condemn male pre-
marital sex, Dowie shows Gallia selecting Gurdon as a husband not
despite but because of his sexual history; he has proved not only that he
– unlike Essex – is sexually active, but also that he is fertile.

Abortion scenes are not common in Victorian fiction, even in the
self-consciously shocking 1890s, and it seems from the reviews that
many of *Gallia's* first readers simply failed to notice this one.[11] Clearly
Dowie was treading very delicate ground here, but the scene and its
repercussions were so central to her plot that she expended great care
in attempting to make the unsayable explicit. When Gurdon returns to
the flat in which he keeps Carla Lemuel to find her feverish and deliri-
ous, Dowie supplies a worldly charwoman to counterbalance his naive
bemusement and inform the alert reader of the cause of her plight:

'I was frightened, and so I thought I would dance and dance ... '
He shook his head vaguely.

'Bein' no stairs to come up and down,' said Mrs Miles in a furtive undertone ... [12]

(*Gallia*, 137–8)

Gurdon's concerned insistence on summoning a doctor is met by Mrs Miles's – to him – inexplicable reluctance, and the doctor – a 'keen, worldly-wise young man' – asks questions which 'caused him some embarrassment' but leave him still 'puzzled' (138). However, when Gallia learns of the incident from Mrs Miles she rapidly reaches the conclusion that this is a positive indication of Gurdon's qualifications for fatherhood: 'I saw that the logical sequence of my own views about the kind of man I wanted to marry read equally as my approval' (139).

This, of course, is a quite extraordinary inversion of received attitudes, even amongst New Woman writers, towards male sexuality. Where Sarah Grand demands equal sexual restraint for men, or George Egerton comparable licence for woman, Dowie accepts an essentialist view of masculine sexual needs but evaluates their significance simply as indicators of male fitness for the female project of successful maternity. The scene of Gurdon's proposal to Gallia provides Dowie with a wonderful opportunity for comic deflation of male expectations. Embarking on the normal confessional course ('you must hear about my life' [192]) Gurdon is brutally interrupted by Gallia's declaration of her reason for accepting him:

'I believe I was already dreaming of marrying you ... when the knowledge of the illness of your mistress came to my ears.'
If a cannon had gone off close to his head, Mark would have been less amazed.

(*Gallia*, 192)

Again we should note the significance of Dowie's choice of words: it is not the *existence* of Gurdon's mistress which is at issue, but her '*illness*' – the fact that he has successfully impregnated her. Essex's rebuff to Gallia's early romantic confessions is amply avenged by her notification to Gurdon of his marital credentials:

I have wanted the father of my child to be a fine, strong, manly man, full of health and strength. A man who is a man, whose faults are manly; who has never been better than a mere man in all his life.

(Ibid.)

Gurdon's story, therefore, consists in tracking what Dowie takes to be the normal course of the averagely sexualized English male, ending in his capture by a New Woman wanting little from him but healthy sperm. The 'ordinary male reader' of 1895 would indeed find himself – perhaps deservedly – unprepared for this.

Dowie's radicalism in *Gallia* resides in her undermining of masculine certainties by treating the male body as object. George Egerton, in the two *Symphonies* stories 'Sea Pinks' and 'A Nocturne', focuses rather on the more complex area of masculine emotion. In both stories, her concern is to undermine attitudinal conventions of male response to women: economic patronage, sexual sophistication, control and autonomy. Both stories adopt the narrative voice of the mature, sexually experienced single man; in both the male narrator encounters 'woman as victim', magnanimously sets aside instinctive sexual predation in favour of disinterested rescue; and in both the man ultimately discovers himself to be not only redundant but left with an enduring sense of lack – as the women vacate the male space, they remove masculine autonomy.

Egerton rarely adopts a male narrative voice (only once in *Keynotes*, and this for an oddly conventional little love story, 'A Little Grey Glove'), yet in *Symphonies* she places these two stories next to each other and structures both as a man relating a highly significant, perception-altering incident to a single, unidentified, male listener. This narrative enclosure within apparently secure masculine space is ironically belied by the prime thrust of the stories, which in both cases rests upon the invasion of male space – both physical and emotional – by a woman.

In 'Sea Pinks' the narrator explains to his listener the presence in his room of these eponymous wild flowers 'fresh from the country'.[12] They arrive weekly, he reveals, from a girl he had found struggling with poverty as a circus-rider in the south of France. The encounter between a worldly, sophisticated man and an innocent young English girl, incongruously placed in the carnivalesque atmosphere of the southern circus, appears set for a conventional tale of rescue followed by seduction. But Egerton reverses the expectations. Inexplicably, the man finds his sexual tendencies dormant, and his pleasure in selflessly escorting her to Paris and paying her passage home. As he finally places her on the boat-train to London, she reveals that she no longer has need of his money, having unexpectedly received some from her brother; ignoring his proffered comradely hand-shake, she kisses him 'right on the mouth' (*Symphonies*, 88) and departs without a backward glance.

He is thus thwarted not sexually but morally, his uncharacteristic generosity and restraint redundant and his hinted desire for a more permanent relationship ('I wouldn't mind having her good-morning always' [87]) denied. Confessing to his listener that he remains 'bothered' by the kiss, he concludes that the weekly arrival of the flowers makes him wish 'she didn't have quite so good a memory' (89).

The story's ending is deliberately, though perhaps not altogether satisfactorily, ambiguous. The thwarted male regrets both that her memory is accurate and that it interprets as 'good' an incident which has left him with a sense of loss and of power-relations reversed. 'A Nocturne' handles the same theme with greater assurance, and with a richly evocative sense of gender complexities as finely written as any of the now better-known *Keynotes* pieces. Here Egerton uses the male voice to convey more directly the sense of masculine anxiety and loss in the face of New Womanhood, setting up a masculine space redolent of *fin-de-siècle* decadence, dandyism and self-indulgence and reducing it, through a brilliantly low-key use of concluding symbolism, to ashes.

The opening words – 'I have rather nice diggings' (90) – stress the importance of the man's personal space and introduce a setting of male autonomy and control, designed for the indulgence of material and sexual tastes. The nameless narrator reveals himself progressively as a collector of first editions, a lover of Eastern shoes, a man of refinement whose tea and tobacco are specially imported, whose porcelain is finest Worcester, whose dressing-gown is an antique Japanese kimono and whose sexuality is aroused by delicate female feet. This enclosed and secure masculine space is, however, ominously situated on the Thames embankment within sight of Cleopatra's needle, allegedly a phallic monument to a *femme fatale*. When the narrator encounters a distressed woman outside his flat at midnight, and magnanimously takes her in from the rain and a suspicious policeman, he introduces into his sanctuary a figure as destructive to contemporary masculine certainties as Geraldine to Christabel's romantic purity.

The story once again begins with woman as victim – she is weakened from starvation and exposure, penniless and homeless – and ends, within the space of twenty-four hours, with the woman empowered and the man diminished. Despite having her helpless in front of him throughout the course of a night and morning, he is unable to appropriate her to any received model of womanhood: 'She was a vexatious sort of contradictory person; there was a tantalizing lack of finality about her' (100). Egerton conveys her narrator's unease at his inability to reduce her to a familiar category – beautiful or ugly, 'devil' or 'saint' –

by dislocating his gaze. Unable to form an overall vision, his eyes evaluate odd parts of her anatomy as separate entities: hair, chin, hands, feet, nose, jaw, ankles, mouth, calves, throat, knees, bosom, back, scalp – all at various points receive commentary or evaluation. Yet the woman refuses incorporation, rejects categorization.

Egerton builds her narrative with great care in order to depict a process of subtly shifting power relations. Taking in a helpless unknown woman, the narrator is initially in a position of absolute power; when she faints from fatigue, he is able to remove her hat and gloves, touching her with a degree of intimacy which only such an extreme situation could permit. While she is unconscious, he allows himself to reflect on the peculiarity of male sexual predilections:

> I belong to the race of men to whom temptation comes in the guise of little feet. An instep or ankle appeals irresistibly to my senses; I acknowledge it frankly ... My friend Foote says, delicately perfumed *lingerie* is his weak spot; his fall is sure at a flutter of lace and ribbon. To be virtuous, he would have to live in a land where the drying of women's frillikins on a clothes-line would be prohibited by law. (94–5)

Egerton thus constructs a scene redolent of sexual suggestiveness – an unconscious woman watched over by a man ruminating on foot-fetishism and underwear theft. But as the woman strengthens physically, the sexual element declines; masculine uncertainty increases as female helplessness recedes. Although for the greater part of the story Egerton deliberately restricts the woman's voice to a few brief explanatory utterances, she lays subtle emphasis on her ability silently but disturbingly to occupy male space. As the night progresses, she physically annexes or consumes the man's most precious personal goods. She drinks his tea ('the best in the market' [95]), smokes his tobacco ('my special baccy' [99]), handles his first editions ('my only heirloom' [100]), wears his kimono ('a gorgeous affair' [97]) and his Eastern shoes ('rather a fad of mine' [96]). His chivalrous impulses begin imperceptibly, Egerton suggests, to encroach on his masculine autonomy.

Male control begins to slip away with the dawn. The narrator's love for his flat and its embankment location is based on a nocturnal aesthetic – 'I never tire of it at night' (90). Morning here signals the loss of control:

> It was one of those beastly mornings, fine under protest, with a sun that looked as if he had been making a night of it. I hate the

mornings ... they are always a sort of ill-natured comment on the
night before. (102)

The comment brought by this particular morning is that the previous
night's power relations are to be spectacularly reversed. For the first
time Egerton allows her woman character to find a sustained voice,
and it is unexpectedly vigorous. Her resumé of the circumstances
which have brought her to such a plight is delivered in ruthlessly
unself-pitying style, punctuated only by a verbal tic of 'don't you
know?' at the end of sentences (in early to mid-twentieth-century
speech an exclusively masculine locution, though perhaps less gendered in the 1890s). To his surprise, the narrator learns that the
morning paper carries a piece of her journalism, and that – with the
help of his introduction to an editor – she can confidently look
forward to future financial independence. Meeting her by chance later
in the day, he learns that for her 'things were going to hum' (108).

As in 'Sea Pinks', the male narrator, at the start of the story
confidently in control, magnanimous in his suppression of masculine
sexual instincts in favour of serving a woman in distress, finds not just
that the rug has been pulled from under his feet but that perhaps he
wasn't really standing on it in the first place. Women, Egerton suggests, are not as readily reducible to male-constructed type as her narrators have assumed. The narrator of 'A Nocturne' confesses at the end of
the story firstly that he has preserved the ash from her cigarettes as his
only tangible memento, and secondly – underlining the symbolic
significance of ashes as the central feature of his physical space – that
his emotional life, anchored as he revealed in his introduction on his
'diggings', has been irrevocably impoverished:

> Sometimes, when the rain beats, and that beastly old river yawns
> like a grave, I stand up at the window and look down. I never felt
> a want in my old digs before. It was jolly to have a woman – a
> woman of that kind, you know – taking an interest in one's first
> editions. (108)

It is a well-judged conclusion, combining the rhetorical flourish of
'yawns like a grave' with the slangily costive 'jolly' to signal embarrassment at the sentimentality which preserves a woman's memory
through her cigarette ash.

Egerton's tone in both stories is wryly elegiac, suggestive of formerly
independent men surprised by loss. By foregrounding the masculine

voice describing fleeting contact with woman, Egerton inverts the usual terms of her significant encounter stories: space here, both physical and emotional, is male; the woman is revealed as autonomous at the expense of masculine security. It is interesting, too, that this discomfiture is signalled through physical female mementoes in male domestic settings – the fresh country flowers in 'Sea Pinks' disturb the narrator's urbane environment; the cigarette ash in 'A Nocturne', carefully preserved in a matchbox, evokes the desiccation at the heart of a suave dilettante existence. The male narrators' attempts to categorize and appropriate the qualities of their encountered women are inadequate in the face of female autonomy – an autonomy which Egerton signals by downgrading the woman's voice in favour of her action.

Dowie's *Gallia*, though entirely different in tone, is also an attempt by a New Woman writer to subvert the fictional conventions of structuring gender relation narratives. By making her New Woman novel his story rather than hers, she deliberately (and highly effectively, as we can see from puzzlement amongst modern as well as contemporary critics) dislocates expectations and creates genuine surprise for readers to match the bemusemant of her male protagonist. Dowie's text is playful, both in its structure and in its toying with extremities of ideology: there is no evidence from her other works or from her biography that she had any great interest in eugenics – unless we take her subsequent expertise in breeding red poll cattle as indicative of darker thoughts. Rather, she is accepting New Womanhood as a given, not promoting it as an ideal, and comically testing masculinity against some of its potential conclusions.

Both Dowie and Egerton, therefore, are breaking fresh ground in their versions of New Woman fiction. Freeing themselves in these texts from the regressive tendencies of earlier works either to destroy or to reintegrate their new woman figures, they construct instead a narrative context in which the radical woman becomes secure and masculinity appears as 'other'. If the New Woman could genuinely be accused of creating a 'crisis of masculinity' it would, surely, be through texts such as these rather than the more familiar, dramatically doom-laden, novels of Sarah Grand, Mona Caird and others. However, as I have argued earlier, both *Gallia* and *Symphonies* appeared at or after the period Gosse identified as the collapse of the New Woman fiction. Their radicalism in re-ordering the scale of gender relations attracted no significant literary followers. On the contrary, as the Edwardian period succeeded the *fin de siècle*, the New Woman as a fictional type began to be appropriated increasingly by male writers who were keen to exploit her sexual potential while confining her activities firmly to the home. Writers such as Wells and Lawrence retrieved masculinity from the dangerous grasp of the emergent feminist, and reasserted sexual service to the male as woman's prime function. Only at the end of our own century does a 'crisis of masculinity' seem to have re-emerged as a consequence of feminism.

Notes

1. Sandra M. Gilbert and Susan Gubar, *No Man's Land Volume 2, 'Sexchanges'* (London: Yale University Press, 1989), xii.
2. Elaine Showalter, *Sexual Anarchy* (London: Virago, 1992), 79.
3. Sandra M. Gilbert, 'Rider Haggard's Heart of Darkness', *Partisan Review*, 13, 1983, 444–53.
4. Thomas Hardy, *Jude the Obscure* (London: Macmillan, 1895).
5. Edmund Gosse, *Saturday Review*, 8 February 1896, 153–4.
6. *Saturday Review*, 23 March 1895, 383–4.
7. Ménie Muriel Dowie, *Gallia* (London; J. M. Dent, 1995), 3.
8. *Gallia*, 8.
9. *Gallia*, 24.
10. George Eliot, *Middlemarch* (London, Penguin, 1985), 67.
11. I should perhaps confess that, when I first read *Gallia* in 1970, I too failed to spot the significance of this scene and so misread the novel.
12. George Egerton, *Symphonies* (London, John Lane, 1897), 64.

6
New Women and the New Hellenism

Ann Ardis

During the great age of English university reform, Hellenism, the systematic study of Greek history, literature, and philosophy, served as a crucial means of both liberalizing classical republican political discourse and establishing the basis for a 'homosexual counterdiscourse able to justify male love in ideal or transcendental terms'.[1] As Linda Dowling has noted, the revisionary Greek ideal lying at the centre of Oxford Hellenism was 'the purest model of Victorian liberalism itself', promising to 'restore and reinvigorate a nation fractured by the effects of laissez-faire capitalism and enervated by the approach of mass democracy' (Dowling, 79, 31). But Oxford Hellenism also 'provide[d] the means of sweeping away the entire accumulation of negative associations with male love which had remained strong through the beginning of the nineteenth century' (Dowling, 79). '[T]riumphantly proclaiming' male love to be 'the very fountain of civic health in a polity that [was] urged to take as its cultural model the ancient city-state of Athens', key figures in the Oxford reform movement such as Walter Pater and John Addington Symonds sought to realize the Platonic doctrine of eros, whereby an older man, 'moved to love by the visible beauty of a younger man, and desirous of winning immortality through that love, undertakes the younger man's education in virtue and wisdom' (Dowling, 79, 81). Arguing that Oscar Wilde's passionate defence of male love as 'pure' and 'perfect' and 'intellectual' during the final moments of his first trial in 1895 can best be understood in the context of this larger history of Victorian Hellenism, Dowling charts the very complex genealogy of Wilde's Platonic language regarding male love in a 'crucial moment in the modern emergence of homosexuality as a positive social identity' (Dowling, 4).

Does the 'New Hellenism' enable or discredit female intellectuality? Does turn-of-the-century Platonic discourse carve out a cultural space for *female* homorelationality²? Dowling's work in *Hellenism and Homosexuality in Victorian Oxford* frames my attempt to begin answering such questions through a discussion of two turn-of-the-century British texts: Olive Schreiner's 'The Buddhist Priest's Wife' and Ethel Arnold's *Platonics* (1894). Consideration of fictional and historical 'New Women' responses to the 'New Hellenism' of the 1890s will require thinking about the 'gendering of intellectuality' in the nineteenth century³ and the casual but nonetheless aggressive sexism of male intellectuals. The issues addressed are 'bigger' than the two fictional texts under discussion here. Still, they offer a useful occasion for extending Dowling's scholarship on the New Hellenism to include consideration of women's responses to a homosocial paradigm of 'philosophy' that 'still informs and governs intellectual life in the West'.⁴

* * *

Making himself as comfortable as he can, in full evening dress, in his friend's tiny room 'up many long flights of stairs', the unnamed male interlocutor of 'The Buddhist Priest's Wife' asks of his female friend, who has summoned him to visit her after seven months' silence:

'But really what have you been doing with yourself all this time? You've entirely disappeared from civilized life. When I was down at the Grahams' in the spring, they said you were coming down there, and then at the last moment cried off. We were all quite disappointed. What is taking you to India now? Going to preach the doctrine of social and intellectual equality to the Hindu women and incite them to revolt? Marry some old Buddhist Priest, build a cottage on the top of the Himalayas and live there, discuss philosophy and meditate? I believe that's what you'd like. I really shouldn't wonder if I heard you'd done it!'⁵

His friend's only response is to laugh, smoke a cigarette, and note that she 'want[s] change' (BPW, 87). They talk briefly about his successful election to Parliament. He acknowledges the inertia that 'creeps over one as one grows older', which has kept him from pursuing a suggestion she once made about a trip to Norway, and he chides her for making nothing of her life, for 'throw[ing her]self away' rather than being 'the most successful woman in London' (BPW 87, 88). Her response to this accusation is brief as well: '"Oh, my life is very full ...

There are only two things that are absolute realities, love and knowledge, and you can't escape them"' (BPW, 88).

This answer does not satisfy him, however, and he pursues his assessment of her life:

'You ought to settle down and marry like other women do, not go wandering about the world to India and China and Italy, and God knows where. You are simply making a mess of your life ... You go squandering yourself on every old beggar or forlorn female or escaped criminal you meet; it may be very nice for them but it's a mistake from your point of view.' (BPW, 88–9)

Without offering her an opportunity to respond, he then describes, by contrast, his own present intention of marrying.

'I intend to marry. It's a curious thing ... that when a man reaches a certain age he wants to marry. He doesn't fall in love; it's not that he definitely plans anything; but he has a feeling that he ought to have a home and a wife and children. ... When I was a young man I used to despise men for getting married; wondered what they did it for; they had everything to lose and nothing to gain. But when a man gets to be six-and-thirty his feeling changes. It's not love, passion, he wants; it's a home; it's a wife and children. He may have a house and servants; it isn't the same thing. I should have thought a woman would have felt it too.' (BPW, 89–90)

Provoked at last to fuller comment, and revealing more to the reader about her feeling for him than her male friend registers, Schreiner's heroine suggests that 'marriage is much more serious' for a woman than for a man. 'She might pass her life without meeting a man whom she could possibly love, and, if she met him, it might not be right or possible' (BPW, 90). Then she describes more fully the woman he should marry, a woman pointedly different from herself in age, appearance, and sensibility.

The kind of woman you want would be young and strong; she need not be excessively beautiful, but she must be attractive; she must have energy, but not too strongly marked an individuality; she must be largely neutral; she need not give you too passionate or too deep a devotion, but she must second you in a thoroughly rational manner. She must have the same aims and tastes that you have. No woman has the right to marry a man if she has to bend herself out of shape for him. She might wish to, but she could never be to him with all her passionate endeavour what the other woman could be to him without trying. (BPW, 91)

Charging him to take his holiday in America rather than Scotland this year, so that he can search there for this woman, Schreiner's protagonist then offers, unsolicited, a long peroration on sexual difference. Like the above description of his 'ideal woman', her abstract theorizing bears more specific reference to this particular relationship than her male interlocutor is ever aware.

'Intellectually we may both be alike', she notes. 'I suppose if fifty men and fifty women had to solve a mathematical problem, they would all do it in the same way; the more abstract and intellectual, the more alike we are' (BPW, 92). But '[t]he nearer you approach to the personal and sexual, the more different we are', she argues. '[S]ex love in its substance may be the same in both of us; in the form of its expression it must differ' (BPW, 92). Although she initially explains this phenomenon through reference to nature, the example she then develops provides social rather than biological reasons for this difference while also answering her interlocutor's initial question about her reason for travelling to India.

'If a man loves a woman, he has a right to try to make her love him because he can do it openly, directly, without bending. There need be no subtlety, no indirectness. With a woman it's not so; she can take no love that is not laid openly, simply, at her feet. Nature ordains that she should never show what she feels; the woman who has told a man she loved him would have put between them a barrier once and for ever that could not be crossed; and if she subtly drew him towards her, using the woman's means – silence, finesse the dropped handkerchief, the surprise visit, the gentle assertion she had not thought to see him when she had come a long way to meet him, then she would be damned; she would hold the love, but she would have desecrated it by subtlety; it would have no value. Therefore, she must always go with her arms folded sexually ... Of course friendship is different. You are on a perfect equality with man then; you can ask him to come and see you as I asked you. That's the beauty of the intellect and intellectual life for a woman, that she drops her shackles a little; and that is why she shrinks from sex so.' (BPW, 92–3)

Once again, however, her male interlocutor fails to register the relevance of most of this commentary to their own relationship. '"It's really very strange to be sitting and talking like this to you,"' he observes casually. '"But you are so different from other women. If all women were like you, all your theories of the equality of men and women would work. You're the only woman with whom I never realize that she is a woman"' (BPW, 93). Reminiscing briefly about how he might have fallen in love with her three years ago – '"if you hadn't always attacked me so incontinently and persistently on all and every point and on each and every occasion"' (BPW, 94) – he excuses himself shortly thereafter, noting that '"it's so fascinating sitting here talking that I could stay all night, but I've still got two engagements"' (BPW, 95). Only at the very end of the story, after she asks him to kiss her and he does so, does he realize what the reader has been piecing together for quite some time: this woman has loved him passionately, has desired not simply his friendship and intellectual companionship but other kinds of emotional and physical intimacy with him as well. And she is leaving for India not only because she may be dying of an unnamed illness but also because of a 'love she could not have', a love he could not give her because he 'never realize[d] that she is a woman' (BPW, 84, 93).

Mark Sanders has argued that the theory of sexual difference Schreiner models in 'The Buddhist Priest's Wife' presents 'the pragmatic suspension of sexual difference customary in intellectual life as an emancipatory gesture'. Foregrounding the protagonist's comment about how intellectual life allows a woman to drop the 'shackles' of her sexual and gender identity 'a little', he uses this story as a springboard into a discussion of Waldo Farber's encounter with a Stranger in *The Story of an African Farm* as a cross-gendered fictionalization of a pivotal moment of intellectual 'awakening' in Olive Schreiner's own life. Given a copy of Herbert Spencer's *First Principles* (1862) by a colonial official staying briefly with her aunt at the rural mission station in the Cape Colony, Schreiner, like Waldo, was transformed by this reading experience: initiated into an intellectual quest that would take this daughter of a missionary far 'away from her orthodox upbringing'.[6] Noting the contrast between Waldo's interaction with a Stranger and Lyndall's (which culminates in an unwanted pregnancy), Sanders suggests that the difference between *The Story of an African Farm's* two narratives of intellectual initiation reveal Schreiner's anxiety 'about female participation in intellectual life'. Her concern about the risks associated, for women, with eroticized intellectual congress – e.g., unwanted pregnancy, abortion – necessitate her autobiographical 'masquerade' as Waldo as she models the 'quasi-erotic' intellectual initiation of a younger by an older man.[7]

As interesting as this interpretation of Waldo's autobiographical resonances for Schreiner is, what Sanders fails to register is Schreiner's analysis of male resistance to female intellectual and sexual mentorship. The anxiety Schreiner expresses about female participation in intellectual life in a story such as 'The Buddhist Priest's Wife' is prompted much more obviously by men's inability to 'realize' the woman in the intellect than by the risks of physical generativity. Rather than being an 'emancipatory gesture', in other words, Schreiner's characterization of 'the pragmatic suspension of sexual difference customary in intellectual life' is deeply painful, even tragic, from the woman's point of view. The male interlocutor's comically orientalized description of his 'friend's' Platonic life in India, married to 'some old Buddhist Priest,' contrasts sharply with the frame-tale's presentation of her unburied corpse and the narrative's bitter indictment of the patriarchal technologies of gender and class that have normalized the male interlocutor's obtuseness – though he himself remains oblivious to both levels of commentary in the text. His mocking parody of the Hellenic ideal of self-development and 'pure', 'perfect', 'intellectual' companionship (to borrow Oscar Wilde's phrasing) reveals only his own inability to grasp what is at stake in the Socratic dyad of an older lover and a younger beloved; it tells us nothing about his friend's ideals. It has been suggested that Schreiner's female protagonist 'hails' her male interlocutor as a 'very cultured, intellectual m[a]n'.[8] But in fact she considers him to be a man who ought to marry precisely because he has 'no absorbing mental work' with which a wife 'would interfere' (BPW, 90). That he views this woman who engages him, but also repels him by her dogged pursuit of knowledge, with amusement, 'as one does an interesting child or a big Newfoundland dog', is not at all to his credit (BPW, 95). Rather, his 'half-amused, half-interested' treatment of her, his impatience with her Bohemianism and his Society commitments explain – though they do not justify – his inability to engage her in a relationship of Platonic eros: to enter, under her guidance, into a 'higher life' of spiritual procreancy.[9]

* * *

Linda Dowling has taught us to hear the echoes of Oxford Hellenism's defense of human potentiality and self-cultivation in Wilde's April 1895 speech about 'pure', 'perfect', 'intellectual' male love and other turn-of-the century defences of/attacks on 'the higher sodomy'. If there are subtle Hellenistic resonances in Schreiner's depiction of a failed (non)relationship between an older female lover and a younger male beloved in 'The Buddhist Priest's Wife', they reverberate even more powerfully and overtly through Ethel Arnold's *Platonics* (1894). Brief consideration of Schreiner's and Arnold's real-life experiences with Victorian academicism can usefully preface a discussion of this text.

Having grown up in South Africa, Olive Schreiner did not encounter what Dowling has so aptly characterized as the 'intense homosociality' of Victorian academic culture first hand until she arrived in England in 1881. Therefore, she could describe the impact that reading Herbert Spencer's *First Principles* for the first time had on her in purely intellectual rather than social terms.[10] Unlike Beatrice Webb, for example, who was similarly enraptured and transformed intellectually by Spencer's work, Schreiner was not confronted personally with his sexism, which Webb describes in her diaries as finding expression in casually demeaning remarks about George Eliot's physical unattractiveness.[11] Insofar as intellectuality was gendered as 'male' in the nineteenth century, English academic culture, in spite of its liberalizing rhetoric, supported rather than subverted bourgeois gender ideology through such judgements of feminity.[12] How much more difficult it must have been, then, for Ethel Arnold to live always on the outside of Oxford's intellectual inner circle.

Ethel M. Arnold was: the granddaughter of Thomas Arnold, the Headmaster of Rugby School to whom 'much of the new and invigorating intellectual atmosphere at Oxford' in the 1850s and 1860s has been attributed;[13] niece to Matthew Arnold; spinster daughter of 'Tom Arnold the Younger, teacher and scholar of English';[14] and sister of Mrs Humphry Ward, Somerville College co-founder and novelist. 'One might assume that being an Arnold would have provided certain personal and professional advantages for Ethel,' Phyllis Wachter has suggested'; yet 'she frequently found herself unsupported by a patriarchal Victorian family focused on her social status instead of her creative potential as author'.[15] Biographical and autobiographical information about Arnold is hard to come by.[16] However, Virginia Woolf's account of Kitty Malone's life in the fourth and fifth essays of *The Pargiters*, the novel-essay portion of *The Years*, can provide us with an adequate sense of life in Oxford for a Master's daughter:

> The difficulties, inconsistencies, and complexities of life in Oxford in the eighties for a girl like Kitty were numerous; and puzzling

enough to perplex a mind that was original enough to ask them, though not original enough to ask them openly. The only question that Kitty could put openly, and was determined to put to her parents on the 1st of September 1880 – the day was marked with a cross on her calendar – was, 'May I leave Oxford and become a farmer in Yorkshire?' But however tactfully she phrased it, she knew the question was so wrapped up in all those other questions – about pouring out tea, and standing at the window in a nightgown, and not going for walks alone, and always calling undergraduates 'Mr', and never meeting them except with her mother, and talking to rowing men about rowing and reading men about reading; it was so involved also with the opinions of great men like Gladstone who thought that women must be chaste, and of Walter Bagehot who thought that they could be labourers but not capitalists, of Mark Pattison who thought that [he *stood*] in special need of 'the restful sympathy which women knew how to give', of Walter Pater who thought that 'it was an insinuation of the Devil that caused this woman to drop her glove', of Oscar Browning who thought that the lowest man is intellectually the superior of the cleverest woman; it was so complicated, further, by the fact that there was no way in which a woman could earn her living; and therefore no way in which she could be independent of such opinions ... [17]

Woolf's Kitty Malone wants to leave Oxford and be a farmer; Ethel Arnold wanted to pursue rather than renounce the life of the mind. If, as Wachter suggests it might be argued, Arnold 'didn't progress beyond the level of the inspired dilettante who dabbled in a variety of avocations from acting and photography to journalism, [literary criticism, fiction-writing], and public speaking on behalf of woman suffrage', her struggle to achieve 'self-actualization, economic independence, and socio-political autonomy' nonetheless epitomizes the struggle of so many middle-class late-Victorian women to reinvent themselves as something other than the docile daughters of educated men.[18]

'Amidst the challenges of a rapidly changing world,' Wachter observes, 'one stabilizing factor for Arnold was the way in which she actively sought the companionship of other women for emotional nurturance, political solidarity, and professional mentorship.' She goes on to suggest that the term 'homorelational' offers a more accurate characterization of the 'full range or spectrum of same-sex relationships' in Ethel Arnold's life than a term such as 'lesbian continuum', because it 'takes the attention away from sexual persuasion and focuses [instead] on gender'. By putting the emphasis on '"relatedness" rather than sex-uality, it offers alternative ways of investigating women's and men's same-sex relationships which otherwise are all too often compared and contrasted to male/female relationships' (xi). In spite of this effort to theorize an alternative to a modern conceptualization of homo/hetero polarity, however, Wachter's discussion of both Arnold's life and *Platonics* nonetheless projects backward onto the 'indeterminate welter of late-Victorian psychosocial categories' an 'as-yet-unthought-of polar-ization of "homosexual" versus "heterosexual"' behaviour.[19] I would like to suggest that *Platonics* offers a fascinating portrait of New Women's responses to the New Hellenism *before* Wilde's trials polar-ized modern gender distinctions and crystallized the New Hellenism's association with homosexual 'deviancy'.

* * *

Once again, Woolf's *The Pargiters* can provide us with a useful point of contrast and historical contextualization. In the fourth essay, which focuses on the differences between Edward Pargiter's and Kitty Malone's academic socialization, Woolf describes the male world of English public schools and universities in the following way.

> The difference between 1530 and 1930 seems to us, at any rate, unmeasurable; [and yet,] when we reflect that during all that time Benedict's had been a college; that young men had sat, more or less, where Edward was sitting in May 1880; had been hearing lectures in the lecture room, and saying prayers in the Chapel, and eating dinner in the hall; it is obvious that a variety, a complexity, an intri-cacy of tradition and theory and ceremony had accumulated whose force, exerted as it was during the impressionable years that lie between ten and twenty, cannot be exaggerated ... (76–7)

Woolf goes on to contrast this with Kitty Malone's private instruction under the tutelage of Miss Lucy Craddock, a 'worthy, plain, industrious old maid' who had 'gone short of firing and clothing and food in order to attend classes at Queens College', and who at last, 'after years of labour', finally 'won the right to live in a bed-sitting room, in an Oxford lodging, teaching girls like Kitty for five shillings an hour' (112, 113). I would contrast the intensely social nature of both Edward's and Kitty's academic experience with Susan Dormer's isolation. The protag-onist of Arnold's *Platonics* is introduced to us as a woman who 'spent herself ... in early life ... in an intensity of devotion to her own people:

her mother, one or two friends, and her husband'. All have died, leaving Susan determined 'to wall up her heart against all further invasion' (2–3). For two years after her husband's death she did just that, 'preserving as her only link with [the world] one intimate woman friend [Kit Drummond], the solitary human being whom she loved' (3). When Kit's brother asks her to join him in Canada, Susan is left absolutely alone on her Northumbrian estate. In her solitude, she reads, seeking from books 'companionship and distraction rather than any definite consolation'. She starts with history: 'training her mind by degrees to see men and events *en bloc*, and to distinguish the enduring elements in human nature under the ever-changing fashions of circumstance.' Next she turns to philosophy: 'reading always voraciously and intelligently, not, as men for the most part read philosophy in the schools, for the sake of the mental discipline, but in the hope of finding the absolute Truth – not realizing that it still is where it was originally planted – at the foot of the rainbow' (4). As the narrator continues to describe Susan's self-education in the opening pages of the novel, the commentary becomes increasingly negative:

> The greater part of what she read she probably did not understand, for the fortress of thought is not to be stormed in any such summary fashion. Still, her reading afforded her mental food and stimulant, and gradually she evolved a philosophy of her own, vaguely realized at first, but passing ... into a passionate conviction, taking the place of all other beliefs and hopes. It seemed to her that individualism, the imprisoning of the soul within the walls of the Ego was at the roof of all the sin and misery of the world, and that she suffered in the past because she had nursed and fostered her individuality instead of setting herself from the first to break down the barriers which separated her soul from the world-soul. (5)

In reality, the narrator observes, Susan's new philosophy was simply 'a modern form' of Christian asceticism. Rather than condoning Susan's newfound conviction through this comparison, however, the narrator condemns it as 'a sort of mental anaesthetic deadening all sensibility, a sort of moral refrigerator freezing all the channels of her once overflowing affections' (6).

Just when Susan 'seemed finally to be succeeding in severing herself absolutely' from all human company, Ronald Gordon – 'man of the world, traveller, dabbler in many things', and heir to the estate across the river (6) – succeeds in breaking down the barriers of Susan's reserve' (7).

'In spite of much vehement disagreement on many questions they found one another increasingly pleasant company.' Two years slip by in which they see one another 'almost every day', while 'all unknowingly the heart which Susan fully believed to be dead awoke to a new and passionate life' (7). Four years have passed, thus, when Kit Drummond writes to say she is returning to England. '"Good things can't last for ever"', is Gordon's pessimistic response to this news. When Susan objects, explaining that '"Kit is my other self"', he protests: '"But I don't want another you! ... I was quite happy with one you. We've got on so well – you and I – so exceptionally well; a third person will be such a bore"' ... '"I want to be your 'best friend'"' (10, 11). But the proposal of marriage he offers to ensure this has disastrous consequences. When Susan explains her refusal on the basis of their unreconcilable differences of opinion –

'You believe in the intensification of each moment of individual life; you are a modern of the moderns, for to you Time holds Eternity in its folds, not Eternity Time. From such a view of life mine is as far as the Poles asunder. Every hour of my life of late years has taught me more clearly that form of any kind is one thing that passes away – that personality, individual, *self*, in a word, perishes, that the universal remains ... ' (17)

– she is devastated by his willingness to jettison the idea of marriage and remain friends. She is devastated, that is, by the dual realization that Gordon's feeling for her has been 'liking' rather than 'love' and that her philosophy has failed her: 'All it had been able to do for her was to lend its formula to her lips, for the better concealment' of her own emotions (22, 21). '"You called me cold and inhuman", she cries after he has left, '"but if you had loved me you would have understood"', and she could have denounced her 'formula' as the 'moral refrigerator' the narrator had characterized it as initially.

Not unlike the relationship in 'The Buddhist Priest's Wife,' Susan's with Ronald Gordon provides both parties with what Oscar Wilde termed, in describing one Oxford friend to another, '*intellectual friction to rouse [one] up to talk and think*'.[20] But in this case the 'Socratic ideal of mental intercourse between male friends'[21] is sabotaged not only by the gender of one of the participants but also by both the narrator's and Susan's critique of disembodied intellectuality and abstraction. This critique is reinforced later in the novel as well, in a scene in which Susan, Gordon, and Kit argue about the value of a picture of a beautiful view. A picture, Gordon argues, '"appeals to one's sense of beauty distilled by memory into a pure essence. If Constable were alive, and I could get him to paint this bit of the park, I should feel every time I look at the picture a shock of feeling keener, because less diffused, than the impression I am conscious of now"' (70–71). Neither woman is convinced. 'He was not often either priggish or commonplace,' the narrator notes; 'and when, as now, he was both, their subtle feminine instinct told them that he must be finding himself on very thin ice indeed' (71). Kit finally responds for both women, though with an abruptness that distinguishes her from Susan: '"I shouldn't care if all the pictures in the world were burnt so long as the things themselves remained"' (71). She goes on to describe herself as a philistine for taking this position. But in fact this whole narrative builds a case against the philistinism of academic culture: against the acculturation of vision, intellect and sensibility that makes it so difficult for an Edward Pargiter to 'express his genuine emotion in a genuine way'[22] and that makes Ronald Gordon claim to privilege aesthetic re-presentations of life over life itself.

Through her representation of Susan and Kit's relationship, Arnold also builds a case against both the male homosociality of academic culture and the hetero-sociality of Victorian middle-class culture. Terry Castle has described the literary history of the lesbian as a history of derealization, of 'ghosting'. Although the pattern of spectralization that she traces through eighteenth-, nineteenth- and twentieth-century European texts is confirmed at the end of *Platonics* when Susan 'come[s] back' to Kit, 'even though it were only from beyond the grave' as Kit reads Susan's unsent letter,[23] we risk historical accuracy, I think, by identifying Susan and Kit as 'lesbians'. *After Oscar Wilde's* trials in 1895, the fluidity and ambiguity of categories such as 'Uranianism', 'sexual inversion', and 'manly love' will be contained through a new, and increasingly scientific vocabulary of gender polarity. Since *Platonics* was published in 1894, however, it is more appropriate to think of Susan and Kit as 'bi-social', a term Margaret Stetz has coined to describe the way in which Wilde himself operated with equal ease in the all-male environment of public school, university and Clubland and in a wide circle of female friendships.[24] In other words, although Phyllis Wachter prefers 'homorelational' to 'lesbian continuum' in describing Susan and Kit's relationship because of the first term's alleged emphasis on behavior rather than sexuality, neither term does justice to the way both women sustained primary emotional bonds with Gordon *and* each other.

When Kit first arrives in Northumbria the morning after Gordon's proposal of marriage to Susan, 'a look of such tenderness, such benign loving-kindness, as almost raised friendship into a sacrament' comes into her face as she tries to comfort the exhausted and distraught Susan, neither knowing nor caring what was wrong 'so long as she might help and comfort' (25–6, 26). When she tells Susan of Gordon's confession of love for *her* and his for him, she refuses to give priority to hetero-relationality. Pressing Susan's 'cold, thin hand' between 'her two strong, warm ones', she claims:

> 'if it's to make any difference between us two – if you're to love me less or to live your life apart from mine, I will give it all up. I couldn't bear it. I loved you first, and for years you have been mother, sister, and friend to me. Nothing in the world not even this strange new feeling which has sprung up in my heart, transforming life, can alter my love for you. Tell me you will be the same to me – that nothing can break the bond between us.' (103–4)

When this does not happen and Susan spends the first year of her marriage travelling with Gordon on the continent, the narrator describes her as being happy 'as far as she could be happy' (109). 'She was genuinely in love with the man she had married; she found him delightful company, and was never bored by him. But there are some women whom no man's love can altogether compensate for the loss of a woman's, and Kit was one of them' (109).

'The passing judgement of the majority of men' on women's friendships 'might be summed up in the words, "Occupy till I come"', Mary Cholmondeley notes in her popular New Woman novel of 1900, *Red Pottage*. And in many cases, her narrator goes on to note, this is in fact what happens. Even when 'they don't come the hastily improvised friendships may hold together for years'. 'Here and there', however,

> among its numberless counterfeits a friendship rises up between two women which sustains the life of both, which is still young when life is waning, which man's love and motherhood cannot displace nor death annihilate; a friendship which is not the solitary affection of an empty heart nor the deepest affection of a full one, but which

nevertheless lightens the burdens of this world and lays its pure hand upon the next.[25]

By contrast with Arnold's characterization of Susan and Kit's relationship, Cholmondeley is very careful *not* to assert the ultimate primacy of a woman's relationship with another woman. Writing in the wake of the scandal of Wilde's trials, perhaps she had no other rhetorical options, given how, in the words of Richard Dellamora, 'the crises of sexual identity and male privilege' of the 1890s ultimately 'issued in the reaffirmation of the naturalness of gender norms, of manly men and womanly women, of marriage, of the return of the middle-class woman to the home, and of the primacy of mothering'.[26] Writing in 1894, however, Arnold describes a relationship between two women that simultaneously challenges both the compulsory prioritization, for middle-class women, of hetero-sociality and Oxford Hellenism's Socratic idealization of 'pure' 'perfect' 'intellectual' love (to borrow Wilde's phrasing once again). Susan's unsent letter to Kit plunges us back into corporeality and the small-scale satisfactions of quotidinal human life:

> when, just now, I knew that my life was over, my eyes seemed suddenly to be opened, and I saw that what I had believed to be the final victory of an idea was, after all, something very different and much more human ... here, on the threshold of Death, the Ego I have tried to kill springs up into an infinitely strengthened life, rebelling passionately against the thought of ceasing to be, craving only the touch a human hand, now and for ever. The door over which is written 'Loving-Kindness,' is the only door which leads to the open. (127)

Platonics thus ends with a renunciation of idealism, of the Socratic model of eros, of both bourgeois hetero-normativity and the male homo-normativity of Oxford academicism. Like Woolf's Kitty Malone, Ethel Arnold lived as a perpetual outsider to Oxford's intellectual inner-circle. Nonetheless, her only novel presents us with a very complicated rejoinder to the New Hellenism: a commentary on women's exclusion from Victorian academic culture, a recasting of the Socratic student–teacher relationship, and a critique of the Platonic ideal of disembodied intellectuality. Read in conjunction with Schreiner's 'A Buddhist Priest's Wife', we begin to understand why New Women might have felt that the New Hellenism dis-enabled rather than encouraged female intellectuality, erased rather than articulated female bi-sociality. And we find further reason to give feminine phenomena 'central importance in the analysis of modernity' – thereby changing our understanding of modernity itself.[27]

Notes

1. Linda Dowling, *Hellenism and Homosexuality in Victorian Oxford* (Ithaca: Cornell University Press, 1994), xiii.
2. The term homorelationality is Phyllis Wachter's, who argues that it is more inclusive than Adrienne Rich's more familiar characterization of a 'lesbian continuum'. Its adequacy as a means of characterizing the female relationships in *Platonics* will be discussed below. Phyllis Wachter, 'Introduction'. Edith Arnold, *Platonics* (London: Thoemmes Press, 1995), ix.
3. Suzanne Clark, *Sentimental Modernism: Women Writers and the Revolution of the Word* (Bloomington: Indiana University Press, 1991), 3.
4. Mark Sanders, 'Towards a Genealogy of Intellectual Life: Women, Autobiography and Fiction in Olive Schreiner's *The Story of an African Farm*'. Unpublished manuscript, 2.
5. Olive Schreiner, 'The Buddhist Priest's Wife' (henceforward BPW), *Daughters of Decadence* (London: Virago Press, 1993), 86.
6. Sanders, 15, 5.
7. Sanders, 25, 14, 5.
8. Sanders 12, quoting BPW 92.
9. Dowling, 149.
10. 'I always think that when Christianity burst on the dark Roman world it was what that book was to me', she writes to Havelock Ellis in a letter dated 28 March 1884. Schreiner, *My Other Self: the Letters of Olive Schreiner and Havelock Ellis, 1884–1920* (Peter Lang, 1992), 39.
11. '"It would never have done for me to marry"', Webb writes that he told her at a 'miserable dinner-party' in December of 1884. '"I could not have stood the monotony of married life and then I should have been too fastidious. I must have had a rational woman with great sympathy and considerable sense of humour" "Rather difficult to find", [Webb] observed in response. "Rational women are generally odiously dull and self-centred". To her goad he responded: "That is a very erroneous generalization: George Eliot was highly rational and yet intensely sympathetic, but there the weak point (which appeared a very important one to me) was physique." "I could not have married a woman who had not great physical attraction," added the withered old philospher, stretching his bony limbs and leaving that patent theory-making machine on the side of the armchair, his upper lip appearing preternaturally long and his eyes preternaturally small."' Norman and Jeanne MacKenzie, eds, *The Diary of Beatrice Webb*, I (Belknap Press, 1982), 100.
12. See Clark, *Sentimental Modernism*: and Deidre David, *Intellectual Women and Victorian Patriarchy: Harriet Martineau, Elizabeth Barrett Browning, George Eliot* (Ithaca: Cornell University Press, 1987).
13. Dowling, 63.
14. Wachter, x.

15. Wachter, x.
16. In writing this essay, I have not had access to Arnold's essay in the *Oxford High School Magazine* and other biographical materials Wachter mentions in her introduction to the Thoemmes Press edition of *Platonics*.
17. Virginia Woolf, *The Pargiters* (London: Harcourt Brace Jovanovich, 1977), 128.
18. Wachter, xi.
19. Dowling, 133.
20. As quoted by Dowling, 124. The physical description of both Gordon and Kit as slim, androgynous figures would also support this association.
21. Oscar Wilde, as quoted by Dowling, 124.
22. Woolf, 83.
23. Terry Castle, *The Apparitional Lesbian: Female Homosexuality and Modern Culture* (New York: Columbia University Press, 1993).
24. Margaret Stetz, 'Oscar Wilde and Women'. Unpublished manuscript, 7.
25. Mary Cholmondeley, *Red Pottage* (Harmondsworth: Penguin, 1985), 130.
26. Richard Dellamora, *Masculine Desire: The Politics of Victorian Aestheticism* (University of North Carolina Press, 1990), 216–17.
27. Rita Felski, *The Gender of Modernity* (Cambridge, Mass: Harvard University Press, 1995), 10.

7
Narrating the Hysteric: *Fin-de-Siècle* Medical Discourse and Sarah Grand's *The Heavenly Twins* (1893)

Ann Heilmann

A synonym for femininity in nineteenth-century medical textbooks, hysteria encodes female rebellion in contemporary feminist theory. This essay examines the way in which Sarah Grand's novel *The Heavenly Twins* (1893) challenges Victorian medicine while also taking issue with the feminist conflation of hysteria and protest. Presenting Charlotte Perkins Gilman's account of female madness through the eyes of the physician husband, Grand drew on contemporary medical discourse in order to undermine patriarchal authority by exposing its destructive impact on female identity. Her strategy of disrupting the doctor's story with the voices of the female narrator and her heroine anticipated that other *fin-de-siècle* hysteric who exploded the narrative frame of her case study, Anna O. By ultimately relegating her character Evadne to the shadow land of the failed rebel, Grand suggested that, while hysteria dramatized the clash between patriarchal law and female experience, thus marking the transition from internalized conflict to externalized anger, its liberating potential was lost unless this externalization did in fact take place. To a writer then in the process of becoming an activist, it was commitment to organized political action, and not the earlier phase of hysterical self-absorption, that was the mark of the successful feminist.

The novel features three female characters whose attempts to struggle free from parental, marital and medical oppression leave one of them dead and another suffering from clinical depression. Evadne learns about her husband's dissolute (possibly syphilitic) past on her wedding day and, under intense pressure from her parents, agrees to live with him on condition that the marriage remain sexless. Angelica (one of the twins of the title) marries in order to exchange her authoritarian father for a more permissive one; she does not think of her husband as a sexual partner at all until she is shocked into 'femininity' (submissive sexuality) after causing a male friend's death. Thus for both women, marriage and sex are associated with punishment and death. This message is sensationalized through Edith, who marries a debauched officer, is promptly struck down by syphilis and insanity, and dies after bearing a diseased child.

Although Edith (the Old Woman) is constructed as Evadne's (the New Woman's) opposite, the two friends change dramatically as a result of their marital tragedies, with Edith becoming more like Evadne, and Evadne turning into a weak-spirited, submissive Edith. While still unmarried, Edith evades all knowledge of life, thus anticipating Evadne's later attitude: 'She did not want to think. When any obtrusive thought presented itself she instantly strove to banish it.'[1] In the face of disease and death, however, Edith is suddenly inspired by a capacity for revolt previously inconceivable for her; metamorphosing into a mad Bertha Rochester, she dreams of stabbing her husband:

> I am quite, quite mad! ... Do you know what I have been doing? I've been murdering him! I've been creeping, creeping, with bare feet, to surprise him in his sleep; and I had a tiny knife – very sharp – and I felt for the artery ... and then stabbed quickly! and he awoke, and knew he must die – and cowered! and it was all a pleasure to me. Oh, yes! I am quite, quite mad! ... I want to kill – I want to kill *him*. (*HT*, 304)

The label and experience of 'madness' liberate Edith as decisively as they silence Evadne. Edith's dream of revenge is enacted, in a more moderate form, by Angelica who (in a further echo of *Jane Eyre*) tries to elude Edith's womanizing husband by hiding behind the curtains of the bay window in the library, but then emerges to hurl a Bible at his face, breaking his nose in the process. Of the three women, Angelica alone is able to deal constructively with periods of intense anger or despair, which in the case of the other two inevitably result in 'mad' spells culminating in fantasies of violence (Edith) or pathological withdrawal (Evadne). Angelica's indifference to social decorum, her exuberance, extroversion and energy allow her to respond to problems constructively, through positive action and physical activity. Thus at the height of a crisis, when she mourns her friend, for whose death she feels partly responsible, she finds relief in putting on her brother's trousers and going for a proto-Lawrentian night-time run through the forest:

> She threw up her arms and stretched every limb in the joy of perfect freedom from restraint; and then with strong bounds she cleared the grassy space, dashed down a rocky step, and found herself a substance amongst the shadows out in the murmuring woods. (*HT*, 530)

Being used, from childhood, to 'talk[ing] things out' with others, she shares her grief with others, as a result of which 'she found herself the better in every way' (*HT*, 532). Anticipating Anna O.'s 'talking cure' made so famous by Freud and Breuer's *Studies on Hysteria* (1895/1955),[2] and linking a treatment which was to revolutionize psychoanalysis to the contemporary feminist demand for healthy outdoor exercise and non-constricting clothes, Grand rewrote the old texts and rest cures of patriarchal medicine which insisted that women's desire for an active public life was itself a form of madness, and that sanity, for women, consisted in a return to domesticity.

While Angelica is saved from serious illness because of her (pro)active approach and her ability to play with gender, Edith and Evadne, unable to struggle free from the norms of femininity, succumb to their 'female malady'.[3] Their different manifestations of madness reflect the female condition of being deprived either of vital knowledge, or of an outlet for action: Edith goes mad as a result of sexual ignorance, Evadne's hysteria is rooted in the promise exacted by her first husband, Colonel Colquhoun, not to get involved in any social or political movement during his lifetime (*HT*, 345), and is compounded by her fear of the dimension her pent-up rage could take:

> I can be the most docile, the most obedient, the most loving of women as long as I forget my knowledge of life; but the moment I remember I become a raging fury; I have no patience with slow processes; 'Revolution' would be my cry, and I could preside with an awful joy at the execution of those who are making the misery now for succeeding generations. (*HT*, 672)

Too frightened of her anger and its destructive potential (Edith's madness), too conscious of social problems to banish them altogether from her mind, stuck in a second marriage which allows for even less

mental freedom than her first, while robbing her (sexually, in reproductive terms, and medically) of control over her body, Evadne with-
draws into mental illness. The most disturbing reflection of her
disintegration is the fact that her voice and perspective are filtered
through a male consciousness, with the last Book moving from a third-
person narrative to a first-person account delivered by her doctor and
second husband.

Though he appears to be a positive character, Dr Galbraith's twin
roles of physician and husband suggest grim analogies with Charlotte
Perkins Gilman's 'The Yellow Wallpaper', published a year before *The
Heavenly Twins*. Written from the opposite angle, the story provides
chilling insights into a marriage in which the husband is so 'careful
and loving' that he 'hardly lets [his wife] stir without special direction'.[4] Read in conjunction with Gilman's text, the patriarchal authority behind Galbraith's concern for Evadne becomes transparent, for
even if he doesn't reduce her to his 'blessed little goose' (YW, 15), he
counts her as one of his children (*HT*, 672, 675). In both texts, the
doctor-husband's medical regimen contributes to his wife's condition,
and both women experience pregnancy as particularly alienating
because of the additional control their husbands gain over their bodies.
But while Gilman's narrator uses her madness to break free from her
husband, hypnotizing and paralysing him with her Medusa's gaze and
crawling (walking) over him when he has fainted, Evadne directs her
anger and despair against herself. Whereas 'The Yellow Wallpaper'
ends with the wife's declaration of independence ('I've got out at last
... so you can't put me back!', YW, 36), Evadne has grown so attached
to her shadow existence that she no longer wants to 'get out', asking
Galbraith to let her 'live on the surface of life, as most women do' (*HT*,
672). A comparative reading of the two texts throws into relief the different encodings of female madness in turn-of-the-century feminist
fiction, subversion in Gilman's story contrasting with disempower-
ment in Grand's.

Faced with Galbraith's appropriatory gaze, Evadne is frozen into a
frame defined by his perspective, with their first encounter foreshad-
owing the parameters of their later relationship: while visiting her
aunt, he discovers a girl asleep in an arm-chair, and appraises her facial
features with a mixture of voyeurism and scientific detachment. His
attitude anticipates the way in which he will later dissect Evadne's
'case' and seek to enter the recesses of her mind – an activity whose
phallic symbolism was well-established by the end of the nineteenth
century when, as Elaine Showalter and Elisabeth Bronfen have pointed

out, dominant images and metaphors in culture and art represented women as boxes ('cases'/case studies) whose mystery could only be lifted if they were opened and penetrated, with the writer's pen, the painter's brush, the doctor's knife, or the psychoanalyst's gaze.[5]

Throughout the text, Galbraith keeps coming across Evadne's sleeping body, the object of his ever more intensified gaze; at one point he even watches her through a telescope and, convinced that 'her whole attitude ... appealed to [him] like a cry for help', sets off for her house in great agitation, only to find her 'perfectly tranquil ... with no trace of recent emotion' (*HT*, 587). His telescopic appropriation of Evadne echoes aspects of Jean-Martin Charcot's use of the camera at the Salpêtrière; like Charcot, Galbraith seeks for dramatized external poses which would reflect his patient's inner mysteries.[6] Eroticizing his medical interest in Evadne, he constructs her as a Lady of Shalott figure because this image 'appeals' to him, just as the pictorial representation and dramatic performance of feminine hysteria appealed to the nineteenth-century medical establishment more generally.

However, since Grand's discourse on female madness foregrounds the instability of, and changing power relations between, the figures of male doctor and female hysteric, she resists the temptation to construct Galbraith as a straightforward villain and Evadne as his passive victim. Both Galbraith and Sir Shadwell Rock, the medical celebrity he consults, earnestly wish for Evadne to recover, and their holistic treatment, with its emphasis on the stimulation of body *and* mind, represents a significant departure from real-life Victorian doctors' punitive and invasive medicine. Contemporary treatments meted out to the female hysteric, ranging from the rest cure to clitoridectomy, leave little doubt about the primarily disciplinary function of medical interventions on the female body; thus Silas Weir Mitchell noted that

> The moral uses of enforced rest are readily estimated ... The result is always ... a remarkable and often a quite abrupt disappearance of many of the nervous symptoms ... [T]he physician ... should ... seize the proper occasions to direct the thoughts of his patients to the lapse from duties to others, and to the selfishness which a life of invalidism is apt to bring about.[7]

As a result of Mitchell's rest cure, Gilman (whose depression was rooted in her loss of identity following her marriage and the birth of her daughter) 'came so near the border line of utter mental ruin that [she] could see over'.[8] Whereas Mitchell wanted to castigate the mind and

destroy women's selfish will, Isaac Baker Brown, performing clitoridec-
tomies in the 1860s, wanted to castigate the body and destroy
women's sexual desire.[9] Hysteria was associated with unrestrained
female sexuality as well as with sexual resistance to marital intercourse;
thus the leading British physician William Acton warned a feminist
patient that her refusal to carry out her wifely duties left her husband
in imminent danger of impotence.[10] Exceptionally well read in the
medical literature of the time, Grand constructed *The Heavenly Twins* as
a counter-narrative to the master discourse of Victorian medicine, suggesting that, while husbands' health was not impaired by their part-
ners' sexual withdrawal, wives suffered serious damage to their mental
health as a result of their husbands' prohibition of meaningful work.
Colonel Colquhoun dies from a heart attack, not from the after-effects
of impotence, but Evadne falls permanently ill the moment she makes
her fatal promise.

By encouraging Evadne to take an active interest in intellectual and
socio-political matters, Galbraith sounds a new note in medical treatment, but ultimately Grand considers him unable to disengage himself
from the dominant ideology. Thus echoes of real-life doctors and their
patriarchal authority over their women patients surface in his belief
that 'steady moral influence' is required to 'awaken the conscience' of
hysterics to their 'depraved' ways (*HT*, 575). Although professing sympathy for the women's movement, he clings to the belief that it is only
by first fulfilling their 'natural' role as wives and mothers that women
can gain the mental equilibrium required to 'distinguish' themselves as
feminists. Consequently, the moment Evadne becomes pregnant, her
biological function as a mother takes precedence over anything else: 'a
new interest in life was coming to cure her of all morbid moods for
ever' (*HT*, 660). Even though his own experience flatly contradicts his
medical diagnosis, he insists that '[n]othing could have been healthier
or more natural than her pride and delight' in her maternal role (*HT*,
667). In reality, Evadne's mental state deteriorates considerably during
pregnancy, culminating in an attempt to poison herself and her baby.
Far from providing an incentive to take an interest in the outside
world, motherhood encloses her once and for all within the domestic
sphere. After the birth of their son, who even in his name ('Donino')
reproduces his father ('Don') while their daughter remains nameless,
the transformation from 'raging fury' to meek and dependent child-
wife is complete. Like Edith at the beginning of her marital career,
Evadne now sees her life's purpose in fulfilling an exclusively home-
bound role:

I will do nothing but attend to my household duties and the social duties of my position. I will read nothing that is not first weeded by you of every painful thought that might remind me. I will play with my baby by day, and curl up comfortably beside you at night, infinitely grateful and content to be so happily circumstanced myself ... (*HT*, 672)

As Lyn Pykett has pointed out, Evadne's mimicry of hyperfemininity signals resistance through withdrawal,[11] but as a mode of protest it is ineffective since her voice is lost and she fades into a simulacrum of ladyhood. While Angelica and Galbraith play an important role in *The Beth Book* (1897), Grand's sequel to *The Heavenly Twins*, Evadne appears only in her official function, as 'Lady Galbraith', acting as a silent shadow to her husband during dinner parties, and failing to respond to the one rhetorical question addressed to her.[12] Ending *The Heavenly Twins* with Evadne's silence and Galbraith's acknowledgement of his failure, Grand reaffirms the impression that male medicine is detrimental to women's mental health.

This is further accentuated by the novel's dual narrative structure which pointedly draws attention to the discrepancies between feminist and medical readings of female breakdown. Thus Galbraith's account is preceded, and undermined, by an editorial note which deploys the same textual strategy of hiding damning criticism behind ostensible praise which is used to such effect in 'The Yellow Wallpaper' ('He is very careful and loving, and hardly lets me stir without special direction'). In the guise of commending Galbraith, the text points to the gaps in his knowledge, suggesting that his incomplete understanding of the case and his personal bias led to diagnostic errors, and advising readers to approach the first-person narrative with caution:

The fact that *Dr. Galbraith had not the advantage of knowing Evadne's early history* when they first became acquainted adds a certain *piquancy* to the *flavour* of his *impressions*, and *the reader, better informed* than himself with regard to the antecedents of his 'subject,' will find it interesting to note both the accuracy of his insight and the *curious mistakes* which it is possible even for a trained observer like himself to make by the *half light of such imperfect knowledge* as he was able to collect under the circumstances. His record, which is minute in all important particulars, is specially valuable for the way in which it makes apparent the changes of habit and opinion and the modifications of character that had been brought about in a very short time by *the restriction Colonel Colquhoun had imposed* upon her. In some respects it is hard to believe that she is the same person. But *more interesting still, perhaps, are the glimpses we get of Dr. Galbraith himself in the narrative*, throughout which it is easy to decipher the simple earnestness of the man, the cautious professionalism and integrity, the touches of tender sentiment held in check, the *dash of egotism*, the healthy-minded human nature, the capacity for enjoyment and sorrow, the love of life, and, above all, the perfect unconsciousness with which he shows himself to have been a man of fastidious refinement and exemplary moral strength and delicacy; of the highest possible character; and most lovable in spite of *a somewhat irascible temper and manner which were apt to be abrupt at times.* (HT, 554, emphasis added)

The first sentence establishes the unreliability of the first-person narrator, highlighting the essentially constructed nature of his account by drawing on a vocabulary which pinpoints its sensory (emotional) rather than scientific basis ('piquancy', 'flavour', 'impressions'). By emphasizing the reader's superior knowledge, Grand challenges the doctor's privileged status as a master narrator, alerting her readers to the need to scrutinize his 'performance'. She thus reverses the power dynamics, especially in the case of female readers, by encouraging them to study *his* 'case' while he is engaged on examining Evadne's. While casting doubt on the accuracy of Galbraith's observations, Grand carefully directs her readers to her own, feminist reading of Evadne's mental illness as a result of the promise of passivity exacted by her first husband. At the same time Grand implies that Evadne's second marriage contributed its part, signalling her disapproval of Galbraith's character by ending her exaggerated eulogy with a damning remark on his temper and by framing her editorial note with his professional and personal failings. What thus emerges is a complex multiple narrative whose surface structure is destabilized by the feminist narrator's critique of male science. As the spokesman of nineteenth-century medicine Galbraith constructs marriage and motherhood as beneficial, whereas Grand exposes both as damaging to women.

Grand takes care to emphasize that Evadne is anything but a 'cold-blooded' woman with no sexual desire; even years into her marriage, her senses are still 'troubled' by the close proximity of her husband (HT, 344). However, Galbraith's assumption that her depression is caused by sexual frustration is not borne out by the text, since she does not recover as a result of her second marriage. The only time we see her in radiant health is when she is working as a nurse during a smallpox epidemic: 'She was the life of the camp, bright, cheerful, and active, never tired apparently, and never disheartened' (*HT*, 599). At a time of transition, when the medical establishment was moving from the doctrine of the non-existence of sexual pleasure, which criminalized sexually active women (William Acton),[13] to the opposite position, which pathologized spinsters (Sigmund Freud), feminists like Grand pointed out that what drove women mad was not the absence of sex, but the lack of a meaningful and fulfilling occupation.

The consequences of denying women a self-determined life are demonstrated by Evadne's retreat into fantasy. Anticipating Anna O.'s 'private theatre' described in Breuer's case study, Evadne turns to daydreaming, only to find that, gradually, the dreams take over:

I began to be intoxicated. My imagination ran away with me. Instead of indulging in a daydream now and then, when I liked, all my life became absorbed in delicious imaginings, whether I would or not ... I lived in my world apart. If people spoke to me, I awoke and answered them; but real life was a dull thing to offer, and the daylight very dim, compared with the movement and brightness of the land I lived in – while I was master of my dreams ... By degrees they mastered me; and now I am their puppet, and they are demons that torment me. (*HT*, 626–7)

As Laura Marcus notes in her contribution to this collection, daydreaming was a complex and ambivalent concept for Freud and Breuer, associated as it was both with the creative imagination of the artist (constructive) and with feminine pathology (destructive). Profoundly influenced by male psychoanalytic discourse, while simultaneously aware of the way in which fantasy provided women with an outlet for their repressed desire for an active and/or creative life, female analysts like Anna Freud and Lou Andreas-Salomé constructed (their own) daydreaming as a signifier of female sexuality (interiority) *and* a symptom of women's rebellious impulses (exteriority). It is against this background that daydreaming, as a marker of autobiographical experience, became a metaphor for female resistance in *fin-de-siècle* feminist writing. Thus Gilman, who at the onset of puberty had been forbidden by her mother (the patriarchal substitute for the missing father) to indulge in the dream world which she had inhabited for years, drawing on this 'richer, more glorious life ... inside' at a time when she was increasingly coming to resent her brother's somewhat fuller life, outside, in her writing later encoded madness as the outer sign of women's 'captive imagination', representing their withdrawal into an alternative, inner, reality as the inevitable outcome of their social confinement to the world within.[14] Similarly, Grand projected political qualities into Evadne's retreat into fantasy.

What is striking in Grand's story are the similarities between Evadne's breakdown and some aspects of Anna O.'s case study. Like Evadne, Anna O. has a 'powerful intellect' and 'great poetic and imaginative gifts' and, as with Grand's character, her energy, will-power and craving for intellectual stimulation and an occupation, when frustrated, degenerate into 'suicidal impulses' and nervous symptoms, her amnesias (repression of memories) corresponding to Evadne's all-too-conscious repression of all painful knowledge. With her sexuality 'undeveloped', Anna O., too, seeks relief in a fantasy world of the senses. Breuer writes that '[t]his girl, who was bubbling over with intellectual vitality' and who, like Evadne, temporarily recovered from her depression while looking after the sick,

> embellished her life in a manner which probably influenced her decisively in the direction of her illness, by indulging in systematic day-dreaming, which she described as her 'private theatre'. While everyone thought she was attending, she was living through fairy tales in her imagination; but she was always on the spot when she was spoken to, so that no one was aware of it. She pursued this activity almost continuously while she was engaged on her household duties ...[15]

Although at first able to switch back and forth 'on the spot', Anna O. goes through a complex process of mental disintegration, with a gradual falling away of language, and the emergence of hallucinations and non-organic paralyses. Paradoxically, Anna O. and Evadne are simultaneously incapacitated *and* empowered by their hysteria, which enables them to 'abreact' (deal with, subvert) their anger. Thus Evadne's somnambulism (her immersion in a dream world and loss of a sense of reality) provides her with an excuse for breaking the male-written codes of ladyhood, allowing her to walk through a disreputable part of London, unaccompanied, and at night, to the great consternation of Galbraith, who follows her, ostensibly in order to protect her, but really to spy on her. Unable to rebuff Galbraith's advances in daytime reality, Evadne repulses a night-time pursuer while Galbraith looks on as if glancing into a mirror: for the man who propositions

Evadne is also a gentleman, and as such the dark double of Galbraith. Similarly Anna O., the indefatigable nurse during her father's last illness and paragon of domesticity, takes to her bed, subverting the law of the father by refusing to speak his language, and reviving at night, under hypnosis, to give an uninhibited account of her 'real' feelings: 'in the day-time', Breuer writes, she was 'the irresponsible patient pursued by hallucinations, and at night the girl with her mind completely clear' who, '[a]fter giving ... energetic expression to the anger she had held back ... woke from her hypnosis ... [with] the disturbance vanished, never to return.'[16]

A creative work of mythological dimensions, *Studies on Hysteria* was first published in 1895, two years after the international success of *The Heavenly Twins*, and was not fully available in English until 1955.[17] Evadne's case study is therefore not a feminist response to a specific medical text; instead, Anna O.'s story constitutes Freud's (via Breuer's) literary (re)construction of female hysteria and transference through the medium of science at a time when this medium was increasingly being challenged by feminist writers who deconstructed hysteria as failed rebellion, debunking medical case studies as the product of male doctors' counter-transference (as a result of their erotic fantasies of feminine frailty). In this instance at least, psychoanalysis reflected the themes, though not the political direction, of women's writing, with both cultural arenas creating powerful myths of female hysteria as subversion.

Bertha Pappenheim, the woman behind the sign (Anna O. – the Alpha and Omega of womanhood), was treated by Breuer in the early 1880s, half a decade before Charlotte Perkins Gilman consulted the less congenial Silas Weir Mitchell, and some fifteen years before Grand herself suffered a number of breakdowns and rest cures in the 1890s and early 1900s.[18] Though Breuer ended his case study on a cautious note of success, Pappenheim's recovery was not the foregone conclusion as which he presented it under pressure from Freud. In reality, Pappenheim continued to suffer from severe nervous symptoms and morphine addiction, with prolonged hospital stays considered necessary until 1887, five years after Breuer had 'officially' terminated his treatment, the very year in which Gilman took up her rest cure, and a year before Grand started writing *The Heavenly Twins*.[19] Like Gilman, Pappenheim eventually cured herself; and like Grand, she developed into a feminist writer and activist with social purity proclivities, moving into journalism, political pamphleteering and narrative writing after a sustained career as a social worker, translating Mary

Wollstonecraft's *Vindication of the Rights of Woman* in 1899, founding the *Jüdischer Frauenbund* (League of Jewish Women) in 1904, and, like Grand's character Ideala, devoting herself to the rescue and rehabilitation of prostitutes.[20] Pappenheim and Gilman remained violently opposed to Freudian psychoanalysis for the rest of their lives.[21]

Bertha Pappenheim, Sarah Grand and Charlotte Perkins Gilman: the mental breakdowns of these three feminist writers and activists, who broke free from patriarchal and medical discourses in three different Western countries at roughly the same time, reflect the conditions and pressures under which the New Woman laboured towards the close of the nineteenth century. Infusing their narrative writing with autobiographical experience and drawing strength from literature in living their political activism, they all suggested that it is the lack of intellectual and professional opportunities, compounded by medical and sexual oppression, which impairs women's physical and mental health, rather than the repression of their sexual desire. In *The Heavenly Twins*, Evadne's compliance with her first husband's prohibition to work imposes a rest cure which lasts a life-time. Like the narrator in Gilman's 'The Yellow Wallpaper', and like Bertha Pappenheim in Breuer's study of Anna O., Evadne is driven mad by the images that take over her mind. A few years before the birth of psychoanalysis feminist writers and activists on both sides of the Atlantic were thus articulating a socio-political counter-narrative to the Freudian construction of hysteria as a quintessentially sexual neurosis.

Notes

1. Sarah Grand, *The Heavenly Twins* (London: Heinemann, 1908; first published in 1893), 168. Further references to the novel will appear in the text as *HT*.
2. Josef Breuer, case study of Anna O., in Josef Breuer and Sigmund Freud, *Studies on Hysteria*, trans. James and Alix Strachey (Harmondsworth: Penguin, 1974), 73–102. First complete English edition 1955, first German edition 1895.
3. Elaine Showalter, *The Female Malady: Women, Madness and English Culture, 1830–1980* (London: Virago, 1987).
4. Charlotte Perkins Gilman, 'The Yellow Wallpaper' (London: Virago, 1988), 12. First published in 1892. Further references to this story will appear in the text as *YW*.
5. Elaine Showalter, *Sexual Anarchy* (London: Bloomsbury, 1991), 134; Elisabeth Bronfen, *Over Her Dead Body: Death, Femininity and the Aesthetic* (Manchester: Manchester University Press, 1992), 3–14.
6. See Showalter, *The Female Malady*, 147–55, and *Hystories: Hysterical Epidemics and Modern Culture* (London: Picador, 1997), 30–7.

7. Silas Weir Mitchell, [from] *Fat and Blood: And How to Make Them* (1877), in Catherine Golden (ed.), *The Captive Imagination: a Casebook on The Yellow Wallpaper* (New York: Feminist Press, 1992), 48–50.
8. Charlotte Perkins Gilman, 'Why I Wrote "The Yellow Wallpaper"?' (1913), in Ann J. Lane (ed.), *The Charlotte Perkins Gilman Reader* (London: Women's Press, 1981), 20.
9. Showalter, *The Female Malady*, 75–8; Isaac Baker Brown, [from] *On the Curability of Certain Forms of Insanity, Epilepsy, Catalepsy and Hysteria in Females* (1866) and *On Some Diseases of Woman Admitting Surgical Treatment* (1866), in Sheila Jeffreys (ed.), *The Sexuality Debates* (New York: Routledge & Kegan Paul, 1987), 11–41; Pat Jalland and John Hooper (eds), *Women From Birth to Death: the Female Life Cycle in Britain 1830–1914* (Brighton: Harvester, 1986), 250–65.
10. William Acton, [from] *The Functions and Disorders of the Sexual Organs* (1875), in Jeffreys, *The Sexuality Debates*, 63–4.
11. Lyn Pykett, *The 'Improper' Feminine: the Women's Sensation Novel and the New Woman Writing* (London: Routledge, 1992), 175.
12. Grand, *The Beth Book* (Bristol: Thoemmes, 1994), 415, 351. First published in 1897.
13. Acton, *The Functions and Disorders of the Sexual Organs*, 61.
14. Gilman, *The Living of Charlotte Perkins Gilman* (Madison: University of Wisconsin Press, 1990), 23–4. First published in 1935. See also Golden, *The Captive Imagination*.
15. Breuer and Freud, *Studies on Hysteria*, 74. For previous references see 73, 80.
16. Breuer and Freud, *Studies on Hysteria*, 80, 73, 88.
17. The first English translation by A. A. Brill, *Studies in Hysteria: Selected Papers on Hysteria and Other Psychoneuroses*, published in New York in 1909, excluded Anna O.'s case. See 'Editor's Introduction' to Breuer and Freud's *Studies on Hysteria*, 31.
18. Gillian Kersley, *Darling Madame: Sarah Grand & Devoted Friend* (London: Virago, 1983), xi–xii.
19. For Anna O. see Breuer and Freud, *Studies on Hysteria*, 102; Lisa Appignanesi and John Forrester, *Freud's Women* (London: Virago, 1993), 76–7; and Mikkel Borch-Jacobsen, *Remembering Anna O.: A Century of Mystification*, trans. Kirby Olson in collaboration with Xavier Callahan and the author (London: Routledge, 1996), 9–10, 21–5. For Gilman see Denise D. Knight (ed.), *The Diaries of Charlotte Perkins Gilman*, 2 vols (Charlottesville: University Press of Virginia, 1994), vol. 1, 385. For Grand see Kersley, *Darling Madame*, x.
20. Appignanesi and Forrester, *Freud's Women*, 77–80.
21. See Borch-Jacobsen, *Remembering Anna O.*, 27; Gilman, *The Living*, 314, and Ann Lane, *To Herland and Beyond: the Life and Work of Charlotte Perkins Gilman* (New York: Pantheon, 1990), 323, 352.

8
Staging the 'Private Theatre': Gender and the Auto-Erotics of Reverie

Laura Marcus

> The young woman who writes and the young man who writes are alike dissatisfied; but the woman writes in order to have something, the young man in order to be relieved of something.
>
> (Laura Marholm, *The Psychology of Women*)[1]

The phrase 'private theatre' comes from Freud and Breuer's *Studies in Hysteria* (1895), in which it is used by one of Breuer's women patients, Bertha Pappenheim, known as 'Anna O':

> This girl, who was bubbling over with intellectual vitality, led an extremely monotonous existence in her puritanically-minded family. She embellished her life in a manner which probably influenced her decisively in the direction of her illness, by indulging in systematic day-dreaming, which she described as her 'private theatre'. While everyone thought she was attending, she was living through fairy-tales in her imagination, but she was always on the spot when she was spoken to, so that no one was aware of it. She pursued this activity almost continuously while she was engaged on her household duties, which she discharged unexceptionally ... this habitual day-dreaming while she was well passed over into illness without a break.[2]

One of the tasks Breuer and Freud set themselves in *Studies on Hysteria* was to demonstrate that the roots of hysteria lie 'in an excess rather than a defect'. According to Breuer's 'energetic' model of mental and 'nervous' life, affect or excitation liberated by active mental work is also used up by this work. In states of abstraction and dreaminess, on the other hand, 'intercerebral excitation sinks below its clear waking level', a state which passes over into sleep. If in this 'state of absorption', 'a group of affectively coloured ideas is active', it is put at 'the disposal of abnormal functioning, such as conversion [hysteria]'. While Anna O.'s 'private theatre' is at one moment seen as an aspect of a creative and active imagination, in which 'energetic mental work is carried on', at the next it becomes identified with 'habitual reverie', the first step towards 'pathogenic auto-hypnosis'.[3] The double perspective indicates a more general uncertainty as to the normality or abnormality of creativity and imaginative life. This issue was explored in the numerous studies of genius, creativity and pathology at the turn of the century, as well as in psychoanalytic debates and writings, the best known of which is Freud's essay 'Creative Writers and Day-Dreaming' (1907).

For Breuer 'being in love' and 'sick-nursing' (the latter almost always the province of the unmarried daughter of the house) are the 'two great pathogenic factors' leading to hysteria:

Hysteria and feminism were, a number of recent critics have argued, two sides of the same coin – two forms of protest in the nineteenth century against women's lack of freedom and self-determination. Time and again in the early case histories of psychoanalysis we find references to the women patients' confinement in the home – often confinement to the sickroom of one or other parent. Their attempts to develop lives and careers outside the domestic sphere – often through classes and lectures of various kinds – are almost uniformly thwarted by illness, either their own or that of family members.

For Breuer 'being in love' and 'sick-nursing' (the latter almost always the province of the unmarried daughter of the house) are the 'two great pathogenic factors' leading to hysteria:

> neither 'absence of mind' during energetic work nor unemotional twilight states are pathogenic; on the other hand, reveries that are filled with emotion and states of fatigue arising from protracted affects *are* pathogenic. The broodings of a care-ridden man, the anxiety of a person watching at the sick-bed of someone dear to him, the day-dreams of a lover – these are states of this second kind. Concentration on the affective group of ideas begins by producing 'absence of mind'. The flow of ideas grows gradually slower and at last almost stagnates; but the affective idea and its affect remain active, and so consequently does the great quantity of excitation which is not being used up functionally ... . This is the way in which pathogenic auto-hypnosis would seem to come about in some people – by affect being introduced into a habitual reverie.[4]

Throughout *Studies on Hysteria* we find an ambivalence towards reverie and the 'private theatre'. On the one hand there is perceived to be a continuity between daydreaming and hysterical illness, and a concern that the doubling effected by daydreaming – the fact of living simultaneously in real and fantasy worlds – results in a pathological state of 'double consciousness' (*double conscience*). Anna O., Breuer writes, 'was in the habit, while she was in perfect health, of allowing trains of imaginative ideas to pass through her mind during her ordinary occupations. While she was in a state that favoured auto-hypnosis, the affect of anxiety entered her reverie and created a hypnoid state for which she had amnesia'.[5] On the other hand, Anna O.'s ability to create a 'private theatre', and to construct and narrate 'stories', is also seen to have played a part in her cure. Symptoms and affects can be 'removed' precisely because Anna O. is capable of recounting her stories, 'which acted as a psychic stimulus' and so brought about 'release and relief'.[6]

At the close of *Studies in Hysteria*, Breuer explores the workings of 'double consciousness', 'the habitual co-existence of two heterogeneous trains of ideas'. He suggests that it is women's conventional tasks, 'monotonous, simple and uninteresting occupation[s]', that lead to habitual reverie. Daydreaming is also linked to suggestibility by literary products: 'an interesting set of ideas, derived for instance from books or plays, forces itself upon the subject's attention and intrudes into his thoughts'.[7] Breuer implies not only a link between femininity and reading but an understanding of daydreams as inhabited by literary forms of representation and 'ready-made phantasies'. Freud, as Jean Laplanche and J.-B. Pontalis write, 'always held the model fantasy to be the reverie, that form of novelette, both stereotyped and infinitely variable, which the subject composes and relates to himself in a waking state'.[8] Breuer makes the link between reverie and fiction in *Studies in Hysteria* through repeated references to the 'scenes' and 'book[s] of pictures' of the patients' memories and reminiscences. This bears in particularly complex ways on the case of Anna O., whose illness and cure were so intricately bound up with daydreaming, storytelling and, ultimately, story-writing.

To alleviate the monotony of her life, Anna O., prior to her illness, indulged in 'systematic day-dreaming'. When, following her father's illness and death, she became ill herself, her 'psychical disturbance' manifested itself not only in somatic symptoms but in the presence of 'two entirely distinct states of consciousness ... which alternated very frequently and without warning and which became more and more differentiated in the course of the illness'.[9] The only relief from the hallucinatory '*absences*' she suffered in one state of consciousness was obtained by narration during the states of auto-hypnosis which succeeded them. As Breuer notes, the daily pattern of her mental states was a version of the schedule established during the period in which she was nursing her father. Moreover, the stories Anna O. was able to tell often took as their 'starting-point or central situation ... a girl anxiously sitting by a sick-bed'. 'The stories were always sad', Breuer notes, 'and some of them were charming, in the style of Hans Andersen's *Picture Book without Pictures*, and, indeed, they were probably constructed on this model.'[10]

These stories became an essential part of the 'talking-cure', as 'Anna O.' entitled the analytic procedure, although the deterioration in her mental condition for a time transmuted her evening narratives from 'more or less freely-created poetical compositions ... into a string of frightful and terrifying hallucinations'. For almost a year, moreover, she relived, during her hypnotic states, the events of the year preceding the one in which she was in fact historically situated, each day narrating the events of the day exactly one year previously, as if her consciousness were shaped by the temporality and form of a diary. (The veracity of her memories was in fact checked against the diary her mother had kept of the events of the previous year.) Breuer refers to his evening visits to his patient, during which he 'relieved her of the whole stock of imaginative products which she had accumulated since my last visit. It was essential that this should be effected completely if good results were to follow'.[11]

But Bertha Pappenheim also found other ways of 'discharging' her imaginative life. She had written down the 'sad' and 'charming' stories she had composed while under Breuer's treatment, and at the end of 1882, while she was still ill but no longer seeing Breuer, she read some of her own fairy tales to her cousin, Anna Ettlinger, who encouraged her literary work. In the later 1880s, she published anonymously a first collection entitled *Little Stories for Children*; a second collection of stories appeared in 1890. In 1899, she published a play, *Frauenrecht (A Woman's Right)* and a translation of Mary Wollstonecraft's *Vindication of the Rights of Women*. In 1900, the first of her polemical articles was published. Although she continued to produce literary works, she became increasingly involved in political and social work, a central figure in the Jewish women's movement in Germany, and a founder, in 1904, of the League of Jewish Women.

These later aspects of Bertha Pappenheim's experience do not enter into Breuer's case-study of the hysteric 'Anna O.', whose clinical biography closes abruptly in the early 1880s. There was thus no occasion for Breuer to explore the paths Bertha Pappenheim's life had taken, nor the relationship between the 'stories' elaborated during her illness and those that she produced for publication, an issue which would have borne interestingly on those questions of creativity and psychopathology that so absorbed psychoanalysis in the first decades of the twentieth century.

It is striking that at least two of Freud's closest women followers and collaborators, Lou Andreas-Salomé (1861–1937) and Freud's daughter Anna, were concerned, in their earliest contributions to psychoanalytic debate, with questions of daydreaming, autoeroticism and narcissism. Both Andreas-Salomé and Anna Freud took the daydreamer as their self-definition, describing their childhood and adolescent years as bound into a continuous process of storytelling, of auto-narration, which, as Lisa Appignanesi and John Forrester note, culminated in detailed written histories of their invented worlds.[12]

Lou Andreas-Salomé wrote in her autobiography of a childhood 'full of lonely reverie', and repeatedly returned, in her autobiographical and fictional texts, to the ways in which much of her childhood was spent in the creation of an imagined world, peopled by characters whose faces she had seen in passing, and whose lives she invented on the basis of these glimpses in the streets or through windows. (This form of fiction-making is strikingly echoed in Virginia Woolf's essay 'Street Haunting', in which Woolf likens the act of reading to the social relations that characterize the modern city: 'one is forced to glimpse and nod and move on after a moment of talk, a flash of understanding, as, in the street outside, one catches a word in passing and from a chance phrase fabricates a lifetime.'[13]) As Angela Livingstone writes: 'Lou was ... always to see herself as engaged in a special kind of egoistic and proto-artistic activity, the half-inventing of a better-shaped world from the actual world's transitory and disorderly data; the half-transforming into something of her own everything that was proscribed and alien.'[14]

Anna Freud's first professional paper, 'Beating Fantasies and Daydreams' (1922),[15] was written and delivered following her reading and translation of the Dutch psychologist J. Varendonck's *The Psychology of Daydreams*, a work modelled on *The Interpretation of Dreams*, in which Varendonck uses his own daydreams as material.[16] Her paper also took up some of the issues explored in Freud's 'Creative Writers and Daydreaming' (1908), and was a direct response to his essay 'A Child is Being Beaten' (1919), in which he explores a beating fantasy common to his patients which, in Anna Freud's words, 'is discharged in an act of pleasurable autoerotic gratification'. Freud argues that the fantasy – a scenario which can be expressed in the sentence 'a child is being beaten' – goes through different stages of development and syntax, but that the wish underlying all its stages could be articulated as 'My father loves only me', a wish expressed in the language of the anal-sadistic organization as an act of beating. Anna Freud's essay was also profoundly influenced by her discussions with Andreas-Salomé, whose thinking and writing at this time were centred on fantasies, daydreams and anal eroticism.

In 'A Child is Being Beaten', Freud refers to four male and two female patients or analysands for whom this fantasy was significant. One of the female cases was almost certainly Anna Freud. (We must leave aside the complexities of a situation in which the analysand reveals the desire for her father to the analyst who is her father.) In her essay, Anna Freud quotes Freud's brief account of two female cases, for whom 'an elaborate structure of day-dreams ... had grown up over the masochistic beating fantasy ... mak[ing] possible a feeling of satisfied excitation, even though the masturbatory act was refrained from'.[17] 'I have been able to find one daydream', Anna Freud writes, 'which seemed especially well suited to illustrate this brief remark ... formed by a girl of about fifteen.' The girl was in fact herself, though this is never acknowledged: she writes as if she were producing the case history of a patient. The occlusion of first by third person narrative suggests both the structures of primal fantasies (as in 'A Child is Being Beaten'), which are not, to borrow Laplanche's and Pontalis's phrase, 'weighted by the ego', and a more defensive reversal of subject positions.

Anna Freud recounts in some detail a structure whereby the day-dreamer struggles over some years to 'retain the [beating] fantasy as a source of pleasure and, at the same time, to give up the sexual gratification which could not be reconciled with the demands of her ego'. The beating fantasy became less frequent as the guilt with which it was associated led increasingly to unpleasure rather than pleasure. At about the same time, when the girl was somewhere between eight and ten, she 'initiated a new kind of fantasy activity which she herself called "nice stories" in contrast to the ugly beating fantasies ... it was inconceivable that a figure playing a part in a nice story could even appear in the beating scene'. The 'nice stories', she writes, 'deserve to be called "continued stories" in view of the constancy of the acting figures and the entire general setting'.[18] The most significant of these 'continued daydreams' was triggered by the girl's reading, in her fourteenth or fifteenth year, of 'a boy's storybook', which contained a short story set in the Middle Ages. (Anna Freud uses the fact of the boy's story to make the case for 'bisexuality' rather than a 'masculinity complex'.) The girl took possession of the figures and 'further spun out the tale, just as if it had been her own spontaneous fantasy product'. In her story, a fifteen-year-old noble youth (the age of the daydreamer) is captured by a knight who holds him prisoner, alternately threatening and nurturing him during the long imprisonment: 'All this takes place in vividly animated and dramatically moving scenes', Anna Freud writes, barely concealing her pride in her own creation.

Analysis revealed to the daydreamer what the reader of the essay by now realizes: that the masturbatory beating fantasies and the 'nice stories' are far from distinct. Both revolve around the interplay between a strong and weak person, and both enact scenarios of punishment and humiliation, although 'the nice stories admit the occurrence of unexpected affectionate scenes precisely at the point where the beating fantasy depicts the act of chastisement ... While the beating fantasy ... represents a return of the repressed, the nice stories on the other hand represent its sublimation'.[19]

The essay thus establishes the mutual dependence of beating fantasies and daydreams (nice stories). A coda recounts the 'development and fate of one of these continued day-dreams. Several years after the story of the knight first emerged, the girl put it in writing'. But 'while the actual writing was done in a state of happy excitement, similar to the state of daydreaming, the finished story does not elicit any such excitement'. There is also a 'renunciation of the daydreamlike pleasure gain at specific climaxes', Anna Freud writes. The written story spreads the load of pleasure over the whole, rather than concentrating it into 'a single great climax at the end of the written tale'. Moreover, the act of writing is seen as a defence against 'excessive preoccupation', an exorcism of obsession: 'The daydream of the knight was in fact finished, as far as she was concerned, after it had been written down.' This is, then, a 'full discharge' which will not be followed by further releases of 'accumulated excitement'.

The essay closes with the claim that the shift from fantasy and daydream to writing was 'an important developmental step: the transformation of an autistic into a social activity'. The dangerous pleasures of private fantasy are thus transmuted into the aesthetic and ambitious strivings of the author: 'For the better she succeeds in the presentation of her material, the greater will be the effect on others and therefore also her own indirect pleasure gain.' The final part of the essay thus enacts the 'sublimation' it describes, seeking to end the dangerous circulation of the fantasy material it has brought to the surface and preventing, as it were, this particular nice story – the birth of the author as social subject – from collapsing back into ugly fantasy. What the essay cannot explore is its own status as an autobiographical text disguised as a scientific document, or the pleasures attendant upon the redescription of the fantasy materials it simultaneously hoards and discharges.

I have turned to Anna Freud's 1922 essay because it so fully opens up the topic of daydreaming, fantasy, auto-eroticism and literary product. I now want to return to the *fin de siècle* and, in passing, to Lou Andreas-Salomé's Russian-born contemporary, the painter Marie Bashkirtseff (1859–84), who died in Paris of tuberculosis at the age of twenty-five, and whose journals caused a sensation when they were published (albeit in expurgated form) in France in 1887, and in England and America in 1890. Hugh Stutfield, writing in *Blackwood's* in 1897, described Bashkirtseff's journal as 'a kind of secret Bible' in which 'the tired and discontented women of the time ... read a few sentences every morning, or at night before going to sleep'.[20] It would seem that the journals fill the transitional and trangressive space between sleeping and waking.

Bashkirtseff became a significant representative figure of *fin-de-siècle* femininity, perceived, like Lou Andreas-Salomé, as a type of the 'modern woman'. Stutfield links her with George Egerton, castigating both for their introspection and 'morbid ego-mania – the literature of hysteria'. Bashkirtseff was destroyed, Stutfield has it, by her own ambition and by her nervous disposition, which is also the destructive temper of her times. Moreover, she reveals her 'inner life' in her journals, those documents which, as the private become public, are both retentive and confessional – and which, *pace* Laura Marholm, could be said to stem from the desire both to have something and to be relieved of something. The journals are, in addition, the writings of adolescence, frequently perceived as the age of reverie. According to G. Stanley Hall, whose monumental study of adolescence appeared in 1904: 'Inner absorption and reverie is one marked characteristic of this age of transition'; 'Puberty is the birthplace of the imagination. This has its morning twilight in reverie.'[21]

Adolescence, I would suggest, is also one of the ages of the New Woman. The 'New Woman', like the adolescent, is frequently figured as a transitional figure. Ambiguously sexual, poised between worlds, the adolescent and the New Woman stand at the dawn of a new age – in a period, moreover, in which the individual's lifespan and the century's age are each other's favourite analogies. In other, non-progressivist models, women remain adolescents throughout their lives, existing almost permanently, in Stanley Hall's words, 'in what is really a suppressed semi-erotic state'.[22]

Adolescence, Julia Kristeva has argued, figures interiority for modernity: '"psychic interiority" is a creation that affirms itself magnificently in the nineteenth-century psychological novel ... . the adolescent character serves as a standard of measure within this involution of baroque man, who is neither within nor without, into nineteenth-century psychological man.'[23] I now wish to turn to the question of interiority and the New Woman, by way of Havelock Ellis and his account of 'Auto-Erotism', the term he coined and discusses at length in his *Studies in the Psychology of Sex*. Ellis writes:

> It was the wish to group together all the far-flung manifestations of the inner irresitible process of sexual activity that underlay my own conception of *auto-erotism*, or the spontaneous erotic impulse which arises from the organism apart from all definite external stimulation, to be manifested, or it may be transformed, in mere solitary physical sex activity, in dreams of the night, in daydreams, in shapes of literature and art, in symptoms of nervous disorder such as some forms of hysteria, and even in the most exalted phases of mystical devotion.[24]

Ellis adds that: 'the conditions of modern civilization render auto-erotism a matter of increasing social significance. As our marriage-rate declines, and as illicit sexual relationships continue to be openly discouraged, it is absolutely inevitable that auto-erotic phenomena of one kind or another ... should increase among us both in amount and intensity.'[25]

Let other pens dwell on the more recherché forms of 'auto-erotism' explored by Ellis. We will, however, pause briefly to consider the bicycle, the vehicle of the New Woman, and its role 'in exciting auto-erotic manifestations'. Ellis suggests that 'Sexual irritation may ... be produced by the bicycle in women', though he takes issue with the view upheld by 'most medical authorities on cycling', 'that when cycling leads to sexual excitement the fault lies more with the woman than with the machine'. There may or may not have been a sexual charge attached to popular representations of the New Woman on her bicycle. What interests me in Ellis's account are the contrasting images of auto-eroticism as external or (as in the production of daydreams) as internal stimulation: the distinction between 'auto-erotism', we could say, as friction or as fiction.

The friction/fiction divide is one, I would suggest, that informs twentieth-century debates over female sexuality as clitoral or as vaginal – the former characterized (as in the Freudian analyst Marie Bonaparte's account) as external and masculine-identified, the latter as internal and properly feminine.[26] Freud's accounts of female development chart the shift from the clitoris to the vagina as the site of pleasure. In this model, 'becoming a woman' entails an interiorization of sensation and sexuality. The friction/fiction distinction would also seem to be an aspect of the dual image of the New Woman. While in popular representations she is often figured as aggressively seeking stimuli in the outer world (movement, experience, education), there is another image of the 'New Woman' as dreamer, turned inward to sensation and feeling.

In Ellis's account, the external, or 'voluntary mechanical', production of sexual excitement is contrasted with 'spontaneous' sexual emotion – 'Schrenck-Notzing knows a lady who is spontaneously sexually excited on hearing music or seeing pictures without anything lascivious in them; she knows nothing of sexual relationships. Another lady is sexually excited on seeing beautiful and natural scenes, like the sea; sexual ideas are mixed up in her mind with these things, and the contemplation of a specially strong and sympathetic man brings the orgasm on in about a minute. Both these ladies "masturbate" in the streets, restaurants, railways, theatres, without anyone perceiving it.'[27] As in much turn of the century sexological material on auto-eroticism and masturbation, as well as in the literary texts of the period, there is a particular fascination with the production of private dreams in public places.

While for Ellis these ladies manifest an eroticism which shades into 'hyperaesthetic weakness', the phenomenon is also closely allied to 'that form of auto-erotism . . associated with revery, or daydreaming'.[28] Ellis footnotes several psychological studies of reverie and daydreaming, particularly focused on adolescents and young women, including research into the 'continued story', 'an imagined narrative, more or less peculiar to the individual, by whom it is cherished with fondness … . The growth of the story is favoured by solitude, and lying in bed before going to sleep is the time specially sacred to its cultivation'.[29] We have seen the representation of the 'continued story' in Anna Freud's account – a form of narrative which could be traced through from *Jane Eyre*, with her 'tale that was never ended', to the uses of 'feminine' forms of stream of consciousness and interior monologue in modernist fiction.

The most significant elements of Ellis's discussion of 'Auto-Erotism' in the present context are the connections he makes between sexuality, dreams, daydreams and art, and the intensity of his focus on the 'spontaneous erotic impulse which arises from the organism apart from all definite external stimulation'. The biologistic context for this claim is Ellis's understanding of 'internal secretions' as the key to sexual identity: 'a woman is a woman because of her internal secretions'.[30] The point of stressing the absence of 'definite external stimulation' in the arousal of erotic impulses is to drive sexuality into (or to construct it out of) the interior, to introject it. As Freud notes, in his *Three Essays on the Theory of Sexuality*, the essential feature of the term 'auto-erotism' for Ellis is that it describes 'an excitation which is not provoked from outside but arises internally'.[31]

Ellis's biologistic account of the 'inner foci' and 'intimate recesses' of the body is inseparable from models of sexuality, identity and aesthetics as profoundly interiorized and subjectivist. This drive to inwardness (characterized by Max Nordau, in the most negative account of fin-de-siécle subjectivism, as 'ego-mania'[32]) is also manifest in much of the writing by and about women at the turn of the century. For Andreas-Salomé, women are characterized by a narcissism which represents not an absence of relationship to an external world but a feminine self-sufficiency and completeness; she also observed that Narcissus' mirror was a pool, and thus not a man-made and bounded artefact, but a part of the natural world with which the subject merges.[33] Laura Marholm characterized George Egerton as 'a subject without an object',[34] while the emphasis of theorists such as Stanley Hall and Marholm is on what women generate from within. For these conservative thinkers, education, as I have suggested, is represented as an irrelevant external stimulus – as a kind of 'friction' – diverting women from their true role and destiny in motherhood.

The writers we label 'New Women' novelists responded in diverse ways to this interiorization, though there is a shared link between constructions of female inwardness and representations of daydream, fantasy and reverie. George Egerton, for example, hollows out the space of women's interiority through fantasy in 'A Cross Line', though the modern woman's desire to become, in Marholm's phrase, 'a substance in herself' has turned into having 'a substance in herself' by the end of the story, when Egerton's heroine realizes she is pregnant.[35]

The passage from reverie and daydreaming to writing is represented in detail in Sarah Grand's *The Beth Book*. The novel (which could be seen as a rewriting of *Madame Bovary*) constructs a moral chart of good and bad fantasizing. Bereft of the 'wholesome companionship of boy and girl' and of 'the rational plans and pursuits she had been accustomed to make and to carry out with the boys', the young Beth has 'nothing to substitute but dreams; and on these she lived, finding an idle distraction in them, until the habit grew disproportionate, and began to threaten the fine balance of her other faculties ... To fill up her empty days, she surrounded herself with a story, among the crowding incidents of which she lived, whatever she might be doing'.[36]

After her marriage to a boorish doctor, Beth finds herself without peace or privacy until she discovers a 'secret chamber' in the attic of the house her husband is renting: 'Everything about her [in this room] was curiously familiar, and her first impression was that she had been here before. On the other hand, she could hardly believe in the reality of what she saw, she thought she must be dreaming, for here was exactly what she had been pining for most in the whole wide world of late, a sacred spot, sacred to herself, where she would be safe from intrusion.' In this sacred and secret spot, she begins first to read – biographies and autobiographies and the lives of authors, not the three-volume novels favoured by her husband: 'Her mind, which had run riot, fancy-fed with langourous dreams in the days when it was unoccupied and undisciplined, came steadily more and more under control, and grew gradually stronger as she exercised it' – and then to write. Leaving her husband, she exchanges her secret chamber for an attic room in London, writes and publishes a novel, but finally abandons fiction-making for a life of 'active service' and public oratory.

The Beth Book thus follows the path delineated by Bertha Pappenheim, representing the passage from reverie and daydreaming to writing and from thence to political/social activism. Yet to read the psychoanalytic and literary texts of the period associatively is to find Grand's trajectory from reverie/reading to writing to being-in-the-world troubled by the circularities of the hoardings and discharges of, to take the most striking example, Anna Freud's narrative of fantasy and its renunciation. The exit from the private theatre could be read as another wishful staging, while daydreaming continues to function both as a guilty secret pleasure and as the site of women's resistance, transgression and autonomy.

The most complex issue, which I must leave open, is that of the uses of dream, daydream and fantasy in turn of the century writing to explore sexual and gendered identities, confusions and reversals, including cross-dressing. 'For the first time I had a daydream or a story with a female main person in my head', Anna Freud wrote to Lou Andreas-Salomé in 1922 – a 'nice story', perhaps, of 'proper' feminine identification which also suggests, by contrast, those spaces in which women (and men) are other than, and others to, themselves.

Notes

1. Laura Marholm, *The Psychology of Woman*, trans. Georgia A. Etchison (London: Grant Richards, 1899), 54.
2. Sigmund Freud and Joseph Breuer, *Studies in Hysteria*, The Penguin Freud Library vol. 3 (Harmondsworth: Penguin, 1974), 74.
3. Ibid., 296.
4. Ibid., 296.
5. Ibid., 314.
6. Quotations from the case history compiled by Joseph Breuer, and the report of her treatment in Bellevue Sanatorium, Appendix D23 in Albrecht Hirschmuller, *The Life and Work of Josef Breuer*, 282–3.
7. *Studies in Hysteria*, 83.
8. Jean Laplanche and Jean-Bertrand Pontalis, 'Fantasy and the Origins of Sexuality', reprinted in *Formations of Fantasy*, eds Victor Burgin et al. (London: Methuen, 1986), 22.
9. *Studies in Hysteria*, 76.
10. Ibid., 82.
11. Ibid., 86.
12. Lisa Appignanesi and John Forrester, *Freud's Women* (London: Weidenfeld & Nicolson, 1992), 243.
13. Virginia Woolf, 'Street Haunting', in *The Crowded Dance of Modern Life*, ed. Rachel Bowlby (Harmondsworth: Penguin, 1993), 78.
14. Angela Livingstone, *Lou Andreas-Salomé* (London: Gordon Fraser, 1984), 21.
15. Anna Freud, 'Beating Fantasies and Daydreams' (1922). Revised version (to which page references refer) in Anna Freud, *Introduction to Psychoanalysis: Lectures for Child Analysts and Teachers 1922–1935* (London: Hogarth Press, 1974), 137–57.
16. J. Varendonck, *The Psychology of Daydreams* (London: George Allen & Unwin, 1921).
17. 'Beating Fantasies and Daydreams', 138.
18. Ibid., 144.
19. Ibid., 152–3.
20. Hugh Stutfield, 'The Psychology of Feminism', *Blackwood's* 161, January 1897, 109.
21. G. Stanley Hall, *Adolescence: its Psychology* (1904) (New York and London: D. Appleton, 1925), 313.
22. Ibid., 572, 578.
23. Julia Kristeva, 'The Adolescent Novel', in *Abjection, Melancholia and Love*, eds John Fletcher and Andrew Benjamin (London: Routledge, 1991), 14. See also Mary Jacobus' superb essay, 'Narcissa's Gaze: Berthe Morisot and the

Filial Mirror', in *First Things: the Maternal Imaginary in Literature, Art, and Psychoanalysis* (New York and London: Routledge, 1995).

24. Havelock Ellis, 'Auto-Erotism', in *Studies in the Psychology of Sex*, vol. 1, 3rd edn (Philadelphia: F. A. Davis, 1920).
25. Ibid., 164.
26. See Marie Bonaparte, *Female Sexuality* (1949), trans. John Rodker, (New York: Grove Press, 1962).
27. Ellis, 'Auto-Erotism', pp. 183–4.
28. Ibid., p. 184.
29. Ibid., p. 185.
30. Havelock Ellis, *Man and Woman*, 5th edn (London: Walter Scott, nd), vi–vii.
31. Sigmund Freud, 'Three Essays on the Theory of Sexuality', Penguin Freud Library 7 (Harmondsworth: Penguin, 1977), 97, n.2. For psychoanalysis, by contrast, 'the essential point is not the genesis of the excitation, but the question of its relation to an object'.
32. See Max Nordau, *Degeneration* (London: William Heinemann, 1895), esp. 241–65.
33. See esp. 'The Dual Orientation of Narcissism' (trans. By S. Leavy of 'Narzissmus als Doppelrichtung' (1921)), *Psychoanalytic Quarterly*, vol. 31, nos 1–2, 1962, 1–30.
34. Laura Marholm, *Modern Women*, (London: John Lane, 1896), 80.
35. George Egerton, 'A Cross Line', in *Keynotes*, (London: John Lane, 1894), 1–36.
36. Sarah Grand, *The Beth Book* (1897), (London: Virago, 1980), 264.

9

'Scaping the Body: Of Cannibal Mothers and Colonial Landscapes

Rebecca Stott

The New Woman flourished in the 1880s and 90s, a period also dominated by the Scramble for Africa and the high point of what Patrick Brantlinger has termed the production of the myth of the Dark Continent. Just as the periodical press was full of articles on the Woman Question so they were also full of articles on the Africa Question, articles from explorers and colonial administrators about its exploration and its political management. Both subjects of public interest were mediated through discourses of evolutionary progress: what marks out the 'civilized' from the 'barbaric', the natural from the unnatural? In this essay I want to explore some of these connections between the myth of Africa as monstrous woman, intensifying and consolidating in the 1880s and 90s, and the myth and fears about the New Woman growing in the same period, and finally to show how both are determined and shaped by evolutionary debates about the 'nature' of the natural world. I will try to suggest ways in which the two myths leak into each other.

Patrick Brantlinger writes: 'Africa grew "dark" as Victorian explorers, missionaries, and scientists flooded it with light.'[1] It grew darkest of all in the final decades of the nineteenth century. However, as this mythologized landscape becomes dark it also becomes distinctly feminized in this period. As it became darker (imagined in the words of Brantlinger as 'a centre of evil ... possessed by demonic darkness'[2]) and simultaneously more feminized, its darkness cast its femininity as increasingly monstrous and 'unnatural'. The peculiarly enduring myth of the Dark Continent, produced by Western writers about Africa in this period, is a distinct fusion of discourses of race, science and gender. Many questions about the nature of gender, of acute importance to European writers troubled by the presence of the New

Woman, became part of what we might call the 'fabrication' of the myth of the Dark Continent.[3]

Descriptions of landscape as female body are not new or peculiar to the late nineteenth century. They are part of a Culture/Nature binary embedded in Western thought in which nature plays female to a masculinized culture. Here my concern is not with feminizations of landscape *per se* but with the feminization of African landscape seen as part of the complex structures of colonial discourse produced in the closing decades of the nineteenth century. Peter Hulme, in *Colonial Encounters* has usefully defined colonial discourse as: 'an ensemble of linguistically-based practices unified by their common deployment in the management of colonial relationships.'[4] Elleke Boehmer argues that colonial discourse can also be described as the means by which Europeans came to understand 'the bizarre and apparently unintelligible strangeness with which it came into contact'.[5] If we begin with these definitions, then the fact that so many descriptions of African landscape are feminized forces us to consider the ways in which these linguistically based practices might be gendered, and secondly the ways in which they might be deployed in the management of Western relationships between men and women as well as colonial relationships.

Imperialist literature of this period – adventure stories in particular – often establish the heroic status of the explorer through casting him in a kind of sexual relation to the landscape, conquering or penetrating dangerous, unknown continents. In such a narrative the landscape plays the role of the virginal female body waiting to be taken. What is more interesting is that the female body-to-be-taken in this narrative (the land) is based upon Western mythical and stereotypical models of femininity which are often deeply problematic and contradictory in themselves. Africa might be constructed as virgin territory (passive, fertile, untouched by others, unknowing) or *femme fatale* (dangerously seductive, potentially violent, unpredictable, all knowing), or monstrous mother (sexually knowing, malevolent and cannibalistic) and in some adventure narratives mythologized 'Africa' is characterized by wild swings between the different types.

In the Stanley–Livingstone exploration stories, for instance, which helped to shape so many early popular ideas about Africa as the Dark Continent, surgical metaphors are one of the dominant means of describing the actions and status of the explorers, 'opening up' the new land for scientific observation. In 1889, H. Waller in an essay called 'The Universities' Mission to Central Africa' described Livingstone as a 'hard, unflinching instrument, who had gone through lands and tribes and tough problems, and had cut furrows in a wilderness of human life which no one had heard of or dreamed of'.[6] The surgical associations of 'unflinching instrument' merge into farming allusions as the 'instrument' becomes a plough ('furrows'), but both actions involve cutting into a passive landscape. Henry Morton Stanley in the bestselling *In Darkest Africa* (1890) described himself triumphantly as having: 'marched, tore, ploughed and cut [his] way for one hundred and sixty days through this inner womb of the true tropical forest'.[7] Here metaphors are two-a-penny: marched (military), tore (heroic?), ploughed (farming) and cut (surgical/scientific) and indicate the instability and multiplicity of the explorer's perception of his own role. The sexual allusion here, though, is startling: was the metaphor of virgin forest so widely used that no one might find the ideas of slashing and cutting at a womb offensive? It appears not.

Cutting and dissection metaphors were being used some time before the publication of Stanley's book in 1890 and are doubtless part of the developing myths of the explorer as anatomist, cutting into the unknown body (here African landscape) in the name of science. Twelve years earlier, in 1878, when Stanley's violence towards the Bambireh tribe in 1876 was still sending shock waves through the Geographical Society, Francis Galton, founder of the eugenics movement, wrote an article about the affair in which he questioned Stanley's right to assume a warlike attitude to native tribes, yet he also asked the readers of the *Edinburgh Review* to think about how Stanley would be regarded by history. After all, he claimed, Stanley had 'dissected and laid bare the very heart of the great continent of Africa', and besides this great achievement, 'the death of a few hundred barbarians, ever ready to fight and kill, and many of whom are professed cannibals, will perhaps be regarded as a small matter'.[8] Galton's argument rests upon two assumptions: deaths may be justified in the name of science, and cannibals, especially 'professed' cannibals have it coming to them anyway. In Galton's mind cannibalism cancels the humanity of the victims of Stanley's violence. I shall return to cannibalism later.

In *Imperial Eyes: Travel Writing and Transculturation*, Mary Louise Pratt defines this description of colonial landscape as a virgin-to-be-taken or unveiled the 'monarch-of-all-I-survey trope' and claims that it began in the 1860s with British explorers searching for the Nile. At the heart of the monarch-of-all-I-survey trope is the aerial view: the explorer, traveller (whether real or fictional) describes Africa as laid out invitingly beneath him. Pratt provides three defining characteristics of the trope: the landscape described is aestheticized; the landscape is invested with a density of riches and meaning and a relationship of mastery is established. The promontory position that the explorer/writer assumes, she speculates, may have been prompted by a sense of threatened identity and mastery which overwhelmed the explorer in the colonial landscape. Pratt's analysis of this trope is limited because it is part of a much larger project in which she plots out the processes of 'transculturation' in colonial cultures.

However, Pratt does not have the opportunity to look at the complex and unstable metaphorical layering of so much colonial discourse, nor at the transformation of such metaphors *within a single text*. Where the landscape is feminized in colonial discourse, it is not always described as a virgin. Sometimes, when the landscape represents a threat to the explorer its femininity is demonized (seducing *femme fatale*), or when the explorer imagines himself as scientist the landscape is desexualized (corpse-to-be-dissected) and when this happens the oscillations between types of femininity create significant tensions and ambiguities. The discomfort arises in part from an unease on the part of the explorer, uncertain of his role and position in relation to the landscape.

Pratt suggests that 'hyphenated' white male writers (men 'whose national and civic identifications were multiple and often conflicted'[9] because they were Anglo-Pole like Conrad, or Anglo-American like Stanley) and women writers tend to abandon the 'legitimising rhetoric of presence'[10] characteristic of colonial discourse. In this essay I will look at the representations of African landscape in three colonial texts in order to examine Pratt's contention: Rider Haggard's *King Solomon's Mines* (1887), Conrad's *Heart of Darkness* (1899) and Olive Schreiner's *The Story of an African Farm* (1883), all texts in which the monarch-of-all-I-survey trope is immensely complicated by enormous representational swings between contradictory images of womanhood (virgin, whore, mother, monster). Joseph Conrad is, of course, one of Pratt's named 'hyphenated' white men but Olive Schreiner, whom Pratt does not mention, is in many ways more complicatedly 'hyphenated' than Conrad, as a woman writer, as a white settler born in South Africa, and a New Woman.

Mary Louise Pratt tends to present the monarch-of-all-I-survey trope (Africa as body to be unveiled) as static, as consistent throughout individual texts and characteristic of colonial discourse as a whole. In texts by both Conrad and Haggard, however, 'Africa', initially fantasized as passive virgin, is replaced by a terrifying and threatening experience of

Africa as active and malevolent monster. The monarch-of-all-I-survey trope *is* characteristic of the early parts of these novels, *but cannot be sustained*. Early in Haggard's *King Solomon's Mines*, for instance, Haggard uses the trope to almost comic effect. The travellers come up over a ridge and see Sheba's Breasts glittering in the distance. Quatermain comments:

> I am impotent before its very memory ... These mountains placed thus, like the pillars of a gigantic gateway, are shaped after the fashion of a woman's breasts, and at times the mists and shadows beneath them take the forms of a recumbent woman, veiled mysteriously in sleep. The bases swell gently from the plain, looking at that distance perfectly round and smooth; and upon the top is a vast hillock covered with snow, exactly corresponding to the nipple on the female breast ... Sheba's Breasts had scarcely vanished into cloud-clad privacy when our thirst – literally a burning question – reasserted itself.[11]

This *is* a classic monarch-of-all-I-survey scene, yet it is uneasy, full of tension. Pratt's defining characteristics are all present: the land as veiled woman, the aestheticizing of landscape, the density of riches invested in the landscape and the relation of mastery established in the aerial view. But nonetheless the unease is caused in particular by a collision between models of femininity – landscape/body conceived of as virgin (to be taken, conquered, enjoyed) and landscape/body as mother (protective, nurturing, in position of power). The explorers, like Stanley in the extract I quoted earlier, are uneasy about their relation to the landscape.

Whilst Quatermain may imagine that this landscape has thirst-quenching properties hidden in its veiled 'breasts', the maternal qualities of this fantasized 'bodyscape' are not realized, however. In the following chapter the men shelter in the 'nipple', (a cave in the tip of the mountain). Here one of their own number dies from cold and they find the petrified corpse of another explorer who had taken shelter there many years before. Where the aerial view had oscillated uncomfortably between constituting the landscape as virgin or mother, here the bodyscape is confirmed as monstrous, a maternal body in which breasts deny nourishment and are so cold that they can freeze bodies to death.

As the novel progresses this feminized 'Africa' does indeed become darker, and its femininity becomes increasingly monstrous as a consequence. The African landscape of *King Solomon's Mines* is littered internally with the petrified bodies of past kings and past explorers. In the novel's gothic denouement the two heroes are trapped in a labyrinth of tunnels underground where the bodies of past rulers are being gradually transformed into stalactities, as if they are gradually being digested within the body of this feminized landscape. Indeed, such descriptions are reminiscent of scenes from modern horror films such as *Alien* and *The X-files* series in which the heroes encounter monstrous alien mothers brooding over their eggs or offspring in underground caverns dripping with slime or in which human bodies are being gradually digested as part of a food system for their young. In Haggard's novel, as the journey progresses the position of mastery over this giant body simply cannot be sustained. Landscape is gradually revealed to be a kind of incestuous, potentially cannibalistic and monstrous mother. The imperialist fantasy of consumption is replaced by the nightmare of being consumed.[12]

In Conrad's much later novella of 1902, *Heart of Darkness*, a similar, though more complex transformation, occurs in the gendered configurations of landscape. Once again a group of men travel into the 'dark continent', hopeful, with a mission. But, unlike Haggard, Conrad avoids the aerial view, the monarch-of-all-I-survey trope, right from the start. Marlow is tempted by the map of the Congo in the shop window but what he sees in the map is not an invitation to possess but rather a warning: 'an immense snake uncoiled, with its head in the sea, its body at rest curving far over a vast country, and its tail lost in the depths of the land.' Marlow writes that the river 'fascinated [him] as a snake would a bird'.[13] The snake hypnotizes the bird in order to consume it. This malevolent, hypnotic quality of the landscape is sustained and intensified as the novel progresses.

> And outside, the silent wilderness surrounding this cleared speck on the earth struck me as something great and invincible, like evil or truth, waiting patiently for the passing away of this fantastic invasion (33)

> And the stillness of life did in the least resemble a peace. It was the stillness of an implacable force brooding over an inscrutable intention. It looked at you with a vengeful aspect. (48–9)

One of the most dominant words used to describe the landscape in this novel is 'brooding', one of those much-used Conrad adjectives that have a multitude of associations: brood over, bad feeling, hang closely over, meditate resentfully or incubate eggs like a chicken or snake. The maternal incubation here is monstrous because it is incubating revenge through a kind of demonic cannibalism, the digestion of life into the body. Kurtz is the living sign of this monstrous incubation:

> The wilderness had patted him on the head, and behold, it was like a ball – an ivory ball – it had caressed him and – lo! – he had withered; it had taken him, loved him, embraced him, got into his veins, consumed his flesh and sealed his soul to its own by the inconceivable ceremonies of some devilish initiation (49).

Once again the potential consumer, the imperialist, is assimilated into an African wilderness that caresses, seduces and finally cannibalizes him.

Cannibalism, then, is an issue in texts by both Haggard and Conrad, not only manifested in the anxieties of the characters that they might be attacked by cannibals, but embodied in the landscape itself. Dorothy Hammond and Alta Jablow note that cannibalism is an important theme in British writing about Africa after mid-century: 'in the imperial period writers were far more addicted to tales of cannibalism than ... Africans ever were to cannibalism.'[14] Stanley's best-selling tales of African exploration are full of references to cannibalism, references which increase as he moves further into 'unexplored' territory. But Nigel Rigby has shown that Stanley introduced the themes for the purposes of sensationalism – his diaries show that his insistence on cannibalism was neither supported by evidence nor was it a trait of the Africans that much bothered him at the time.[15] Cannibalism comes to represent the nadir of barbarism, a marker between civilized and uncivilized man. Although many of the studies of European accounts of cannibalism in encounters with the New World and Africa do not pay much attention to the question of gender in relation to cannibalism, it would seem that in the spectrum of transgression the cannibal mother is one of the most extreme forms of the myth, enacting multiple transgressions simultaneously. By 1900 the cannibalistic mother begins to figure more prominently as part of the myth of the Dark Continent as exemplified in extreme form in this extract from a novel by Paul Vigne d'Octon of 1900, strangely reminiscent of the way in which Conrad describes the wilderness's revenge on Kurtz:

> This is Africa, man-eater, soul-destroyer, wrecker of men's strength, mother of fever and death, mysterious ghost which for centuries has

sucked the blood of Europeans, draining them to the very marrow, or making them mad.

Peter Hulme defines cannibalism as 'the image of ferocious consumption of human flesh frequently used to make the boundary between one community and its others' within European colonialism.[16] Further he speculates that the threat that the image offers 'although figured as the devouring of human flesh, is in fact addressed to the body politic'. In other words cannibalism can work as a kind of projection onto those outside the structure, a projection of the 'violence on which that body politic is inevitably based, the exploitation inseparable from divided societies'.[17] Cannibalism, then, can be both a marker of boundaries (of the absolutely 'other') and a projection of the violence of assimilation implicit in the colonial enterprise onto those who suffer it.

But what can the cannibal mother embedded in the myth of the Dark Continent tell us about the cultures in which such nightmares were produced – not Africa, but Europe? What can the cannibal mother of colonial discourse tell us about Western conceptions and constructions of femininity in the last decades of the nineteenth century? In an important essay published in 1989,[18] James Eli Adams argues that one of the most profound impacts of evolutionary theory on Western thought was that it challenged traditional concepts of nature as benign mother. If nature was indeed *Mother* Nature then what kind of mother was this who was hideously overproductive and yet could allow her children to die (even consume them) in the process of natural selection? Adams draws attention to the cannibal 'Nature red in tooth and claw' of Tennyson's *In Memoriam* (1850), teeth and claws red with the blood of her own children. The second part of Adams's thesis is that such new concepts of the monstrosity of nature forced new conceptions and nightmares about what constituted 'natural' femininity and the 'nature' of motherhood itself.

Adams's concern is with Tennyson and Darwin and their struggle with the potential monstrosity of Nature imagined as 'mother', although he does speculate briefly that the production of *femme fatale* figures in the final decades of the century may have been stimulated by evolutionary theory's forced reconfiguration of femininity. However, many representations of monstrous or neglectful mothers are to be found both in fictional and non-fictional attacks on the New Woman and in mythical form in Western representations of Africa as Dark Continent. The narrative of a Nature which is expected to be benign and maternal, but is revealed to be monstrous, barbaric, a multiple transgressor (incestuous and cannibalistic) is played out over and over again in *colonial discourse*. Colonial discourse, 'an ensemble of linguistically-based practices unified by their common deployment in the management of colonial relationships' may also have worked to endorse Western ideas of gender roles, dependency and power. The myths of the New Woman, the Dark Continent and new concepts of Nature brought about by evolutionary theory mutually reinforce each other. Their intricate connections are more a result of a kind of cultural 'seepage' of narratives than of linear cause and effect.

One of the most powerful means of attack on the New Woman in this same period was that of the charge of unnatural woman, unnatural because of her supposed rejection of motherhood and marriage. The New Woman was considered monstrous and unnatural by the more sensational conservative press because of her supposed rejection of motherhood and by the imagined voraciousness of her desires. However, feminist positions on the role of woman as mother in this period were more complex than the representations of a sensationalist press. One of the primary areas of shared concern between feminists and those who championed imperialism were questions of racial superiority, racial purity and racial motherhood.[19] Sally Ledger in *The New Woman: Fiction and Feminism at the Fin de Siècle* draws attention to the irony of the fact that whilst the New Woman was criticized for being a 'bad mother' and the breeder of a degenerate 'race', many New Women were actively campaigning for the continuance of the 'race' through the championing of motherhood, support of the empire and purity campaigns.[20]

Ledger singles out Olive Schreiner for particular attention here as a supporter of empire and of motherhood, particularly as she seems to want to challenge Schreiner's status as a feminist icon. She has four main 'charges' (her own term) to level at Schreiner: charges of incipient imperialism, of homophobia, of a near deification of the concept of motherhood and finally racism.[21] My business here is not to stand in defence of Olive Schreiner against such charges but rather to endorse Ledger's acknowledgement made elsewhere in her book that Schreiner's position is complex and variable.[22] Schreiner's interest in motherhood and the way in which she explores the contradictions of motherhood in her own descriptions of a feminized South African landscape are indeed complex. I do not want to argue like Pratt that Schreiner's version of the Dark Continent myth is going to be different from those of her male counterparts either *because* she is a woman or *because* she is a settler. Ledger rightly challenges Gilbert and Gubar's collapsing of patriarchy and imperialism (women are the colonized in a patriarchal hierarchy) and asserts that we must acknowledge, however uncomfortably, that some Western feminists might also have been racist supporters of imperialist ideologies. My task here is similar to that of Vron Ware:

> not to bring white women to account for past misdeeds, nor to search for heroines whose reputations can help to absolve the rest from guilt, but to find out how white women negotiated questions of race and racism – as well as class and gender.[23]

Schreiner's representation of African landscape is of interest here because it is shaped in part by her understanding of the politics and psychology of motherhood as institution and her knowledge of nineteenth-century science, particularly evolutionary theory. Schreiner was deeply influenced by the work of Darwin and Herbert Spencer and much of her utopian and political writing is filtered through an evolutionary frame. In 1887 when she was writing *Woman and Labour*, for instance, she wrote to Havelock Ellis: 'My sex paper is purely scientific in principle. It is an attempt to apply the theory of evolution to elucidate sex problems.'[24]

Motherhood is a persistent concern of Schreiner, as Ledger demonstrates, a recurrent preoccupation in her writing, not, in my view, in the form of a near-deification (Ledger), but rather as a political problem to be resolved. While she does sometimes idealize maternity, she is also deeply critical of motherhood as institution and inclined to describe mothers in monstrous terms. In *Woman and Labour*, for instance, Schreiner describes women as bloated parasites, reduced by social evolutionary conditions to the position of something like a field bug 'to the passive exercise of their sex functions alone'. She is quick to insist that it is a historically specific aberration, a monstrosity *caused* by centuries of patriarchal family structures, not inherent in all women. For Schreiner the natural world had a good deal to tell of strange and bizarre couplings between the sexes. Her notes to this section of her book are peppered by references to the sexual and reproductive habits of a variety of different creatures, including barnacles. She had clearly read Darwin's four-volume work on barnacles, published in the early 1850s, which presented as an example of sexual peculiarity in the natural world, a species of barnacle in which the male lived as a tiny parasite within the huge bloated body of the female barnacle, absorbed within its flesh and entirely dependent upon it. In another example she writes of a certain species of tick in which it is the female who fastens herself to a living creature and sucks its blood, 'having become a mere distended bladder'. Sex-parasitism cuts both ways, she insists. 'The whole question of sex-parasitism among the lower animals is one throwing suggestive and instructive sidelights on human social problems' (85).

Schreiner's ambivalence about motherhood, her oscillations between sentimentality and revulsion, is partly, I believe, due to her knowledge that Nature produced a host of different possibilities of sexual and reproductive couplings. All are 'natural'; some appear monstrous. In *Woman and Labour*, however, she is concerned to show how sexual parasitism and degeneration of the human female heralds the end of civilization when observed with an evolutionary framework. Schreiner is compelled to argue, as many of her peers also argued, that the education and the work of women would be the saving of the race. It is women's dependency that is monstrous, their inactivity. If women are monstrous parasites they have evolved that way through social conditions. But from a Social Darwinist perspective such evolution must be reversed through social intervention or the continuance of the species itself will be threatened.

How did Schreiner's knowledge of Darwin and the natural sciences inform her representation of the African landscape in *The Story of an African Farm* (written in 1883, two years before *King Solomon's Mines*) and how did she negotiate the reconfiguration of Mother Nature brought about by theory? In *Woman and Labour* she is interested in the evolutionary future of women and she uses evolution only to support her pessimistic prophesies of the evolutionary *future* of the race. In *The Story of an African Farm*, however, her interest is in the evolutionary *past*. Her descriptions of the South African landscape are full of references to natural *history*, the evolutionary past of nature inscribed upon its rocks in the form of fossils. She has a minute and specialized knowledge of the landscape she describes.

There is a monstrous mother in this text – Tant Sannie, Lyndall's grotesque step-mother. She dreams of sheeps' trotters; she snorts horribly in her sleep. She dreams of consuming men. This is the monstrous man-eating mother of Darwinian nightmares – interestingly in this text *not* transfigured into landscape. The landscape itself is quite different:

The full African moon poured down its light from the blue sky into the wide, lonely plain. The dry, sandy earth with its coating of stunted karoo bushes a few inches high, the low hills that skirted the plain, the milk-bushes with their long finger-like leaves, all were touched by a weird and almost oppressive beauty as they lay in the white light.[25]

Each description of African landscape in the novel is a variation on this leitmotif. Milk, skirts, fingers – all point to a landscape which is feminized, but not eroticized. Instead it is described as lonely, exposed and caressed by moonlight. The *moonlight* is cast as a maternal presence in the text but at the same time the landscape appears to be aligned with the two sleeping and motherless children, Em and Lyndall. This is an aerial view but not described as a master-of-all-I-survey trope, because the aerial view is not that of the mastering imperial eye, but of the moonlight.

The landscape is often figured as a child, particularly a child exposed to the burning sun which is always figured as harsh and pitiless. In the drought:

the earth cried out for water ... pitiless sky ... the sun looked down from the cloudless sky, till the karoo-bushes were leafless sticks, broken into the earth, and the earth itself was naked and bare; and only the milk bushes, like old hags, pointed their shrivelled fingers heavenward, praying for the rain that never came. (44)

The landscape is naked, leafless, old, like an old 'hag', a mother past lactation, but crying like a child for water to a pitiless sky. More and more often this landscape is aligned with the suffering child rather than the neglectful mother. It is itself motherless. It is a feminine presence, which like Lyndall herself, despairs for want of mothering. It is not cannibalistic, nor man-eating, it does not seduce its children, but it is unable to mother because it is itself unmothered. Rachel Blau DuPlessis describes Lyndall as 'torn between being a childless mother and being an unmothered child, held, mute and impotent, in an incomplete transition from the pupa'.[26] The landscape shares these qualities with Lyndall; it too is thirsty, exposed, motherless, impotent and mute.

Both Conrad and Haggard describe the African landscape as mute, but its muteness is malevolent: 'Could we handle that dumb thing or would it handle us?' Marlow asks.[27] In Schreiner's *The Story of an African Farm* the landscape is rich with memory, but has been silenced. Waldo exclaims:

'if they could talk, if they could tell us now!' he said, moving his
hand over the surrounding objects – 'then we would know something. This "kopje", if it could tell us how it came here! The
"Physical Geography" says ... what are dry lands now were once
lakes, and what I think is this – these low hills were once the shores
of a lake; this "kopje" is some of the stones that were at the bottom,
rolled together by the water ...' (48–9).

Its silence is only partial, however, for later in the novel Waldo claims
that the stones have begun to speak to him, to whisper secrets:

> Sometimes I lie under that little hill with my sheep, and it seems
> that the stones are really speaking – speaking of the old things, of
> the time when the strange fishes and animals lived that are turned
> into stone now; and the time when the little Bushmen lived here, so
> small and so ugly ... It was one of them, one of those old, wild,
> bushmen, that painted those pictures there ... Now the Boers have
> shot them all, so that we never see a yellow face peeping out of
> among the stones ... But we will be gone soon, and only the stones
> will lie on here, looking at everything like they look now. (50)

Schreiner's knowledge of geology and evolutionary theory enables her
to write a landscape that has a history, and has memory. It has not
always been like this. At some point in its history it was wet and fertile
and that pre-colonial history is still to be traced on the present landscape. The stones of the silenced landscape whisper a different story
from the official colonial versions of history – they speak of barbarism,
of slaughter, of the wiping out of culture. They tell alternative truths.
Thus for Schreiner the feminized landscape, imagined as a geological
receptacle of the past, is the site of a pre-colonial history that will
outlive all of them. If Schreiner's landscape is maternal, its neglectful-
ness, its silence and its passivity are all understood and presented as
the result of the history of abuse it has witnessed and suffered, and the
wiping out of the old things. But these rocks are also the guardians of
pre-colonial history, knowledge and culture. The colonial landscape,
like the state of modern motherhood, has been debased by time and
evolution, not raised by it.

In later writing, notably the allegorical *Three Dreams in a Desert*, the
landscape is described in almost identical terms to the landscape in
The Story of an African Farm. Out of this barren landscape a figure rises,

carrying a suckling male child. This figure, in the words of Gerald Monsman is 'heroically idealised' and enacts 'the monumental drama of the race and gender'.[28] In the second dream, set on the banks of an African river, the woman is told to put down the suckling child. She resists because she wants to carry him to the land of Freedom but Reason insists because, he says, he will weaken her resolve to continue the fight towards liberation and because his dependency needs to be broken.

> 'In your breast he cannot thrive, put him down that he may grow.'
> And she took her bosom from his mouth, and he bit her, so that the blood ran down on to the ground.[29]

Schreiner's writing here inscribes the relationship between mother and son/lover as mutually dependent and destructive. If we transpose Schreiner's feminist tract into a colonial/imperialist context, is it not possible that Schreiner herself may have seen the potential of the story to be read as a liberation narrative addressed not only to feminist New Women incarcerated in Pentonville, but also to be read in South Africa itself? However, this liberation narrative casts the mother figure in a hugely complex role. This allegorical woman, rising from the landscape itself, puts down her child, rejects him, not through vengeance or negligence itself, but because she comes to understand that this abandonment is necessary for the future of women. The mother figure of the allegory is at the centre of a vision of the *future* and yet in *The Story of an African Farm* the maternal landscape is debased, but is also the receptacle of all that is valuable in the pre-colonial *past*. This maternal landscape is unable to mother because it has been the subject of the abuses of power carried out in the name of empire-building.

Peter Hulme argues that cannibalism, seen as an important part of colonial discourse, enacts a kind of projection of the violence implicit in the assimilations of colonialism onto the victims of that assimilation. In other words, when applied to representations of landscape, what is being done to the African landscape (assimilation) becomes the chief threat of that landscape (that it will consume those who are trying to consume it). The early feminization of landscape as virgin, implicit in the sexual relations of the master-of-all-I-survey trope of colonial discourse, makes the demonization of femininity inevitable as Africa becomes darkest of all in the last decade of the nineteenth century. The darkest point of the myth of the Dark Continent is surely its representation as a cannibal mother, a cannibal mother in part shaped by refigurations of femininity brought about by evolutionary theory and in part by the myth of the New Woman and her supposed rejection of motherhood and its imagined repercussions for the 'race'. Hulme argues that cannibalism is used by Western writers as a marker of an absolute boundary between 'civilized' and 'savage', 'human' and 'inhuman'. But where it is gendered as cannibal *mother* in the descriptions of landscape in Haggard and Conrad, it also seems to express the impossibility of demarcation in the colonial encounter. There are no clear edges, no definable bodies. This is not just a world of eat or be eaten, rather a world of slippage in which all these processes of consumption and assimilation are happening *simultaneously*. The consumer is consumed while consuming.

What Schreiner brings to the trope of the cannibalistic landscape is a politicization of maternity, an informed construction of the complex interconnections of dependency and power embedded in the structures of the family as created by Western capitalism. The mother may be in a position of power over her children because of their dependency upon her, and she may abuse that power; this is likely to happen where she herself suffers from the powerlessness of her dependency upon patriarchal power, or where she herself has been inadequately mothered. Cyclical abuses of power seem to Schreiner to be characteristic of the complex dependencies of both motherhood as Western institution and colonialism. Schreiner's African landscape is also feminized but its feminization, even its construction as mother, is politicized through Schreiner's more subtle, though sometimes contradictory, understanding of the complex structures of power and interdependency embedded in motherhood and in colonialism.

Notes

1. Patrick Brantlinger, 'Victorians and Africans: The Genealogy of the Myth of the Dark Continent' *Critical Inquiry* 12 (Autumn 1985), 166.
2. Brantlinger, 175.
3. See Rebecca Stott, *The Fabrication of the Late Victorian Femme Fatale* (London: Macmillan, 1992).
4. Peter Hulme, *The Colonial Encounter: Europe and the Native Caribbean, 1492–1797* (London: Methuen, 1986), 2.
5. Elleke Boehmer, *Colonial and Postcolonial Literature* (Opus, 1996), 50.
6. H. Waller, 'The Universities' Mission to Central Africa', *Quarterly Review* CLXVIII (1889), 229–30.

7. Quoted in General William Booth, *In Darkest England and the Way Out* (London: Salvation Army, 1890), 9.

8. F. Galton, 'Stanley's Discoveries and the Future of Africa', *Edinburgh Review*, CXLVII (1878), 167 and 171.

9. Mary Louise Pratt, *Imperial Writing and Transculturation* (London and New York: Routledge: 1992), 213.

10. Pratt, 209.

11. Rider Haggard, *King Solomon's Mines* (1885; rpt London, Paris and Melbourne: Cassell, 1898), 38.

12. Critics such as Judith Wilt and Patrick Brantlinger have pointed to the rise of what has come to be termed 'imperial gothic'. In much adventure fiction, the empire becomes an alternative gothic space in which anxieties peculiar to the time can be explored, where a gothic overreacher/explorer stumbles onto something powerful and uncontrollable which is unleashed by his intrusions. Such a reading is significant because it shows how an ancient narrative form, gothic, can be transformed over time and transposed from gothic castle to colonial landscape. Both threaten to engulf, trap and consume the adventurer. But such readings do not account for the complex overlaps between race, science and gender within the texts.

13. Joseph Conrad, *Heart of Darkness* (1902), (Harmondsworth: Penguin Modern Classics, 1981), 12.

14. Cited in Patrick Brantlinger, 'Victorians and Africans: the Genealogy of the Myth of the Dark Continent', *Critical Inquiry* 12 (Autumn 1985), 184.

15. Nigel Rigby, 'Sober Cannibals and Drunken Christians: Colonial Encounters of the Cannibal Kind', in *Journal of Commonwealth Literature*, vol. 27: 1 (1992), 178.

16. Peter Hulme, *The Colonial Encounter: Europe and the Native Caribbean, 1492–1797* (London: Methuen, 1986), 86.

17. Hulme, 87.

18. James Eli Adams, 'Nature Red in Tooth and Claw: Nature and the Feminine in Tennyson and Darwin', in *Victorian Studies* 33:1 (Autumn 1989), 7–27. Reprinted in Rebecca Stott, ed., *Tennyson* (Harlow: Longman, 1996), 87–111.

19. See Sally Ledger, *The New Woman: Fiction and Feminism at the Fin de Siècle* (Manchester, Manchester University Press, 1997), 64.

20. Ledger, 69.

21. Ibid., 76.

22. Ibid., 72.

23. Vron Ware, *Beyond the Pale: White Women, Racism and History* (London: Verso, 1992), 43.

24. 6 April, 1887, S. C. Cronwright-Schreiner, ed., *The Letters of Olive Schreiner*, London: Unwin, 1924, 113.

25. Olive Schreiner, *The Story of an African Farm* (1883), Harmondsworth: Penguin, 1986), 35.

26. Rachel Blau DuPlessis, *Writing Beyond the Ending: Narrative Strategies of Twentieth Century Women Writers* (Bloomington: Indian University Press, 1985), 27.

27. *Heart of Darkness*, 38.

28. Gerald Monsman, *Olive Schreiner's Fiction: Landscape and Power* (New Brunswick: Rutgers University Press, 1991), 56.
29. Olive Schreiner, 'Three Dreams in a Desert', in Elaine Showalter, ed., *Daughters of Decadence: Women Writers of the Fin-de-Siècle* (London: Virago, 1993), 314.

10
Capturing the Ideal: Olive Schreiner's *From Man to Man*

Carolyn Burdett

W. T. Stead, journalist and commentator on the reality and fiction of New Womanhood, gave a special place to his friend Olive Schreiner in the pages of his 1894 review of 'The Novel of the Modern Woman'.[1] Schreiner's only published novel was, of course, *The Story of an African Farm*; its heroine, Lyndall, the novel's 'first wholly serious feminist heroine'.[2] Lyndall speaks – although she does not manage to enact – a language of progress which identifies marriage and maternity as amongst the chief bars to women's emancipation: 'I am not in so great a hurry to put my neck beneath any man's foot; and I do not so greatly admire the crying of babies', Lyndall says as a counter to her cousin Em's not-yet-disabused enthusiasm for married life.[3] Lyndall is, like her author, a modern: she scorns the worthlessness of crafting for six weeks a footstool that 'a machine would have made better in five minutes' (*SAF*, 186). Her analysis of the constructedness of gender identity is so strikingly modern that, when Schreiner's work was redis-covered by the women's movement of the next century, Lyndall could be quoted 'straight', her words as relevant to the position of women in the second half of the twentieth century as they were at the end of the nineteenth. There has been no question that what Lyndall speaks is the truth; the problem for Schreiner's present feminist critics is what happens to the woman who does so.

For Lyndall's Napoleonic ambition ('"[Napoleon Bonaparte] was the greatest man who ever lived ... when he said a thing to himself he never forgot it. He waited, and waited, and waited, and it came at last"' (*SAF*, 47)) has only the briefest of flowerings. Her feminist aspiration thwarted by biological destiny, she dies in a Boer cart from a fever con-tracted while sitting, weak after a difficult birth, by the new grave of her dead baby. Like other principled, and suffering, fictional New

Women who were to come after her, Lyndall refuses a conventional resolution to her plight.[4] She rejects her lover's offer of marriage, fearing in it imprisonment to a man for whom she feels no intellectual or spiritual kinship. But she also, at the same time, refuses the progress and modernity she so eloquently evokes. She will not try to escape to a more intellectually hospitable world: '"I will not go down country"', she insists, '"I will not go to Europe"' (*SAF*, 239). Instead, Lyndall goes to the Transvaal, the heart of Afrikaner-colonized South Africa, a place which affords her no respite from a stifling, Calvinistic and narrowly conventional, colonial life. Lyndall feels suffocated: returning to the farm after her first absence, she says to her cousin Em, who is to inherit the farm: '"If I were you, when I get this place I should raise the walls. There is not room to breathe here; one suffocates"' (*SAF*, 183). Metaphorically, Lyndall *is* suffocated, and her fate is an early death.

The remedy for female suffocation Schreiner offers in her later, non-fictional account of women's lot, *Woman and Labour*, is, again, the exemplary modern one, summed up in the text's famous refrain: '*Give us labour and the training which fits for labour!*'[5] It is, of course, a remedy for Western, middle-class women (a point Schreiner makes explicitly in opening her book with an anecdote about an African woman's self-conscious acceptance of her grim conditions of life. For the toiling African woman, the time for emancipation is not yet come.) Western women will inevitably need to turn to public and professional tasks in order to find social and personal fulfilment in modernity. Traditional forms of female labour are shrinking, Schreiner argues, and, if women are to escape the blighting effects of enforced idleness, they must find their way into new types of socially meaningful activity. *Woman and Labour* puts a trenchant liberal case – for equality of opportunity and an end to restrictive and protective educational and professional practices – but gives it an evolutionary spin. Modern changes mean that women bear fewer children and perform less domestic labour; if they fail to find new forms of work, Schreiner argues, they will be socially useless and parasitic and, from this state, only degeneration can result. The history of evolutionary change makes it *necessary*, not just desirable, or even right, that women seek to join the public worlds of education, the professions and politics.

It comes as some surprise to turn from these texts, which were responsible for Schreiner's reputation as one of the most important voices for female emancipation in the decades around the turn of the century, to her major fictional project of these years, the unfinished novel *From Man to Man*, which was published after her death, in 1926.

For *From Man to Man* – the novel in which Schreiner hoped her mature reflections would find their most achieved imaginative form – seems deliberately to eschew the vision of women's entry into what had been exclusively masculine realms. What it presents us with instead are the objects and tasks and aspirations of a very traditional feminine world. The reason for this, I will argue, is to be found in the problems posed for Schreiner's thinking about change and progress and the position of women by South Africa.

From Man to Man tells the story of two sisters, brought up on a farm in the Eastern Province of the Cape Colony. The eldest, Rebekah, is intense and intellectual; she is deeply interested in natural history and in human justice. She also wants to be in love and to be a wife and mother. At the beginning of the main part of the book (which follows a 'prelude' telling of five-year-old Rebekah's experiences on the day her sister is born), Rebekah is about to marry her cousin, Frank, and go with him to Cape Town. As the novel progresses, we learn that, despite the sons she gives birth to and the small study-room in which she thinks and reads, Rebekah is deeply unhappy. What appears to be domestic harmony in her suburban home and its blooming garden disguises the torment and humiliation of marriage to a philandering man. Eventually, she discovers Frank sneaking out at night to have sex with a servant-girl, and also discovers that the girl is pregnant with Frank's child. Thereafter, things change, although not visibly so. Rebekah redraws the terms of her marriage: she remains in Frank's home, caring for him and their four sons, but she no longer has a sexual relationship with him. She also adopts his illegitimate daughter and pays for her own and the girl-child's keep by farming a small land-holding, bought with money given to her by her father when she married. When the novel breaks off, another character, Mr Drummond, has entered Rebekah's world – a man who, it is intimated, will properly deserve her love.

Bertie, Rebekah's younger sister, is habitually called 'Baby-Bertie', a family endearment which serves to emphasize her simplicity and innocence. She is wholesomely domestic and she is also very beautiful. She is seduced by the English tutor who comes to teach her at the farm and, as a consequence, is rejected by the man she falls in love with, Frank's brother, John-Ferdinand. Thereafter, she is pursued by the gossip of mean-minded women and eventually taken to London by a man who has effectively bought her. She there enters a strange, night-marish existence as a kept woman, which is only brought to an end by a further crisis in which she is thrown out onto the street. The last we hear of Bertie, she has been taken away by another man who values her only in terms of her sexual credit, sealing her fate as a prostitute.

In a letter to Havelock Ellis, Schreiner writes of *From Man to Man*: 'The worst of this book of mine, is that it's so womanly. I think it's the most womanly book that ever was written, and God knows I've willed it otherwise.'[6] Schreiner is right; it *is* a womanly book. Rebekah moves from the Eastern Province farm of her childhood to her Cape Town house, immersed in the times and rhythms of a domestic and feminine life vividly established in the novel's opening phrase: 'The little mother lay in the agony of childbirth.'[7] Even the long passages meant to represent Rebekah's intellectual and emotional worlds, where narrative plot comes almost to a halt for nearly fifty pages as Rebekah argues to herself about cruelty and justice and art, are punctuated by reminders of her domestic existence: the socks in the basket to be darned, small noises from her nearby sleeping children, her aching, recently pregnant body (*FMM*, 171–227).

The difficulty of Rebekah's life is not, however, thwarted feminine ambition, but rather the collapse of an emotional structure supposed to sustain the woman in her dedication to family – namely, the love and fidelity of her husband. The New Woman fiction has often been castigated by feminist critics for its inability to make narratives which imagine something other than heterosexual marriage as the route to happiness and fulfilment – and, because the latter invariably fails, to ward off depression and pessimism.[8] Near the beginning of *From Man to Man*, Rebekah, anxious for the wellbeing of her beautiful, but unintellectual sister, Bertie, herself lays out the fearfully restricted prospects – and the hideous risks – for feminine fulfilment in the world of the domestic:

> "Some women, with complex, many-sided natures, if love fails them and one half of their nature dies, can still draw a kind of broken life from the other. The world of the impersonal is left them: they can still turn fiercely to it, and through the intellect draw in a kind of life – a poor, broken, half-asphyxiated kind of life, not what it might have been ... but still life. But Bertie and such as Bertie have only one life possible, the life of the personal relations; if that fails them all fails." (*FMM*, 121)

From Man to Man seems, in this sense, a typically pessimistic New Woman novel. Its plot ties together the fates of the two sisters: Bertie, sweet and loving, who is seduced and haunted by malicious gossips until she falls into prostitution in a dismal London; and Rebekah, intellectual and complex, who comes to recognize her own marriage as a form of prostitution, wedded to a man who knows little of value beyond his own sexual greed and a respect for appearance and convention. Schreiner prefigures the enmeshment of the sisters' lives – and thus the parallel between marriage and prostitution – in the closing image of the 'Prelude' which precedes the main story, where the girl Rebekah and her new-born sister end the day sleeping together, their hands so firmly interlocked that the nurse cannot part them (*FMM*, 73).

Lucy Bland, amongst other feminist critics, has pointed out that a keynote of the New Woman fiction links together selfish male sexual behaviour and the double standard of morality which characterized Victorian marriage.[9] By the 1880s, prostitution was seen as the most vivid sign of this link. The equivalence between marriage and prostitution was made explicit in, for example, Mona Caird's 1888 *Westminster Review* article, 'Marriage', and was elaborated on in much of the New Woman fiction.[10] Some targeted the folly of the romantic ideal and its associated female sexual ignorance (George Egerton's young woman protagonist, in the story 'Virgin Soil', who berates her mother for sending her unprepared to the marriage-bed of an experienced and remorseless sensualist, is a disturbing example[11]); others – Schreiner included – were clear that the only remedy for prostitution, in all its guises, lay in women's economic independence from men.[12]

But although Schreiner was explicit about the centrality of the topic and trope of prostitution in *From Man to Man* – she wrote as late as 1907 to her husband, Samuel Cronwright: 'You will see if you read my novel, that all other matters seem to me small compared to matters of sex, and prostitution is its most agonizing central point'[13] – we never have its narrative working out in the novel. The last we directly hear of Bertie, she has been taken from the gloomy boarding house in the London suburbs which had been her refuge after being rejected by the man who kept her. We know things will not go well with her. Her prostitute identity has already been confirmed by the woman who, during one of Bertie's ghostly city perambulations, reminds her of Rebekah, but who responds to Bertie's tentative touch of her arm with a hardening of her face which places Bertie beyond the pale: 'For an instant she looked at Bertie and took it all in – the beautiful round white face with its fringed eyes, the fifteen-guinea French bonnet tied a little askew ... the ungloved hand with the rings. All her face hardened' (*FMM*, 375). But we never have narrative confirmation of Bertie's fate.

The story breaks off after we have been returned to Cape Town and Rebekah who is living according to conditions she had imposed on her husband, Frank, more than five years earlier (which amount, in effect, to her sexual, emotional and financial independence from him). If we leave *From Man to Man* there, as a novelistic contribution to the ongoing critique of sexual double standards, then I think it cannot be anything other than disappointing. We do not even have the scene Schreiner describes in a letter to Karl Pearson of 1886, where Rebekah finds her fatally ill (presumably syphilitic) prostitute sister, and takes her to die in her own house. Reproached by her husband because of the scandal, she 'asks why she should not take out her dead and bury it in the sunlight – she who for 14 long years herself had been living as a prostitute'.[14] As it stands, though, the unfinished narrative simply does not make the links.

The last seventy or so pages of *From Man to Man* seem, however, to be doing something rather different about which there *is* more to say, in particular about Rebekah's renegotiation of her marriage with which the existing novel ends. Her relative independence seems to be fairly successful, although it is a peculiar kind of independence. As I explained earlier, it consists of living 'as if' Frank's wife, attending to his material needs and looking after their children and the child of his adulterous liaison with Rebekah's servant woman, while financially supporting herself and her adopted child by farming a small land-holding situated just beyond Cape Town's suburbs. The past agonies of her husband's infidelities can now, at most, make her feel 'a faint adumbration of pain' (*FMM*, 447).

It seems clear that Schreiner had intended Rebekah's hard-won contentment to be a costly compromise (she sacrifices sexual love) and one shaken by a resurgence of real pain upon her meeting and falling in love with the character who – briefly though he appears in the book – is its fictional portrayal of New Manhood, Mr Drummond. The ending of the novel provided by Schreiner's husband, Cronwright, as well as the version of the story Schreiner told to Pearson, both elaborate on the 'undying' – but physically unconsummated – love that develops between Rebekah and Drummond. The signs of their affinity are also obvious in the existing narrative as, for example, when Rebekah first sees Drummond's hand as he is sitting next to her at a concert and seems to recognize it; later, she realizes that the hand it reminded her of was her own (*FMM*, 446).[15] But we get very little of that part of the story; what we are left with is the compromise only.

There are at least two reasons why it appears an uncomfortable or even failed compromise for Schreiner's twentieth-century feminist critics. First, it leaves Rebekah firmly within the sphere of the domestic, identified as she is, in the novel's two final existing chapters, primarily by her role as mother. Secondly, we quickly learn that the deal she has struck – the terms on which she continues to live with the man who had forced her systematically to dismantle her fantasy of marriage-as-love-and-integrity – includes her adoption of Sartje, the child of her husband's affair with Rebekah's coloured servant. It is the discovery of this affair that precipitates the crisis through which Rebekah gains independence (the crisis is 'resolved' by Rebekah's ultimatum to her husband which bars him from future sexual relations with her). In this sense, her relinquishing of romantic fantasy is also a drama about racial boundaries. At the point she realizes that the servant girl is carrying Frank's child, Rebekah acts: the girl is dismissed, the room she had occupied in the backyard is literally and symbolically whitewashed. Sartje, we learn, Rebekah adopted as a baby and is 'treated in all ways as her own child, except that it was taught to call her mistress' (*FMM*, 411).

Put this baldly, the narrative seems to replicate a distressingly familiar colonial structure. The scene in which Frank understands that Rebekah has learnt of his sexual misdemeanour in the backyard – he sees the servant girl's empty room, and smells the fresh whitewash – is as chilling an image of differential social power and its effects as a piece of literature might present. Frank's response to the prospect of an illegitimate child is predictably brutal – he gives it only a fleeting thought, and then to hope that the infant might succumb to the high mortality rates amongst the coloured population about which he had read in a newspaper. But Rebekah's response seems predictable too: it is the coloured woman – and not, for instance, the pimply adolescent who was one of Frank's former conquests – who marks the limit of her attempt to accommodate herself to her husband's sexual incontinence.

However, in making the object of Frank's sexual appetite a woman of colour, Schreiner is quite deliberately embedding the novel's gender politics in their South African context. What was, by around the middle of the nineteenth century, already being called the Cape's coloured population, is a complex grouping of the Cape's indigenous peoples, the Khoi and the Bushman or San (with some mixture of European or Xhosa ancestry),[16] and the descendants of slaves and ex-slaves, many of whom were born of sexual relations between white slave-owners and slave women, and then, even more commonly, between white men and Dutch-speaking Cape-born women of mixed parentage.[17] Frank's sexual liaison in the backyard thus evokes a past in which sexual, racial and class exploitation are bound together in the horror of slavery. It is this that Rebekah cannot bear: not the fact that adultery with a woman of colour is 'a grosser and more brutal thing' than with a white (it might seem so '"in the eyes of the world"', Rebekah says, '"but not in mine"' (*FMM*, 287), but that Frank's desire is so ephemeral, predatory and exploitative – little different, in other words, from the dismal past.[18]

It is thus exactly Rebekah's uncomfortable compromise with which the novel ends, and the way in which it foregrounds the issue of racial divisions in South Africa, which had become the heart of Schreiner's project in *From Man to Man*. Schreiner worried for years about whether she could make *From Man to Man* work: 'You know, I think in this book I *will* say what I want to say. I mean I've sometimes felt as if I couldn't make this book say everything I wanted to say as *An African Farm* said what I wanted to say then.'[19] Schreiner began writing the novel when she was a young woman, living in an intellectually stifling colonial culture, and longing to 'pluck for herself the strange bright fruits of art and knowledge' that the metropolis promised.[20] She continued to work on it for much of the remainder of her life, certainly for long after she had decided that England was no longer 'home', and that the ideal of English civilization carried within it forms of violence.[21] Any sense of what the changing world might mean for women becomes more and more tied to the novel's South African setting and consequently to the issues of race and power in South Africa which were increasingly the focus of Schreiner's emotional and political concern. It is because Schreiner *doesn't* write a novel about white, professionally aspirant middle-class femininity – because she writes this 'womanly' book which explores a positive maternity as much as prostitution – that she can begin to deal seriously with the ways in which a feminist response to modernity is inextricable from the issues of race, national identity, power and exploitation that so strikingly and visibly dominated South Africa. It is this reassessment of her feminism in the light of South Africa's modernity – and the reasons why maternity is so central to it – that I will now explore.

Schreiner's account of her dramatic entry into modern thought – had by reading Herbert Spencer's *First Principles*, which had been lent to her by a stranger seeking refuge on a stormy night at an aunt's isolated house in Basutoland – overstates the contingency of her deliverance from the 'complete blank atheism' of her youthful freethinking into belief in evolution.[22] The libraries and booksellers of colonial South Africa gave her access to a good deal of the work influencing social debate in England; and when she arrived in England in 1881 she was able to enter an intellectual, and increasingly a political, world in which evolutionary thinking had become paradigmatic.

As I suggested earlier, in *Woman and Labour* Schreiner explicitly uses evolution as the basis for female progress: woman's labour has changed; the time is now right for her to find new forms of it. In *From Man to Man*, however, Schreiner's engagement with evolutionary theory is put to different uses. In Rebekah's extended disquisition on social Darwinism, she accuses the social theorist who advocates survival of the fittest as the mechanism of social progress of '[sheltering] yourself under the name of science. Are you not, and one-eyedly, perverting the teaching of great minds, as the priestly in all ages pervert and make falsehood' (*FMM*, 209). In the place of one 'natural law' – of grim evolutionary struggle – Rebekah offers another: 'love and expansion of the ego to others has governed life', a love exemplified by mother-love (*FMM*, 209–10). The guiding 'first principle' of social life, according to Spencerian evolution, that 'to interfere with [the great law of the survival of the fittest] is to interfere with nature's one plan for attaining perfection' (*FMM*, 209), is refuted by this love: 'through all nature, life and growth and evolution are possible only because of mother-love' (*FMM*, 210).

On any reckoning, this is a very different reading of evolution from the progressive message of *Woman and Labour*. Read within the themes of the novel, however, the good-evolutionary force of mother-love Schreiner evokes is not an unfortunately naive naturalization. Rather, it signals a thematic bridge between two moments in the novel which, together, make a serious narrative attempt to set the aspirational programme of female emancipation in the context of South Africa and *its* modernity. In South Africa, after all, 'progress' ('nature's one plan') increasingly looked like trauma – particularly as, with the discovery of gold in the Transvaal in the mid-1880s, the infrastructure of a modern industrial state began to be developed. While the freeing up of traditional social organization could be experienced as liberating in England, industrial progress in South Africa meant land dispossession, familial and tribal upheaval, social disintegration and horrific exploitation.[23]

I now want to look at these two moments in the novel in some detail and to suggest that, in the imagined, as well as the literal, space of

South Africa, the narrative of progress which Schreiner could use to such effect in her non-fictional argument about woman's emancipation, *Woman and Labour*, had to be recast, in order to have any hope of addressing the ruthlessly unbinding forces of modernization. The first of these moments in the novel concerns the 'missionary maternity'[24] evoked in the child Rebekah's fantasy world – a world put together from the shards of colonial culture. The second is Rebekah's maternal capacity to reinvent her colonial upbringing for the education and future of her own children.

The Prelude of *From Man to Man*, 'The Child's Day', charts one day in the life of the five-year-old Rebekah, the day on which her sister Bertie is born, together with a stillborn twin. Struggling to find her way amidst the mysteries of life and death, the young Rebekah embarks on a long daydream in which she tells stories to an imagined baby of her own. These stories are drawn from the Bible, from English poetry, and from Dissenting songs and literature; they are fragments which are not fully understood by Rebekah but out of which she struggles to make something meaningful. In her reading of the Prelude, Laura Chrisman describes two of the most striking fragments – a story of the Indian 'Mutiny' and a story of the Roman invasion of Boadicea's Britain – as exemplifying a 'missionary maternity'. The stories combine themes of mothering and of imperialism in a manner which is 'nothing if not ambiguous and contradictory'.[25] In other words, Chrisman argues, the text hovers between confirmation and criticism of empire. What I want to emphasize, however, is the way in which the ambiguity *belongs* to Rebekah. She does not quite know what to make of the elements of her own very colonial upbringing; she does not quite understand how the scraps of English culture which make up her education are meaningful in her South African world. For instance, she quotes Cowper, promising her imaginary child that she will teach it the poem: '"Rome, for Empire far renown/Tramps on a thousand states" ... I could understand it all, except for "For-Empire" and "far-renown". I don't know what "far-renown" is – or "for-empire" – ' (*FMM*, 54–5). Such problems of understanding, or translation, are underlined later in the novel when the grown-up Rebekah reflects on another instance of her quest to make sense of the world and remembers feeling let-down when, as a young girl, she had ordered some science primers from a bookseller in Cape Town. Her intense pleasure when they arrived had given way to distress as she realized that the examples in the botany and the geology did not make sense in her world. Written as they were 'for people in

England ... the plants and rocks and fossils mentioned she could not find in Africa' (*FMM*, 173).

In the penultimate of the novel's existing chapters, however, Rebekah has moved beyond these problems of translation which characterize her attempts to understand English knowledge and culture in the context of South Africa. Instead, she will use her experience of South African life to challenge and mediate that knowledge. In the chapter, she responds to an outburst from one of her sons against having to walk publicly beside his half-sister, Sartje (he is ashamed because she is not white). Rebekah's response takes the form of a series of reflections and stories, in which the evolution of civilization is a process fecund and mysterious, and where Europe features not as its pinnacle, but as *parvenu*. Her reflections culminate in a series of vignettes in which her own childhood experiences provide the source of a knowledge and wisdom she will pass on to her sons.

The vignettes begin with a memory of a favourite childhood fantasy in which she is Queen Victoria and imagines:

'that all Africa belonged to me, and I could do whatever I liked. It always puzzled me when I walked up and down thinking what I should do with the black people; I did not like to kill them, because I could not hurt anything, and yet I could not have them near me. At last I made a plan. I made believe I built a high wall right across Africa and put all the black people on the other side, and I said, '"Stay there, and, the day you put one foot over, your heads will be cut off"' (*FMM*, 435)

This wall across South Africa – the child's fantasy of apartheid *avant la lettre* – 'had slowly to fall down', Rebekah tells her rapt children. The process by which Rebekah learns that the black Africans she had wanted to divide off and expel 'were mine and I was theirs' (*FMM*, 438), is *identification*. At seven years, Rebekah overhears an account of a war in which Africans, armed with spears, fought colonialists armed with cannon, in which a young black woman passed spears to the men, calling them 'to come on and not to be afraid to die', until the cannon 'blows her away too with the others' (*FMM*, 436). At nine years, she listens to her mother and old Ayah discussing an African woman's suicide and infanticide. The child Rebekah can only intuit the sexual drama that had driven the woman to such an act, but mourns for her. As a woman she, too, will come to contemplate taking together her own and her children's lives in the grip of a similar jealous despair (*FMM*, 436–7).

The importance of empathic identification has its own complex place within the history of modernity. By the end of the eighteenth century, for instance, the imaginative identification with another which characterized the man of good heart in Henry Fielding's fiction had become, in the guise of sensibility, feminized and devalued. By the twentieth century, however, identification has all too often looked like appropriation. Rebekah's identifications with black women, and in particular with their caring and mothering, presuppose a possibility of communication across cultural boundaries which, as Jacqueline Rose puts it, in an article about another South African writer, Bessie Head, has come to be seen as masking 'a moment of self-aggrandizing blindness' otherwise known as universality.[26] The fact that this has tended to block out what might be important or good about universalizing impulses is, in part, what Rose wants to address.

Schreiner evokes universality as a quality of femininity and especially of maternity. Rose's title, 'On the "Universality" of Madness: Bessie Head's *A Question of Power*', puts 'universality' in scare quotes in order to suggest that it is a corrupted term. Maternity, too, has at times become a corrupted term for feminist critics in the twentieth century. In part this is because of the naturalization and moralization of maternity which justified efforts to exclude women from privilege and power. Schreiner herself puts this as powerfully as anyone when, in *Woman and Labour*, she parodies the argument that women should be content to be child-bearers, given motherhood's importance, its sacral nature, by pointing out that objections to women's work rarely extend to the punishing slog of the poor, but only to the well-rewarded and independent woman: 'it is not toil, or the amount of toil, crushing alike to brain and body, which the female undertakes that is objected to; it is the form and amount of the reward.'[27] Perhaps even more important than such ideological manipulation of the image of a natural and moral maternity, though – especially for the history of the late-nineteenth-century New Woman – is the extent to which maternity is associated with imperialism and eugenics.[28]

Rose argues that the 'corrupted' terms of her title – 'universality' and 'madness' – might also be indispensable ones;[29] similarly, *From Man to Man* suggests that maternity is indispensable as a means to express the values of patient creativity, of attention to the needs of the other, of the *process* of enculturation, otherwise known as nurturing, so patently needed in colonial South Africa. The identifications haltingly experienced by the child Rebekah recognize an emotional, interior life for Africans, to set against the colonial stereotype which denied such interiority (Schreiner was quite aware of such stereotyping; she made explicit use of it in *Trooper Peter Halket of Mashonaland*, where Peter cannot comprehend that the African women who are coerced into sleeping with him may have emotional lives of their own). Mothering here is explicitly set against the violence of a colonial imagination, exemplified in the wall which has to fall down as Rebekah recognizes human kinship through suffering.

Schreiner's unfinished novel thus registers the impasse of modern (white, middle-class) feminism in the context of South Africa. In South Africa there were no spaces for its progress which did not open out onto the question of European modernity's reliance on other countries for their economic position and national self-fashioning. Most of Schreiner's fiction features absent or weak mothers and dead babies; her decision to make mothering central to *From Man to Man* may look like a retreat from modernity but if it is, it is one, I would argue, that is principled by an awareness that progress looked very different in South Africa than it did in England, and had to be imagined differently. Like so much of the New Woman fiction, female renunciation is painfully central to *From Man to Man*, but it is, nevertheless, a narrative which tries to imagine a future for its woman protagonist; as Gerald Monsman comments, Rebekah 'will learn, work, wait'.[30] Maternal identity is central to that process and its vital creativity. What seems certain is that, at the end of the nineteenth century, what progress meant for women, how maternity might figure in that progress, and how both looked from the point of view of a colonial woman increasingly troubled by the making of modern South Africa, made up some tremendously testing questions. Africa, so often used as evidence for the story of western civilization's move from darkness to enlightenment, becomes, in Rebekah's hands, evidence of that story's true costs – all too clearly for the colony, certainly, but also for Europe itself.

The long chapter in *From Man to Man* where Rebekah witnesses her husband sneaking out into the backyard to the servant-girl's room is largely taken up by a letter she writes to him, in which she tells him what his history of sexual perfidy has meant to her. The chapter is called 'You Cannot Capture the Ideal by a Coup D'Etat'. It charts the final fantasy Rebekah has to relinquish about her marriage: that, if only she could say it clearly enough, and Frank could listen, her *reasoned case* would prevail and she would be understood at last. Rebekah's terrible lesson, and perhaps Schreiner's too, is that sometimes reason does not work, and that to tackle the problem head-on is to miss it. It is to Schreiner's credit, her own learning, working, waiting, that she tried to find ways to tackle testing questions; and it is no condemnation of her that, unable to complete her most precious book, she could not finally make her way to answers – about the shape and nature of progress – which only seem a little clearer a hundred years later.

Notes

1. Stead describes Schreiner as 'The Modern Woman, *par excellence*, the founder and high priestess of the school'. W. T. Stead, 'The Book of the Month: the Novel of the Modern Woman', *Review of Reviews* 10 (1894), 64.
2. Elaine Showalter, *A Literature of Their Own: British Women Novelists from Brontë to Lessing* (London: Virago, 1978), 199.
3. Olive Schreiner, *The Story of an African Farm*, (1883; Harmondsworth: Penguin, 1971), 184. Subsequent references to this work, abbreviated as *SAF*, will appear in the main text.
4. Perhaps the most notorious of examples of this aspect of the New Woman literature is Grant Allen, *The Woman Who Did*, (London: John Lane, 1895).
5. Olive Schreiner, *Woman and Labour* (1911; London: Virago, 1978), 33.
6. Olive Schreiner to Havelock Ellis, 2 February 1898, Richard Rive (ed.), *Olive Schreiner: Letters 1871–1899* (Oxford: Oxford University Press, 1988), 149.
7. Olive Schreiner, *From Man to Man* (1926; London: Virago, 1982), 33. Subsequent references to this work, abbreviated as *FMM*, will appear in the main text.
8. The classic feminist case against the New Woman novelists' pessimism is made by Showalter, 182–215.
9. Lucy Bland, *Banishing the Beast: English Feminism and Sexual Morality 1885–1914* (Harmondsworth: Penguin, 1995), 145–6.
10. Mona Caird, 'Marriage', *Westminster Review*, 130, 2 (1888). Caird draws on contemporary anthropology in order to examine what she describes as 'our modern idea of *possession* in marriage' (189). Sarah Grand used an associated idea – of the sexually dissipated, syphilitic male, entrapping a woman in marriage – in her popular 1893 novel, *The Heavenly Twins*.
11. George Egerton, 'Virgin Soil', *Discords* (1894), rpt. as *Keynotes and Discords* (London: Virago, 1983), 145–162.
12. See, for example, Schreiner's response to Edward Carpenter's 1894 article on marriage, later included in his *Love's Coming-of-Age*: 'You don't perhaps dwell QUITE enough on the monetary independence of women as the first condition necessary to the putting of things on the right footing', Olive Schreiner to Edward Carpenter, 8 October 1894, Rive, 241.
13. Schreiner to Cronwright, 20 March 1907; included as an appendix, *FMM*, 491.
14. Schreiner to Karl Pearson, 9 July 1886, Rive, 93.
15. See appendix to *FMM*, 505–7, for Cronwright's version of the story's ending. For the version Schreiner tells Pearson, see Schreiner to Pearson, 9 July 1886, Rive, 91–5.

16. In colonial terminology, Hottentot and Bushman. These are already difficult terms, registering as they do, colonial and imperial naming, but the naming is complicated further by the fact that the term San was often used as a derogatory term by Khoikhoi groups to describe cattleless outsider groups, and thus implicated too in tensions and hostilities between indigenous African peoples. 'Khoisan' is frequently used as an embracing term which, at its best, registers the difficulty of distinguishing peoples so profoundly affected by colonial history. See Elizabeth Elbourne, 'A Question of Identity: Evangelical Culture and Khoisan Politics in the Early Nineteenth-Century Eastern Cape', collected seminar papers from the Institute of Commonwealth Studies, *The Societies of Southern Africa in the Nineteenth and Twentieth Centuries*, 18 (October 1990 – June 1991).

17. The Dutch East India Company allowed the importation of slaves into the Cape from the mid-seventeenth century from parts of Africa and Asia and from Madagascar. A good account of the complex and heterogeneous nature of the so-called coloured population can be found in Timothy Keegan, *Colonial South Africa and the Origins of the Racial Order* (London: Leicester University Press, 1996), 15–25. 'Coloured', of course, became one of the central classificatory terms of the South African state in the twentieth century; as such, it has earned opprobrium, but it also identifies important elements of group resistance and cultural productivity. Thanks to Ken Parker for telling me that this tension is most readily articulated by members of the coloured community in South Africa by the appended phrase 'so-called'.

18. Elsewhere, when Schreiner discusses the 'Cape coloured' population in her collection of essays about her country of birth, *Thoughts on South Africa*, she explicitly makes the 'half-caste', or coloured, stand as a living sign of the depredations of a slaving past. See 'The Problem of Slavery', *Thoughts on South Africa* (1923; Parklands: A. D. Donker, 1992).

19. Schreiner to Havelock Ellis, 6 November 1890; appendix, *FMM*, 489.

20. The phrase is Virginia Woolf's, about George Eliot; Woolf, *Women and Writing*, ed. Michèle Barrett (London: Women's Press, 1979), 160.

21. 'England is dead for me', Schreiner wrote to Havelock Ellis after returning to South Africa in 1889. Schreiner to Ellis, 5 April 1890, Rive, 168.

22. Schreiner was sixteen when this happened; she wrote to Havelock Ellis: 'I always think that when Christianity burst on the dark Roman world it was what that book was to me.' Schreiner to Ellis, 28 March 1884, Rive, 36.

23. Schreiner protested about the political implications of the new economic power in South Africa in an article jointly authored with her husband, *The Political Situation* (London: Unwin, 1896).

24. The phrase is Laura Chrisman's, from her reading of *From Man to Man*'s Prelude: Laura Chrisman, 'Empire, "Race" and Feminism at the *fin de siècle*: the Work of George Egerton and Olive Schreiner', *Cultural Politics at the Fin de Siècle*, eds Sally Ledger and Scott McCracken (Cambridge: Cambridge University Press, 1995).

25. Chrisman, 59.

26. Jacqueline Rose, 'On the "Universality" of Madness: Bessie Head's *A Question of Power*', in *States of Fantasy* (Oxford: Clarendon Press, 1996), 99.

27. Schreiner, *Woman and Labour*, 203.

28. See, for example, Chrisman, 45, who argues that female individuation in the New Woman fiction is articulated in relation to 'a highly maternalized imperial feminism, definable as the making of racial bodies (a eugenically inspired concept) ... [and a] maternal and missionary notion of feminism as the making and saving of souls'. As Chrisman points out, however, such ideas could be put to very different ends by different writers.
29. Rose, 100.
30. Gerald Monsman, *Olive Schreiner's Fiction: Landscape and Power* (New Brunswick: Rutgers University Press, 1991), 161.

11
'People Talk a Lot of Nonsense about Heredity'[1]: Mona Caird and Anti-Eugenic Feminism

Angelique Richardson

> *Eccentricity has always abounded when and where strength of character has abounded. That so few now dare to be eccentric marks the chief danger of the time.*[2]

In the words of the late nineteenth-century poet Elizabeth Sharp, Mona Caird's opinions, though they were 'met with acute hostility at the time, contributed a great deal to "altering the attitude of the public mind in its approach to and examination of [the woman question]."'[3] Sharp dedicated her anthology of Victorian Women Poets to Caird, designating her 'the most loyal and devoted advocate of the cause of woman'.[4] I shall demonstrate in this essay the extent to which Caird exposed and opposed the repressive ideas which lay beneath the apparently emancipatory rhetoric of many of her feminist contemporaries.

Caird published seven novels, a number of short stories, a travel book, a number of anti-vivisection tracts and several articles on the Woman Question and other social issues. By her fourth novel, *The Wing of Azrael* (1889), her fiction was attracting wide attention, and she achieved huge success – and notoriety – with her polemical and uncompromising novel of 1894, *The Daughters of Danaus*. Reviewing the novel in the feminist periodical *Shafts* Margaret Sibthorp considered it 'one of the best books the century has produced'.[5] Caird's strident and, as the *Court Journal* put it, 'very clever' article, 'Marriage', published in the *Westminster Review* in 1888, sparked, in the words of the editor Harry Quilter, 'the greatest newspaper controversy of modern times'.[6] It even percolated to the household of those

Figure 13 Happy thought! Let us all have a voice in the matter.
Noble Breeder of Shorthorns. 'Well, you *are* a splendid fellow, and *no* mistake!'
Prize Bull. 'So would *you* be, my lord, if you could only have chosen your Pa and Ma as carefully and judiciously as you chose mine!'
Punch, 20 March 1880

paragons of middle-class domesticity, Mr and Mrs Pooter: 'we had a most pleasant chat about the letters on "Is Marriage a Failure?"'[7] In the words of W. T. Stead, sexual agitator and editor of the *Pall Mall Gazette*,[8] it was 'the famous article in which she scandalized the British household by audaciously asking the question "is Marriage a Failure?"': it elicited 27 000 letters to the *Daily Telegraph*, London's widest-read newspaper, during the months of August and September 1888.[9] Quilter caught the moment with a combination of irony, incredulity and genuine awe:

'seasons changed, summer passed away'. Baldwin fell from the clouds, and Edison's voice was brought us in a box, Imperial diaries came out and were suppressed, grouse were cleared from the moors, and partridges shot in the stubble, but still with the inevitability of fate, the regularity of time, and the persistency of a Scotch lawyer, the three columns of perplexed curates, city barmaids, observant bachelors, and glorified spinsters maintained their hold upon the journal, and their claim on the public attention.

(Quilter, 2)

Caird had reached all levels of society with her searching question.

Unsurpassed in her commitment to the emancipation of women from social and sexual oppression, Caird has largely been neglected by historians and literary critics. When studies of the late nineteenth-century Woman Question and literature refer to her, they tend merely to synopsize her views on marriage and, at best, summarize the plots of her less neglected novels.[10] Some critics have, however, begun a more constructive exploration of Caird's work. In her afterword to *The Daughters of Danaus* Margaret Morganroth Gullette considers Caird a 'missing voice of radical feminism'.[11] Similarly, Ann Heilmann has made a valuable contribution to New Woman scholarship, bringing to light biographical information and noting connections between Caird's far-reaching critique of marriage and motherhood under patriarchal law and second-wave feminism. However, Heilmann does not discuss Caird's interest in, and subversion of, evolutionary discourses which, I contend, lay at the heart of this critique.

In her fiction Caird opposed the repressive and authoritarian code of many late-nineteenth-century eugenists, taking issue with her feminist contemporaries who advocated 'civic motherhood', and exposing the limitations of a (feminist) politics that sought to gain social advancement through a gendered division of labour – arguably the single greatest cause of sexual oppression. Eugenic feminists such as Sarah Grand, Ellice Hopkins and Jane Hume Clapperton sought to rewrite love along rational lines, excising passion and privileging desirable offspring: the eugenization of love.[12] Caird advocated the importance of the individual over what she termed 'arithmetical morality', revealing the social bias of science and the flawed logic of eugenists. Caird believed in the historically-determined rather than biologically determined nature of social evolution, and sought to reveal the socially constructed nature of biological discourse. Both in her fiction and in the periodical press, she openly opposed ways in which Darwinian ideas were being (ab)used to justify barbaric social practices.

Mona Caird quotes frequently from the philosopher and sex egalitarian John Stuart Mill, whose keen sense of history and fervent championing of social and sexual equality permeates her own work. In 'Motherhood under Conditions of Dependence' she wrote: 'in [women] the faculties are discouraged which lead away from the domestic "sphere" ... the whole nature is subjected to hot-house cultivation, in such a manner, as to drive all the vital forces in one sole direction' (135). The influence of Mill's mind and prose on Caird is here palpable. Two decades earlier he had declared: 'in the case of women, a hot-house and stove cultivation has always been carried on of some of the capabilities of their nature, for the benefit and pleasure of their masters' (Mill, *On the Subjection of Women*, 238); likewise, four of the epigraphs to her essays in *The Morality of Marriage* are quotations from Mill. The value which Mill and Caird place on history enabled them to expose the *constructed* aspect of nature and of ideas of *fixed and fundamental* racial difference. In 'The Human Element in Man', Caird declared 'in opposition to the widely-accepted theory that whatever is natural is always right, it would be almost safe to assert, that whatever is natural is certain to be wrong' (232), and defined nature as 'the high priestess of all that is fortuitous and incoherent' (234). In 'Suppression of Variant Types' she emphasized: 'we must on no account admit ... local "human nature" as a constant factor, but must regard it as a mere register of the forces that chance to be at work at the moment, and of the forces that have been at work in the past. Different centuries produce different types of humanity, though born of the same race' (197–8); likewise, in 'Early History of the Family', another essay in *The Morality of Marriage*, she wrote 'all history proves that society is in a state of perpetual motion, and that there is, perhaps, no set of ideas so fundamental that human beings have not somewhere, at some period in the world, lived in direct contradiction to them' (23).

While social purists began by challenging the biological basis of the male sexual urge, they then accepted it as convenient for their biologically deterministic melodrama, which figured men as incorrigible villains, and cast women in the role of heroic bearers of moral biology. Unlike social purists and eugenic feminists, Caird had no truck with the notion that the male sexual urge was a biological fact. Eugenic feminists stressed that males were sexually irresponsible: in fact, the eugenic need for women was predicated on this belief. While Lucy Bland and others have argued that feminists used eugenics as a way of challenging the sexual double standard, Caird saw the problems this entailed and questioned the very foundations on which the institution of motherhood was based. While Grand offered a sustained attack on the sacrifice of virgin brides to syphilitic, older men, it was national health rather than the freedom of the individual that motivated her campaign.

Where Caird receives critical attention she is too often grouped with eugenic New Women writers such as Grand, even though her novels constitute a direct engagement with and overturning of maternalist and eugenic arguments. Caird's late-twentieth-century reputation has thus been determined by what has been a largely homogenizing response to the New Woman. Grand's biographer asserts that 'Caird's views of marriage were very similar to Frances' [Sarah Grand's]'.[13] Likewise, Marilyn Bonnell argues that 'the authors whose visions are most closely aligned with Grand are Ella Hepworth Dixon and Mona Caird'.[14] Caird herself, however, made it clear that she did not share Grand's views: in 1888, she wrote that *Ideala*, Grand's novel of that year, 'has been quoted against me'; its 'general drift ... cannot be said to be favourable to my view'.[15] *Ideala* offers a view of motherhood that was anathema to Caird – its eponymous heroine inspires the narrator 'to paint an allegorical picture of her as a mother nursing the Infant Goodness of the race'[16] – and its championing of biological determinism, and the eradication of the 'weak' (through the eventual prevention of their birth) was clearly at odds with Caird's emancipatory value system. Caird was strikingly aware, and critical of the political agenda which underpinned the hereditarian application of evolutionary theory, as her fiction and journalism repeatedly shows. To give a further example of the homogenizing response to the New Woman, Lucy Bland assumes that Caird shared with her contemporaries 'the imperialist rhetoric of racist "commonsense"'.[17] The assumption that Caird held racist views is inaccurate (see below), and symptomatic of the general lack of close attention from which her work has suffered.

In gauging the extent of Caird's dissent, it is useful to consider temporary social-purist reception of her work. The social purist and staunch opponent of pleasure Ellice Hopkins, for example, met her with hostility (and a certain lack of grace):

> I am aware that neither Mr Grant Allen with his 'hill-top' novels, nor Mrs Mona Caird need be taken too seriously, but when the latter says, 'there is something pathetically absurd in this sacrifice to their children of generation after generation of grown people' I would suggest that it would be still more pathetically absurd to see the whole upward-striving past, the whole notable future of the human race, sacrificed to their unruly wills and affections, their passions and desires.[18]

Caird explicitly and consistently attacked the concept of 'race' and 'race purity' in her fiction, not least through her denunciation of eugenism, and was one of the few prominent opponents of imperial oppression and the exploitation of motherhood. For example, in *The Daughters of Danaus*, the arguments of the hard-line eugenists are, significantly, expressed by Miss Du Prel, the loosest cannon in the book (though well-meaning, she is liable to turn coat at any point, and often contradicts herself). Caird gives eugenism to the ineffectual or disreputable characters in her fiction in order to undermine, denigrate or satirize it. Thus, in her 1915 novel *The Stones of Sacrifice* the eugenist anti-hero Swainson Stubbs's dictum that 'the Race, not the liberty of the unimportant unit, was what mattered'[19] serves as an unequivocal condemnation of racial thinking.

Nurture over Nature

In her criticism of eugenics Mona Caird exposed the predominance of environmental (social) factors in shaping the lives of individuals. At no point for her is heredity straightforward, either to predict or explain. In *The Daughters of Danaus* the differences between the four Fullerton children housed under one roof are testimony to this: 'if it were not that one is born with feelings and energies and ambitions of one's own, parents might treat one as a showman treats his marionettes' (*Daughters*, 38). The reader learns that 'each member of the Fullerton family had unusual ability of some kind'. It is conceded that 'heredity might have some discoverable part in the apparent marvel', but that part is neither clear nor certain (59). And of course the less straightforward heredity was, the less attractive it could be to the eugenists: 'heredity asserted itself, as it will do, in the midst of the fray, just when its victim seems to have shaken himself free from the mysterious obsession'. Conversely 'all the old hereditary instincts of conquest and ownership appeared to be utterly dead in [Fortescue]' (260, 210).[20] Heredity, as Caird could see, could not be counted on – therein lay its one redeeming property.

For Caird, nurture was not subordinate to nature: instead it played a key role in individual and social development, enjoying an active and altering union with the individual, and housing the key to the cause and cure of ill-health. Caird resisted the temptation to reconfigure inheritance plots biologically, giving, instead, a significant role to the environment, and thus countering the rigidity of hereditarian ideas through a viable scientific counter-theory. In *The Great Wave*, Professor de Mollyns declares 'people talk a lot of nonsense about heredity, I maintain it's environment that eventually makes heredity' (43), thus neatly effacing nature in the nature–nurture debate (this twinned pair of opposites was coined by Francis Galton, founder of eugenics). In Caird's fiction, daily surroundings (environment/society) are defined not merely as 'pleasant or unpleasant facts, otherwise of no importance; they were the very material and substance of character; the push and impetus, or the let and hindrance; the guardians or the assassins of the soul' (*Daughters*, 59). As Algitha says in *The Daughters of Danaus*, 'I can't believe, for instance, that among all those millions in the East End, not *one* man or woman, for all these ages, was born with great capacities, which better conditions might have allowed to come to fruition'. Ill-health and low levels of achievement are blamed on present living conditions. Hadria remarks that 'it is no more "intended" or inherently necessary than that children should be born with curvature of the spine, or rickets' (*Daughters*, 209). Intention was a concept which Caird, like Darwin, wrote out of evolutionary narrative.

In *The Daughters of Danaus*, the prevalence of nurture over nature is further explored through the absent Mrs Fortescue, who has killed herself largely because her husband lacked mastery (seeking to rouse his jealousy she became entangled with Captain Bolton, and elopes with him before being overcome with remorse). Caird here offers a parodic account of sexual selection. Mrs Fortescue failed to marry the type for which generations of sexual selection have kitted her out. As the Professor puts it: 'she has the old barbaric notion that a husband was a sort of master, and must assert his authority and rights. It was the result of her training' (*Daughters*, 201). The readers learn that her foremothers aided and abetted brute force in choosing the most aggressive of specimens.[21] However, Mrs Fortescue's desire for a brutal mate cannot be explained in simple terms of heredity: we learn that 'her father and grandfather had both been men of violent and tyrannical temper, and tradition gave the same character to all their forefathers', and that 'having inherited the finer and stronger qualities of her father's race, with much of its violence, she was going through a struggle at the time of our marriage', but it is to 'training and tradition' that she succumbs (203).[22] Thus, her sexual preference is born of imitation rather than heredity. Caird held that very few people underwent evolution in a single generation, that is, showed new traits in their self-development; instead they *imitated* ('Phases of Human Development', 200). Past and present *example* was thus much more influential than genealogical make-up. In *The Stones of Sacrifice* Caird, again, offers a parodic account of women's part in sexual selection: 'mother looks out a selection of men, sifts out the likeliest and puts them on the short leet' (*Stones*, 38). Caird also draws here, and elsewhere, on humour as a political resource; it offered her an effective way of highlighting absurdity in the hope of effecting change.

The idea of selection for fitness is parodied in *The Stones of Sacrifice*: Thorne, leader of the Triumvirate (and staunchly eugenic) party, proposes 'to regulate marriages scientifically in the interests of the race, and to decide the vexed question of woman's position in strict accordance with her function of producing the largest number of healthy people for the State'. If 'natural instinct' is not enough then 'they must be coerced into it by law and opinion'. Thorne (his name signalling nature's capacity for cruelty) is an exponent of eugenic love in its most powerful form. He decrees that 'parents (by which [he] was found to mean chiefly female parents) must sacrifice themselves for their offspring' (*Stones*, 154). As Caird wryly signals, for eugenists marriage was overshadowed by mating as sexual selection replaced sexual passion or notions of the meetings of loving and companionate hearts or compatible minds. In her non-fiction Caird made her arguments explicit. In her address to the Personal Rights Association, she urged:

> If Society is obsessed by a crude and unproved theory of heredity, how are we to resist interference with our marriages, or being treated as hysterical, or feeble-minded, or degenerate, or insane? Genius and originality generally seem pathological to the majority.[23]

Professor Fortescue is an anti-eugenist. For him heredity is not incompatible with choice: 'only after the decision had been made did heredity fix it' (*Daughters*, 102). He advises Hadria 'you have peculiar advantages of a hereditary kind, if only you can get a reasonable chance to use them'. Heredity is of no use by itself; its energy potential needs to be unlocked by the environment. Hadria finds herself wondering 'whether her father had also been born with certain instincts which the accidents of life had stifled or failed to develop. Terrible was the tyranny of circumstance!' (36). Try as the Fullerton children do to force the hand of circumstance, it triumphs by the novel's conclusion. The environment needed a more radical reconstruction than they were able to effect. Sally Ledger argues that both Hadria *and* Caird are intellectually defeated by evolutionist discourse (*The New Woman*, 29); I would argue that the novel exposes social law as the ultimate source of oppression.

Personal rights

Mill wrote in *On Liberty* (1859) 'no one can be a great thinker who does not recognize, that as a thinker it is his first duty to follow his intellect to whatever conclusions it may lead' (121); he continued: 'he who lets the world, or his own portion of it, choose his plan of life for him, has no need of any other faculty than the ape-like one of imitation ... it is only the cultivation of individuality which produces, or can produce, well-developed human beings' (126, 131). In 1868 Thomas Hardy who knew *On Liberty* 'almost by heart', listed chapter three, 'Of Individuality' (from which these quotations are taken), as one of his 'cures for despair'.[24] For Mill,

> at present individuals are lost in the crowd. In politics it is almost a triviality to say that public opinion now rules the world. Those whose opinions go by the name of public opinion are not always the same sort of public: in America, they are the whole white population; in England, chiefly the middle class. But they are always a mass, that is to say, collective mediocrity.
>
> (*On Liberty*, 131)

While Mill was careful to demonstrate that he was not countenancing 'the sort of "hero-worship" which applauds the strong man of genius for forcibly seizing on the government of the world and making it do his bidding in spite of itself', he nonetheless refused to deny to any original thinker the freedom to point out the way (132). Horrified, as Caird would also be, by the sway of custom, a brake on social development and progress (136), he declared that 'precisely because the tyranny of opinion is such as to make eccentricity a reproach, it is desirable, in order to break through that tyranny, that people should be eccentric' (132; this was the passage from which Caird took the epigraph to her chapter on the 'Future of the Home', and with which I begin this essay).

For Mill,

> persons of genius are, *ex vi termini*, more individual than any other people – less capable, consequently, of fitting themselves, without hurtful compression, into any of the small number of moulds which society provides in order to save its members the trouble of forming their own character. If from timidity they consent to be forced into one of these moulds, and to let that part of themselves which

cannot expand under the pressure remain unexpanded, society will be little the better for their genius. If they are of a strong character and break their fetters, they become a mark for the society which has not succeeded in reducing them to the commonplace, to point out with solemn warning as 'wild', 'erratic', and the like – much as if one should complain of the Niagara river for not flowing smoothly between its banks like a Dutch canal. (130)

He continued:

It is not only persons of decided mental superiority who have a just claim to carry on their lives in their own way. There is no reason that all human existence should be constructed on some one or some small number of patterns. If a person possesses any tolerable amount of common sense and experience, his own mode of laying out his existence is the best, not because it is the best in itself, but because it is his own mode. Human beings are not like sheep; and even sheep are not indistinguishably alike.

(*On Liberty*, 132–3)

The despotism of custom is everywhere the standing hindrance to human advancement ... if resistance waits till life is reduced *nearly* to one uniform type, all deviations from that type will come to be considered impious, immoral, even monstrous and contrary to nature. Mankind speedily become unable to conceive diversity, when they have been for some time unaccustomed to see it. (136)

The first page of *On Liberty* bore the words 'The grand, leading principle, towards which every government unfolded in these pages directly converges, is the absolute and essential importance of human development in its richest diversity', a quotation from Wilhelm von Humboldt's *Sphere and Duties of Government*. While Caird and Mill were aware that the State was a necessary and *desirable* departure from the state of Nature (see 'The Human Element in Man', 232), they fought against the right of the state to interfere in the life of an individual unless they impinged on another's freedom: 'there is a sphere of action in which society, as distinguished from the individual has, if any, only an indirect interest; comprehending all that portion of a person's life and conduct which affects only himself, or if it also affects others, only with their free, voluntary, and undeceived consent and participation' (*On Liberty*, 80).

Likewise, Caird problematized the politics of community, and at a time when eugenic feminists were urging its supremacy. In the words of Sarah Grand, love 'lives on duty alone, on care bestowed, on kindly little sacrifices of self in daily life, in the continual essentially human effort to make others happy'; 'individuals *should* suffer – they should glory in suffering and self-sacrifice for the good of the community'.[25] Caird argued instead that individual freedom was of paramount importance, and that the politics of community often denied the individual the possibility of development. This belief is the hallmark of her work and was closely informed by Mill's theories of liberty and the individual.[26] It was *because*, not in spite of, her acute awareness of, and dismay with, 'the modern spirit of competition' that she saw the need to value the individual, who needed protection from the 'full blast of the competitive tempest in which modern life is passed'; likewise she was acutely aware of the difference between 'individual' and 'individualistic', deploring 'the present confused, patriarchal, individualistic, woman's sphere-and-woman's responsibility condition of things' ('The End of the Patriarchal System', 52–3, 53). In 'A Moral Renaissance' (103), she quotes Jane Welsh Carlyle (1801–66), the forthright wit, poet and letter-writer, unhappy wife to Thomas Carlyle, closest friend to the feminist novelist Geraldine Jewsbury and celebrated host to the likes of Tennyson, Browning, Dickens, Forster, Macready, Thackeray, Mazzinia and Cavaignac:

> instead of boiling up individuals into the species, I would draw a chalk line round each individuality and preach to it to keep within that and to preserve and cultivate its identity at the expense of ever so much lost gilt of other peoples 'isms'.

In 'Married Life, Present and Future', Caird declared that without respect for individuality, true socialism was impossible:

> the more intensely mankind learns to feel its unity, its coherence, and more deep must be the reverence for each individual nature. Stolid peace, but not living harmony, is possible without it. The truest socialism means, in this sense, the apotheosis of individualism. (145)

In *The Great Wave* (1931), the stringent anti-Nazi Grierson notes wryly 'to the family as a sacred whole we profane units must be subordinated'; the adjective 'natural' is used 'to condone half the crimes and all the beastliness of mankind' (69). The futility of the sacrifice of the individual to the state dominated Caird's impassioned speech of 1913 in which she explicitly attacked the 'apostles of eugenics' (8). She argued that in protecting 'inalienable personal rights':

> we render increasingly possible all that makes life interesting, dramatic, and truly worth the living: all adventures of the human spirit. A vista of possibilities is thus opened which promises an enrichment in all relations of life, an enlargement of the range of consciousness, and therefore of progress, to which we can actually set no limits. Compare this with the unspeakable boredom of the hurdy-gurdy existence of a State-dominated community! (10)

This speech was the presidential address to the forty-first annual meeting of the Personal Rights Association. Although Caird rarely spoke in public she made an exception on this occasion. By her life and work, she was a life-long and passionate defender of personal rights; it was clearly a fitting forum. The Association had been established in 1871 by Josephine Butler and other Contagious Diseases Acts repealers as the Vigilance Association for the Defence of Personal Rights, and known (until the middle of the following decade) as the 'Vigilance Association'; it became increasingly resistant to Britain's central social-purity organization, the National Vigilance Association (which had stolen its name) and established itself in support of Criminal Law Amendment Act of 1885, a legislative curate's egg, which (in the wake of W. T. Stead's publicized purchase of a 13-year-old girl from her mother (see note 8) raised the law of consent, reformed law on sexual assault, but also came down harshly on brothels and prostitutes and criminalized 'acts of gross indecency between men'. In 1889 the *Personal Rights Journal* (founded in 1881 by the Vigilance Association) dubbed the NVA 'vigilant stampers on the feeble' – stampers who included Millicent Fawcett – and questioned the nature of the 'protection' offered by the Association, which 'cramm[ed] homeless and helpless girls into a hospital where surgical outrage … awaits them'.[27] Unlike social-purity, the Personal Rights Association held on to its goal, the resistance to encroachment upon the individual. In the speech Caird decried the growing belief in 'the idea of *numbers*'; an idea which 'enters largely into the popular idea of right and wrong – what I call arithmetical morality' ('Personal Rights', 4, emphasis in original). This was precisely the morality with which the eugenists were taken, in their call for the greatest happiness of the greatest number, and the self-effacement of the individual in a collective (racial) identity. As Grand put it, 'love, like passion, may have its stages, but they are always from the lower to the higher. And as it is in the particular so it is in the general; it prefers the good of the community at large to its own immediate advantage'.[28] Caird argued that:

> the ancient idea of vicarious sacrifice is as rampant today as it was when the groves of ancient temples echoed with the cries of human victims, burnt on the altars, for the appeasement of the Gods and the good of the community. ('PR' 4)

Caird explained that her decision to take the chair on this occasion had been made in part because of the lack of others who might do so:

> I felt moved to accept the honour on account of the scarcity of wholehearted champions, especially – I regret to hear – among the sex which has always been deprived of personal rights ...

She added:

> Perhaps that is just why they *are* lacking in respect for them! And what a warning this is! The spirit of liberty, it would appear, can be starved to death. Society, having done its foolish best to destroy that spirit in half its members, expects the other half to retain it unimpaired – an obvious impossibility. For interaction of influence is incessant and universal between the two sexes. The career of women having depended not on right but on favour, they have learnt to care little for an abstract idea which has no bearing on their lives. Only the exceptional mind cares for that. But similar conditions would assuredly produce the same result in men. And – we are on our rapid way to similar conditions. ('Personal Rights', 3–4)

Caird saw the suppression of the spirit of liberty as a key factor in explaining contemporary support for the state against the individual, and stressed that it was amongst women that the spirit of liberty was weakest. This argument is illuminating in accounting for the involvement of women with eugenics. Eugenics appealed to women not because, as eugenists held, it was their biological destiny to regenerate the race, but as a result of their social subordination. Caird had addressed the relation between individual oppression and the oppression of others in her collection of essays *The Morality of Marriage*: in 'The Lot of Woman under the Rule of Man', she noted that there was 'doubtless an instinctive desire on the part of many women, who were brought up in the old faith, to prevent their sisters from moving beyond the lines that bounded female existence in the earlier half of the century' (95).

Caird's theory of art

Caird devoted her Prologue to *The Wing of Azrael* (1889) to a discussion of whether art should have a function. She began 'much has been said for and against the writing of "novels with a purpose"', and comes out strongly against the instrumentalizing of art:

> the work of fiction whose motive is not the faithful rendering of an impression from without, but the illustration of a thesis – though that thesis be the corner-stone of Truth itself – has adopted the form of a novel for the purposes of an essay, and has no real right to the name.[29]

Her reasons for this stance, however, are very different from those of the male aesthete's dictum 'art for art's sake'; they are born instead of her profound belief in freedom. For she could see that if art became an organ of morality, it might equally be appropriated by the (im)moral right as by the moral left:

> human affairs are too complex, motives too many and too subtle, to allow a small group of persons to become the exponents of a general principle, however true. An argument founded on this narrow basis would be without value, though it were urged with the eloquence of a Demosthenes.
>
> (*Wing of Azrael*, viii)

Caird does not, however, deny that the author's subjective vision will be a transforming one:

> certain selected aspects of a truth may be – indeed must be – presented to the reader with insistence; for the impressions made upon a mind by the facts of life depend upon the nature of that mind which emotionally urged upon the neutral vision one fact rather than another, and thus ends in producing a more or less *selective* composition, and not a photograph.
>
> (*Wing of Azrael*, viii; emphasis added)

Caird stresses that the process of selection, which does not, in itself, serve a purpose, is not confined to the realm of authorship, instead it is part of the human condition:

> this process – entirely purposeless – takes place in the mind of everyone, though he be as innocent as a babe of any tendency to weave romances ... the eye only sees that which it brings with it the power of seeing, whether 'the eye' belong to one who describes his impression or to him who allows it to be written secretly on his heart. For in the heart of each man lies a recorded drama, sternly without purpose, yet more impressive and inevitable in its teaching than the most purposeful novel ever written.
>
> (*Wing of Azrael*, ix)

In a recent discussion of use, feminism and art, Hilde Hein points out that critics of feminism and feminist art, in objecting that 'overtly political representations have no place in art', miss feminist art's implicit charge that '"conventional art" is equally political, the politics being cast in the "neutral" or masculinist mode that appears invisible'. She argues that in recasting experiences 'as they are undergone by women' feminist artists 'expose both the politics and the gender bias of traditional art and risk rejection of their own work on the ground that it is not art within that traditional definition'.[30] It would seem that while Grand's work falls clearly into a feminist camp insofar as she seeks to write outside a masculine definition of art (for art's sake) Caird, in resisting 'novels with a purpose', did not simply fall into the male camp, which objected to mixing art and politics. In the preface to *The Wing of Azrael* she wrote:

> I have described these unattained ideals of the art of fiction in order to show as convincingly as possible that however much this book may be thought to deal with the question recently so much discussed, there is no intention in the writer's part to make it serve a polemical 'purpose' or to advocate a cause. Its object is not to contest or to argue, but to represent. However much it fails, that is its aim.
>
> (*Wing of Azrael*, xi, x)

Ann Heilmann writes that while this disclaimer 'in a writer so energized and motivated by her politics' can be explained 'as an attempt to disarm potential criticism and counter a dismissal of her narrative work as neurotic, dilettantish, and a mere extension of her journalistic writings ... in constructing herself as an artist rather than a feminist, Caird adopted a traditionally gendered discourse which cast the artist as a man'.[31] I would argue, instead, that it is *because* Caird was so energized by her politics that she presented her fiction-writing self as an artist. Caird's politics were predicated on a validation of self and the subjective, thus her (politicized) art would also validate the self and the subjective. For Caird, didactic writing inveighed against freedom.

As eugenists increasingly took a public stance, Caird came out in public opposition. However, even in her last novel, *The Great Wave*, set at the time of the First World War and written in 1931 in overt opposition to oppressive and exclusionary forms of government and science, as the power of the Nazis was rising, she allowed her plural text, rather than a single authorial voice, to bring home the operation of authoritarian power, taking care not to practise at a textual level the totalitarianism against which she preached. At the close of this novel, we receive, through Nora's staging of an outburst from De Mollyns, further insight into Caird's political values and theory of art. De Mollyns exposes his totalitarian ideology as he remarks:

'if we could but get rid of our clamorous *personal* demands ... our yearning for happiness and companionship and love – old Schopenhauer and the Easterns saw that. If we could realize the end of our troubled dreams promised by the absorption into the One, the Great Unconscious –'.

(*Great Wave*, 511)

While Sarah Grand conceived of her fiction as having an allopathic effect on her readers, Caird conceived of hers as working on a homoeopathic principle.[32] Grand spelt out a new morality for her readers while, in keeping with her 'homoeopathic' theory of art – the depiction of sameness which might produce a 'reaction' in the reader – Caird's work has a certain and quotidian accuracy and has the potential to effect a homoeopathic remedy: cure through imitation.[33] Crucially, at the point in *The Great Wave* where Nora appears to have reached emotional and political hopelessness, we are told:

it often happens that the *homeopathic principle* is useful psychically as well as physically, and Nora had counted upon that fact in letting the talk take this dismal turn. And she had judged correctly. The Schopenhauer form of pessimism, backed up by the doctrine of the degradation of energy, had been too much for Grierson. It caused a *reaction*. He begins to recover. (512; emphasis added)

Applying a homoeopathic principle, Nora briefly stands in as *The Great Wave*'s alternative healer, calculating that through projecting herself into Grierson's (medical/emotional) condition (severe post-war depression), she will restore him to healthy equilibrium. At that moment, Nora becomes a metonymic figuring of Caird's theory of art and health: patients and readers were not to be subjected to author-ial/authoritarian intervention.

Caird's principle of sameness also holds good at a linguistic level: she uses many of the same terms as her opponents, but infuses them with radically different meaning. In her analysis of *The Daughters of Danaus*, Sally Ledger draws on the work of Carroll Smith-Rosenberg, who argues that 'for the marginal or powerless to challenge the dominant dis-course, they must frame their challenge in a language meaningful within the hegemonical discourse'.[34] Ledger writes that any attempt to challenge a discourse through its own language must be disadvantaged since the parameters of debate will have been laid down by that dis-course, 'leaving the challenger hidebound by the vocabulary available in which to frame a challenge', and concludes that 'by contesting the logic of evolutionism in its own terms, Mona Caird's challenge is from its inception radically limited' (Ledger, *The New Woman*, 28). I would suggest, instead, that the most politically effective aspect of Caird's art lies in the fact that she chooses to subvert scientific discourse from within, radically reworking the coordinates of the evolutionary terms with which she is working. While Ledger argues that Valeria's comment on 'feminine' self-sacrifice – 'I suppose we are all inheriting the curse that has been laid upon our mothers through so many ages' – is a mark of the extent to which 'theories of heredity are powerfully inscribed in the novel's discourse',[35] I would argue that Caird is using the language of biological transmission to address and highlight *cultural* transmission, and to expose the fact that most circumstances that are given physiological explanations are actually the result of social sanctions and mores, and have nothing to do with biological evolu-tion. Rather than being what Ledger concludes is 'a thoroughly deter-minist novel', I suggest that *The Daughters of Danaus* sacrifices textual freedoms in order to expose a society oppressed not by biological fact but by social value; a recontexualization of the novel in the broader field of Caird's writing, and the debates in which she was involved, make this clear. And, by her own admission, homoeopathy – cure through imitation or *mimesis* – often brought about the most effective reaction. Caird *reworked* the biological terms of her opponents – terms such as progress, variation, fitness and degeneration along social lines, emphasizing the necessity of improving *social* conditions in order to ameliorate life in the present.

For Caird, race was not fixed: 'the race, therefore, even more than the individual, is clay in the hands of the potter: Circumstance' ('Suppression of Variant Types', 196). By contrast, polygenism, the idea that human races had separate origins, and that Adam and Eve had only begotten the white, western branches of the family, thrived and multiplied from the 1860s, with racialist anthropologist spin-doctors like Robert Knox and James Hunt keen and well placed to egg it on. (Importantly, Darwin, who had unfixed species in *On the Origin of Species* through his evolutionary theory of descent with modification, preferred to term human races 'sub-species', thus tentatively siding with the monogenists.) Caird came down firmly on the side of monogeny: the phrase 'human race' ('Defence'; 'Suppression', 159, 204) or 'the human family' ('The Human Element in Man', 235), occurs frequently in her work, showing that, while she is acutely aware of the need to *value* difference, she is equally aware that humans are neither separate species nor fundamentally or fixedly different. This celebration of *kinship* underpins her treatment of sexual difference also; while her work offers a sustained account of the extent to which the immediate family could become a suffocating site of self-enclosure and material and bodily hardship, she knew just how useful the rhetoric of family could be in order to bring home a broader, indeed universal, kinship: 'men and women are brothers and sisters, bound to stand or fall together; that in trying to raise the position of women, they are serving at least as much the men who are to be their husbands or sons' ('Defence', 191)

Caird opposed separatism, just as she saw the injustice of female subordination: both drove false barriers between members of the same *monogenic* family. She chose to celebrate, instead, the fact that 'for the first time in history, we have come within measurable distance of a union between man and woman, as distinguished from a common bondage' and declared that 'nothing could be more false' than the assertion that the new ideals of social and sexual harmony 'imply sexual enmity'. Instead, she clarified, 'they contemplate a relationship between the sexes which is more close and sympathetic than any relationship that the world has yet seen' ('Defence', 187).

When Caird employs a language of race, she does so to point to a kinship – and a sharing of apparently 'uncivilized' codes of practice – between the apparently civilized and uncivilized which overrides division between the two; her strategic use of mimesis can be seen here at its most empowering. Coming down hard upon the 'half-developed being who now, *faute de mieux*, is known as civilized man' ('Suppression', 197), she writes:

> our present life, in the heart of civilization, is a fierce struggle between elements; between the original idiocy of savage appetite, and the acquired wisdom of less material aspiration. We of the nineteenth century, are at once too civilized and too barbarous to rest content with the half animal, half human standards that form our social organization. The human in us is strong enough to be wounded and outraged by the barbarity wherein we are still plunged; but we are not sufficiently human, as yet, to insist on the extirpation of that savage basis to our existence. Not a breath is drawn by the noblest of the race, which is not drawn involuntarily at the expense of pain or sacrifice to some other being. It is scarcely impossible for any one to escape this curse which rests upon the human family ...
> ('The Human Element in Man', 235)

'The Human Element in Man', the final chapter in *The Morality of Marriage*, offers a sustained argument for the ultimate *kinship* of the human family, drawing on Darwin's resistance to the idea of fixity and fundamental racial division.

Against Grant Allen, Karl Pearson and Sarah Grand

In the 1890s the biologist-cum-novelist Grant Allen and the founder of the science of biometrics, and of the Men and Women's Club, Karl Pearson, flexed eugenic muscles in apparent confidence that natural selection – the struggle for life – would win the day, and eliminate the unwomanly woman who dared to express herself against motherhood. In his vociferously pronatal article of 1890, 'The Girl of the Future', Allen mocked any change which sought to undo 'nature'; 'not all the Mona Cairds and Olive Schreiners that ever lisped Greek can fight against the force of natural selection. Survival of the fittest is stronger than Miss Buss, and Miss Pipe, and Miss Helen Gladstone, and the staff of the Girls' Public Day School Company, Limited, all put together'.[36]

In 'Woman and Labour', Pearson followed suit, dismissing the threat to the social and natural order posed by unfeminine or 'asexual' women:

> the woman with a strong physique and strong intellect cannot become the prevalent type, nor indeed would it tend to social efficiency if she could. Such women cannot transmit the asexualism ... to a numerous offspring: then leave it to the woman whose maternal and sexual instincts are strongest to be mothers of the coming generation, and to transmit those instincts to the woman of the future.[37]

With characteristic verve and intellectual rigour, Caird asks why, if this were the case, these critics were so hostile towards the new varieties of women which appeared to be cropping up: if modern women 'are really insurgents against evolutionary human nature, instead of being the indications of a new social development, then their fatal error will assuredly provide itself in a very short time' ('A Defence of the So-called "Wild Women"', 169).

In *The Daughters of Danaus*, the reader learns that 'it is not the protection of the weak, but the evil and stupid deeds that have made them so, that we have to thank for the miseries of disease'. The only answer is 'a more faithful holding together of all who are defenceless, a more faithful holding together among ourselves – weak and strong, favoured and luckless'. The community must work together in seeking to improve conditions, for 'the weak are not born, they are made' (*Daughters*, 104). (Dowie's eponymous Gallia advocated making better people rather than making people better.)[38]

Divergence between Caird and Grand is nowhere greater than on the issue of the 'unfit', the *bête noire* of eugenists. In her later novels, Grand's attack on the unfit, and on those who contributed towards their survival, through medicine or 'indiscriminate charity', became more insistent. For Beth in *The Beth Book* (1897), nature is a neutral force, external to and independent of society, to which the individual must submit. She takes issue with medical help for the 'unfit', which she holds to be an unwelcome endeavour to hinder Nature's good work:

> Nature decrees the survival of the fittest; you exercise your skill to preserve the unfittest, and stop there – at the beginning of your responsibilities, as it seems to me. Let the unfit who are with us live, and save them from suffering where you can, by all means; but take pains to prevent the appearance of any more of them. By the reproduction of

the unfit, the strength, the beauty, the morality of the race is undermined, and with them its best chances of happiness.

(*The Beth Book*, 442)[39]

Beth's beliefs problematize the argument, made by Bland among others, that eugenics was appropriated by feminists as a pragmatic strategy for emancipation.[40] Eugenic feminism might coexist with the desire to emancipate women from patriarchal law, but it sought to replace that law with an authoritarian health regime. Beth's diatribe is the fullest but by no means unusual exposition in Grand's work of negative eugenics as an act of kindness – a way of making the fit happy. The passage echoes Darwin's reassurance that the world, in spite of natural selection, was a happy place after all: 'we may console ourselves with the full belief, that the war of nature is not incessant, that no fear is felt, that death is generally prompt, and that the vigorous, the healthy, and the happy survive and multiply.'[41] Caird argued exactly the opposite in 'The Human Element in Man':

There are, however, some who go even to this length: holding that we suffer from over-civilization, and that it is folly to protect the weak against the strong, since this policy confuses natural selection and enfeebles the race. They are prepared to defy the fact that, in a community where each man had to be perpetually on the defensive, he would have leisure for very little else, so that art and industry must languish. Then 'Nature' would have a gala time of it! (233)

Playing on contemporary moral panic and fears of racial degeneration, Caird argued that if women had really to sacrifice themselves to the nation, then 'progress' would be impossible because women 'must for ever constitute an element of reaction and decay, which no unaided efforts of men could counteract' ('Defence', 187). Likewise, she refuted 'the common contention that the woman is abnormally weak', observing that, more often than not, such a woman 'began life in perfect health' ('Motherhood', 132). Pronatalism accounted for women's ill health; like peach trees and rose bushes, they were 'weakened by over-production' ('Motherhood', 134–5). If 'all the women of England were confirmed invalids' then this was a social, not a biological, condition (*Daughters*, 221; see also 'Defence', 174). Her use of the term 'decay' interchangeably with 'deterioration' testifies to this (*Daughters*, 44); decay, as distinct from degeneration, is brought about by environmental, not biological, factors.

In *The Daughters of Danaus* we learn that 'Mrs Fullerton showed signs of incomplete development. The shape of the head and brow promised many faculties that the expression of the face did not encourage one to expect' (32). Victorian headshapes were all-important for gauging levels of evolutionary development. While arrested development was a sure sign of degeneration for many evolutionists, the case is less straightforward in Caird's writing. If the luckless Mrs Fullerton is degenerating it is for reasons quite other than heredity – 'a few volumes of poetry, and other works of imagination, bore testimony to the lost sides of her nature' (33). It is through her demanding and thankless function as a mother within patriarchy that she has declined. In exploring degeneration, and situating it within discourses of Lamarckian 'disuse' rather than biological determinism, Caird, once again, subverts with acuity the terms of the discourse she has entered.[42] Likewise, she offers a parodic gloss on phrenology, which had affinities with eugenics.[43]

Motherhood in Victorian Britain

As part of her anti-eugenic feminist project, Caird co-opted evolutionary biology into an alternative narrative which did not give to women the role of policing society as evolution's 'consciousness', but which offered irrefutable evidence that they themselves were subject to evolutionary change, and that their functions and uses might be modified in such a way as to reduce the imperative of the maternal role. In this way women might earn their own bread, not merely through exploited forms of labour, but through unalienated industry. They might reject motherhood not in defiance of, but through the very decrees of evolution, which was, as both Darwin and Caird emphasized, primarily concerned with variety and change. She argued that science wished things in the 'maternal instinct department' left 'as they are. Women are made for purposes of reproduction; let them clearly understand that. No picking and choosing' (*Daughters*, 257). Interrogating the values of science she broached a number of gendered social issues from a perspective which did not reject science but strove to interpret evolutionary theory in a way which adhered more closely to Darwin's original thoughts on variation and change than the interpretations of many of his ardent apostles (see, for example, Darwin, *Origin* 115, 173–5; Caird, 'Phases of Human Development', 202, 210; 'Suppression of Variant Types', 210).

Writing for a society obsessed with health, Caird represents pronatalism as a disease of civilization: 'through these ages of overstrain of every kind – physical, emotional, nervous – one set of faculties being in perpetual activity while the others lay dormant, woman has fallen into a state that is more or less ailing and diseased' ('Defence', 175). She continued:

> Have we not gone far enough along this path of destruction; or must women still make motherhood their chief task, accepting the old sentiment of subservience to man, until they drive yet further into the system the cruel diseases that have punished the insanities of the past; diseases which are taking vengeance upon victims of ill-usage for their submission, and pursuing their children from generation to generation with relentless footsteps? Such is the counsel of Mrs Lynn Linton and her school. Upon the consequences of all this past ill-treatment is founded the pretext for women's disabilities in the present. They are physically weak, nervous, easily unstrung, and for this reason, it is urged, they must continue to pursue the mode of life which has induced these evils. (176)

Once again, Caird turns biological determinism on its head, for the transmission between generations she refers to here is cultural and social rather than biological.

For Caird race and motherhood, locked together in the imperial plan, are instruments of oppression which act on and through the flesh. Significantly, they are depicted in a shared imagery of imprisonment. In *The Stones of Sacrifice*, race is 'the chain of life that linked century to century' (207). The same imagery runs through 'To Mothers', the poem by Charlotte Perkins Stetson from which Caird took the epigraph for the *Morality of Marriage*:

> We are Mothers. Through us in our bondage
> Through us with a brand in the face
> Be we fettered with gold or with iron
> Through us comes the race.[44]

Forged of past cruelty and oppression, chains are not simply links; they bind and encumber. They are, literally, the mark and means of bodily infliction. In *The Daughters of Danaus*, Caird made this explicit. Motherhood is 'the sign and seal as well as the means and method of a woman's bondage': it 'forges chains of her own flesh and blood; it weaves cords of her own love and instinct' (341). Posing questions without offering solutions, Caird's fiction cannot accommodate a positive reading of motherhood. As I have suggested, Caird's adoption of a 'homoeopathic' model of writing, of *mimesis*, leads her to describe what was, rather that what ought to be, in her novels, without offering explicit solutions: a new motherhood would be achieved after an equitable relation between the sexes has been reached, but her emphasis is on the present, not the future. In her non-fiction, she gestured toward the possibility of an alternative, unoppressive, form of motherhood: 'it may seem paradoxical, but it is nonetheless true, that we shall never have really good mothers, until women cease to make motherhood the central idea of their existence' ('Defence', 173). George Eliot, a generation earlier, had demonstrated the tensions of mothering through Mrs Transome and the Princess Alcharisi, Leonora Halm-Eberstein.

In the words of the eugenist Frances Swiney, to woman was committed 'the preservation of life, the conservation of type, the purity of race' (*The Awakening of Women*, 85). Childcare – caring for children independently of a biological relation – did not in itself serve the eugenic plan. According to the eugenist Caleb William Saleeby, childcare which was not based on direct biological relation was 'a total denial of the value of the psychical aspects of motherhood and fatherhood alike' (*Parenthood and Race Culture*, 166). These ideas are challenged in *The Daughters of Danaus*. Hadria can only cherish a child that is *not* her own (373); her biological children bear daily testimony to her life of sacrifice: 'through them I am to be subdued and humbled' (190).

Motherhood is revisited in *The Great Wave*, where the anti-eugenist Grierson asserts that the maternal instinct is 'the fiercest of all instincts', and proceeds to desentimentalize maternal love:

> in the beginning, it presumably secured the advantage of the race (if that's an advantage), but *now* – ! Can one count on it as truly civilizing? Does it make for tolerance, for spacious thinking, for broad sympathy, for understanding and peace and brotherhood? Assuredly not. It makes, as I say, for *its own*. The truly maternal woman scouts the notion of caring for any child not of her own superior flesh and blood. 'What do I care for other people's brats?' I heard a violently maternal woman exclaim, and she gloried in her savagery.
>
> (*Great Wave*, 428–9; emphasis in the original)

Four decades previously, Jude the Obscure had remarked:

> The beggarly question of parentage – what is it, after all? What does it matter, when you come to think of it, whether a child is yours by

blood or not? All the little ones of our time are collectively the children of us adults of the time, and entitled to our general care. That excessive regard of parents for their own children, and their dislike of other people's, is, like class-feeling, patriotism, save-your-own-soul-ism, and other virtues, a mean exclusiveness at bottom.[45]

For Caird, mothers who were prejudiced in favour of their biological children had fallen or risked falling victim to an exploitative, maternalist imperialism in the climate of late nineteenth-century Britain. They were privileging the future over the present, valuing life primarily as it signified race continuity and writing biology into citizenship in ways which not only reinforced but which were predicated on a repressively gendered division of labour. In *The Great Wave* the pronatalist Mrs Verekker declares that her sphere '*more* than satisfies me'; 'I rest the woman's claim not on citizenship or law-making or anything of that sort – what does a true woman want with these? No, I rest it on something much more fundamental'. She pauses before announcing with reverence and deliberation: 'on the sanctity of motherhood.' Herr Wobster enthuses 'Ja, Ja, doppel vote mit twins! Zweimal heilig! Gewiss, gewiss, dass is aber gut: dass ist aber furchtbar gut!' (218); like Sarah Grand, he supports civic maternalism.

An imaginative and devoted advocate of the emancipation of women, Caird worked ceaselessly for the social and political freedom of the individual, and for unconditional release from the law of the father. Her works offer a sustained and multivocal critique of discourses of heredity and, culminating in a condemnation of racial science, they also register shifts in the history of eugenics from an emphasis on positive eugenics (pronatalism) to negative eugenics (the prevention of the 'unfit'). While eugenic feminists such as Grand and Clapperton were exercised by concern for the moral and physical health of the nation, Caird's works stand as a compelling and prescient warning against the dangers of courting biological determinism.

Notes

1. Caird, *The Great Wave* (London: Wishart, 1931), 43.
2. John Stuart Mill, *On Liberty* (1859; Harmondsworth: Penguin, 1985), 132, cited in Mona Caird, 'The Future of the Home', *The Morality of Marriage, and other Essays on the Status and Destiny of Woman* (London: George Redway, 1897), 115. *The Morality of Marriage* is reprinted in Ann Heilmann (ed.), *The Late Victorian Marriage Debate: a Collection of Key New Woman Texts*, vol. I (London and New York: Routledge & Thoemmes Press, 1998). All essays by

Caird cited here are from this volume, unless otherwise stated; the full title
of each essay will be used the first time each essay is cited.

3. Elizabeth A. Sharp, *William Sharp (Fiona Macleod): A Memoir*, vol. I, (London: Heinemann, 1912) 207, cited in Ann Heilmann, 'Mona Caird (1854–1932): wild woman, new woman, and early radical feminist critic of marriage and motherhood', *Women's History Review* 5 (1996), 87 n. 3.

4. *Women Poets of the Victorian Era* (London: Walter Scott, 1890). Caird dedicated *The Wing of Azrael* to Sharp 'with grateful and admiring affection'.

5. *Shafts* (February and March 1898), 24, quoted in Sally Ledger, *The New Woman, Fiction and Feminism at the Fin de Siècle* (Manchester: Manchester University Press, 1997), 24. As Ledger notes, Sibthorp pointed out that nearly all the London dailies and many leading Scottish, English and Irish papers had responded to the novel with anger and contempt. See Gullette, 'Afterword', for further details on the novel's critical reception.

6. Caird, 'Marriage', *Westminster Review* (August 1888); *The Morality of Marriage*, 63–111. See also dedication to Edwin Arnold, in Harry Quilter (ed.), *Is Marriage A Failure?* (London: Swan Sonnenschein, 1888).

7. George and Weedon Grossmith, *The Diary of a Nobody* (1892; London: Everyman, 1940), 116.

8. For Stead's purchase of a thirteen year old girl from her mother, see 'Maiden Tribute of Modern Babylon', *Pall Mall Gazette* (6 July 1885). See also Deborah Gorham, '"The Maiden Tribute of Modern Babylon" revisited: Child Prostitution and the Idea of Childhood in Late-Victorian England', *Victorian Studies* 21 (1978), 353–79; Judith Walkowitz, *City of Dreadful Delight: Narratives of Sexual Danger in Late-Victorian London* (London: Virago, 1992), chapter 3.

9. This article received a large number of reviews, from the *Northampton Mercury* to the *Leamington Chronicle*; see *Westminster Review Advertiser* 6 (August 1888).

10. See, for instance, Lucy Bland, *Banishing the Beast, English Feminism & Sexual Morality (1885–1914)* (Harmondsworth: Penguin, 1995), 126–130; Sheila Jeffreys, *The Spinster and Her Enemies: Feminism and Sexuality 1880–1930*, (London: Pandora Press, 1985), 43. More recently, Ledger and Lyn Pykett have done her more justice: see *The New Woman: 24–34*, and *Engendering Fictions: the English Novel in the Early Twentieth Century* (London: Edward Arnold, 1995), 57–61. Ann Heilmann offers the fullest and most insightful discussion to date of the radical nature of Caird's feminism.

11. Margaret Morganroth Gullette, Afterword, *The Daughters of Danaus* (London: Virago, 1989), 500.

12. See Richardson, 'The Eugenization of Love: Sarah Grand and the Morality of Genealogy', *Victorian Studies* 42 (Winter 1999/2000), 227–55, and *The Eugenization of Love: Darwin, Galton and Late Nineteenth-Century Fictions of Heredity and Eugenics*; Oxford: Oxford University Press, forthcoming). See introduction to this volume, and Barbara Taylor, *Eve and the New Jerusalem* (London: Virago, 1983), especially chapter 1, for Owenite feminists' championing of reason over passion earlier in the nineteenth century.

13. Gillian Kersley, *Darling Madame: Sarah Grand & Devoted Friend* (London: Virago, 1983), 58.

14. Bonnell, 'The Legacy of Sarah Grand's *The Heavenly Twins*: A Review Essay', *English Literature in Transition* 36 (1993), 472.

15. 'Ideal Marriage', *Westminster Review* (1888), 620.

16. *Ideala, A Study from Life* (1888; 2nd edn, London: Richard Bentley, 1899), 300.

17. *Banishing the Beast*, 130.

18. *The Power of Womanhood*, 149. The quote from Mona Caird is taken from 'A Defence of the So-called "Wild Woman"' which appeared in the *Nineteenth Century* 31 (1892), before it was republished in *The Morality of Marriage*.

19. *The Stones of Sacrifice* (henceforward *Stones*) (London: Simpkin, Marshall, Hamilton, Kent, 1915), 154.

20. Cf. Clapperton's *Vision of the Future*, Part II, which has as its epigraph: 'the laws of heredity constitute the most important agency whereby the vital forces, the vigour and soundness of the physical system are changed for better or worse' (77).

21. Cf. Frances Swiney's use of the laws of sexual selection to explain how woman 'has perfected in man all the virile virtues, the best and fairest of womanhood having ever fallen a spoil to the conqueror during the reign of sheer force', *The Awakening of Women, or Woman's Part in Evolution* (London: William Reeves, 1899), 72.

22. For a convoluted way in which the concept of nurture could be used to serve mainstream, negative, eugenics, see the first issue of the *Eugenics Review* (1909) I, 1, where it is posited that some conditions are too unfavourable to sustain any form of desirable life, and that it would there-fore be better for children not to be born into them: 'our asylums, our hos-pitals, are crowded with cases in which the pre-natal conditions have been such that any biologist or other expert well acquainted with them before-hand would have been able to predict their natural consequences' (4).

23. 'Personal Rights: A Personal Address delivered to the Forty-First Annual Meeting of the Personal Rights Association on 6th June 1913 by Mrs Mona Caird' (henceforward 'Personal Rights'), 8–9; see discussion of this society further below.

24. Florence Hardy [Thomas Hardy], *The Life of Thomas Hardy*, 2 vols (1928–1930; London: Studio Editions, 1994), 76.

25. Grand, 'Marriage Questions', *Fortnightly Review* 63 (1898), 386; 385, empha-sis in the original.

26. In a paper given at the University of Exeter (February 2000), 'The Law of Progress and the Ironies of Individualism in the Nineteenth Century', Regenia Gagnier usefully distinguished between models of individualism as they developed in the course of the nineteenth century: the competitive, materialistic, and psychological. The individualism which J. S. Mill and Mona Caird champion fits the last category.

27. *Personal Rights Journal* (January 1889), 4.

28. Grand, 'Marriage Questions', 386.

29. Caird, Preface to *The Wing of Azrael* (London: Trübner, 1889), vii.

30. Hilde Hein, 'The Role of Feminist Aesthetics in Feminist Theory', in Peggy Zeglin Brand and Carolyn Korsmeyer (eds), *Feminism and Tradition in Aesthetics* (University Press, Park: Pennsylvania State University Press, 1995), 451.

31. Heilmann (ed.), *The Late Victorian Marriage Debate: a Collection of Key New Woman Texts* (London and New York: Routledge & Thoemmes Press), 1998, vol. V, xvii.

32. Grand, Foreword, *The Heavenly Twins* (1893; London: Heinemann, 1923), 12, quoted in Marilyn Bonnell, 'Sarah Grand and the Critical Establishment: Art for [Wo]man's Sake', *Tulsa Studies* 14 (1995), 126. See my article 'Allopathic Pills? Health, Fitness and New Woman Fictions', *Women: a Cultural Review* 10 (1999), 1–21.

33. See, for example, Ronald Livingston, who refers to homoeopathy as 'treatment by analogy or mimicry', *Homeopathy. Evergreen Medicine: Jewel in the Medical Crown* (Poole: Asher & Asher, 1991), xxiii.

34. Carroll Smith-Rosenberg, 'Discourses of Sexuality and Subjectivity: The New Woman 1870–1936', in Martin Baum Duberman, Martha Vicinus and George Chauncey (eds), *Hidden from History* (Harmondsworth: Penguin, 1980), 264, quoted in Ledger, *The New Woman*, 28.

35. *The Daughters of Danaus* (henceforward *Daughters*) (London: Bliss, Sands & Foster, 1894), 450.

36. 'The Girl of the Future', *Universal Review* (1890), 52.

37. 'Woman and Labour', *Fortnightly Review*, 568. Cf. C. W. Saleeby: 'a generation of the highest intelligence borne by unmaternal women would probably succeed in writing the blackest and maddest page in history' (Saleeby, *Parenthood and Race Culture: an Outline of Eugenics* (London: Cassell, 1909), 153).

38. Ménie Muriel Dowie, *Gallia* (1895; London, J. M. Dent, 1995), 113.

39. Jane Hume Clapperton, who likewise focused on the future, attacked 'individual philanthropy' for 'support[ing] the weak and help[ing] the unfit to survive'. As she saw it, 'individual philanthropy deliberately selected the half-starved, the diseased, the criminals, and enabled them to exist and propagate'. Noting that this led to a gradual '*degenerating* of the race' she also remarked that it increased the strength and solidarity of human society: *A Vision of the Future, Based on the Application of Ethical Principles* (London: Swan Sonnenschein, 1904), 82. Cf. Strahan: 'the highly artificial life which civilized man has built up or created for himself! Here the weakling, the cripple, and the diseased, which in the natural life would at once succumb, are nursed and protected; they are surrounded with an artificial environment designed to render a continuance of life possible', *Marriage and Disease, a Study of Heredity and the More Important Family Degenerations* (London: Kegan Paul, Trench, Trübner, 1892), 2. Darwin, in *The Descent of Man and Selection in Relation to Sex* (1871; Chichester: Princeton University Press, 1981), observed: 'we civilized men ... do our utmost to check the process of elimination; we build asylums for the imbecile, the maimed, and the sick; we institute poor-laws; and our medical men exert their utmost skill to save the life of every one to the last moment' (I, 168). Such debates were very much in the air at the time; for example, the *Pall Mall Gazette* carried an article detailing the progress and benefits of preventive medicine (9 March 1894), 1–2.

40. See also Lesley Hall, 'Women, Feminism and Eugenics', Robert A. Peel (ed.), *Essays in the History of Eugenics*, Proceedings of Conference organized by the Galton Institute, London, 1997 (London: Galton Institute, 1998). Hall

argues that 'apart from those women who saw themselves as educators des-
tined to preaching the eugenic gospel to other women, the appeal of eugenics to women was through the possibilities it offered, or seemed to offer, for
assisting women's desire to bear and rear healthy wanted children when
they chose to do so, in fact when it could be used to increase their choices'
(48).

41. Charles Darwin, *The Origin of Species, or the Preservation of Favoured Races in
the Struggle for Life* (1859; Harmondsworth: Penguin, 1985), 129.

42. The French zoologist Jean-Baptiste Lamarck (1744–1829) put forward the
idea of the 'inheritance of acquired characteristics' or 'use-inheritance' in
his evolutionary treatise, *Philosophie zoologique* (1809). This theory
attempted to account for the transmutation of species. Lamarckians argued
that only those characteristics which were useful to the organism were
inherited; those that were not useful – which fell into 'disuse' – were not
passed on. See Peter Bowler, *Evolution: the History of an Idea* (1983; Berkeley
and Los Angeles: University of California Press, 1989), 82, and D. R.
Oldroyd, *Darwinian Impacts: an Introduction to the Darwinian Revolution*
(Milton Keynes: Open University Press, 1983), 31, for further detail.

43. For the influence of phrenology on Galton and Spencer see Victor Hilts,
'Obeying the Laws of Hereditary Descent: Phrenological Views on
Inheritance and Eugenics', *Journal of the History of the Behavioural Sciences* 18
(1982), 62–77. See also Marouf Arif Hasian, *The Rhetoric of Eugenics in Anglo-
American Thought* (Athens, Ga: University of Georgia Press, 1997) on the
early interest amongst phrenologists in the effects of breeding.

44. This verse was supplied by *Shafts* (1898), 24, in a review of *The Morality of
Marriage*. Stetson was editor of *The Impress*.

45. Thomas Hardy, *Jude the Obscure* (1895; Penguin, Harmondsworth, 1985),
340–1.

12
The New Woman in Nowhere: Feminism and Utopianism at the *Fin de Siècle*

Matthew Beaumont

Nowhere may be an imaginary country, but News from Nowhere is real news.

Lewis Mumford, *The Story of Utopias.*

Reviewing a reissue of Olive Schreiner's *Dreams* in 1912, Rebecca West revealingly wrote that 'The worst of being a feminist is that one has no evidence.'[1] The 'evidence' for which she was foraging took the form of a female 'genius' – in particular a literary prodigy – whose very biography or life's work could point towards those human possibilities that the abolition of patriarchy would surely realize in the future. This is a suggestive starting-point for a discussion of the politics of the women's movement at the end of the last century, the years in which Schreiner struggled to articulate women's personal and social desires. For West's invocation of an alternative, feminist epistemology, her embattled appeal for an heuristic and proleptic (rather than empirical) type of political 'proof', resonates with the search for emancipated interpersonal relations initiated by certain feminists of the *fin de siècle*.

In England during the late nineteenth century, signs of the political necessity and social efficacy of women's liberation seemed to many feminists to feature, albeit dimly, within the field of vision already. This was not only because suffragists and socialists alike regarded women's liberation as ultimately inevitable – either the result of a slow but certain evolutionary ascent beyond the barbaric inequity of modern civilization, or a consequence of the changed social relations that would rush irrepressibly into the space opened up by the sudden disappearance of the entire capitalist system. It was also as a result of the prevalence in the 1880s and 1890s of a sort of 'lifestyle politics' or, better, politics of fellowship, that actively anticipated nothing less than the total transformation of everyday human relations on the basis of a radical egalitarianism. This premature concern with post-capitalist or post-patriarchal social intercourse was an ideological effect of the political isolation felt by most middle-class socialists and feminists at the time, detached as they were from any mass movement. Reformist in spirit, because rather than in spite of the grandiose nature of its ideals, it emerged from a frustrated sense that the late nineteenth century, obsessed as it was with its own transitional historical status (with the signs of change heralded by the New Unionism, the New Woman and a thousand other 'movements'), was somehow stuck on the brink of that as yet obstinately absent alternative future that it variously desired. 'Drawing bills upon the imagination', to appropriate a phrase used by Eleanor Marx,[2] the politics of fellowship sought compensation in the present for the deferral of its longed-for future of universal fraternalism. It was premised on the conviction that the embryonic image of the egalitarian society could be conceived, and gestated, in the individual choices and interpersonal relations of its adherents and activists – carried 'as a babe in [the] bosom' as one socialist-feminist put it.[3] Like its predecessor, Owenite socialism, the legacy of which had been lost during the rise of reformist feminism in the third quarter of the century, it sought ways of 'constructing a New World inside the shell of the Old'.[4]

Edward Carpenter, gradualist socialist and pioneer of the New Life, as well as friend of Olive Schreiner, exemplifies this political trend,[5] and not least because he argued so forcefully for '[woman's] right to speak, dress, think, act and above all use her sex as she deems best' in the effort to forge a free identity for the future: 'Let every woman whose heart bleeds for the sufferings of her sex, hasten to declare herself *and to constitute herself as far as she possibly can*, a free woman.'[6] This kind of call to arms, precisely because of the strictly personal sphere of activity that it invoked, could not but be influential within the fragmentary women's movement of the time. The suffrage campaign suffered a series of delays and setbacks in the final decades of the century, so feminists' faith in their political potential was somewhat depressed; but the new female mobility ushered in by expanding educational and occupational opportunities simultaneously afforded a feeling of confidence.[7] In just such a contradictory and fractile climate, scored with hope as well as disillusionment, the activity and association of individuals became the crucial vector of emancipatory politics.

Progressive societies such as the Men and Women's Club, founded by Karl Pearson in 1885 to foster discussion of sex, are typical of this pioneering mood.[8] So is the appearance of journals like the feminist *Shafts*, whose articles in the 1890s often encoded disciplinary appeals to its readers, urging them, in Carpenterian tones, to cultivate, for example, vegetarian tastes and 'a less ardent love of their furniture', in order to lay the foundations of the future.[9] For feminist discourse at the *fin de siècle*, as Rita Felski has argued, 'acquired a performative and prophetic function, seeking to bring into existence through its own writing that political community to which it aspired.'[10] The history of the feminist and socialist movements at this time, the epoch of the politics of fellowship as it were, is in part the story of an impossible attempt both to adduce and induce evidence of an as-yet non-existent new world.

Perhaps 'utopianism' is the sign under which this story could plausibly be reconstructed. As a 'counter-factual thought-experiment,' utopian speculation strongly inflects the writings of those late nineteenth-century thinkers who pursued 'proof' of the historical possibility and political desirability of alternative social relations – especially those between the sexes. Engels was aware of the extent to which this 'utopian propensity' permeated discussion of 'the woman question' when in 1884 he addressed the subject of post-capitalist society in *The Origin of the Family, Private Property and the State*. There, in an extension of his critique of the Utopian Socialists to the socialist and feminist utopians of his own time, he bluntly stated that the men and women of the future 'will care precious little what anybody today thinks they ought to do; they will make their own practice and their corresponding public opinion about the practice of each individual – and that will be the end of it'.[11] But in the meantime, despite his attempt to close down speculative debate about the future, on the grounds that it distracted from the strategic concerns of the political struggle, there was no end of it.

This was a historical conjuncture in which middle-class progressives, to paraphrase Walter Benjamin, were nourished by the image of liberated grandchildren rather than that of enslaved ancestors (at least partly because many of their ancestors had been privileged rather than persecuted).[12] The series of sharp economic depressions that dominated the years between the mid-1870s and the mid-1890s, and the general social malaise that they carried in their wake, made the capitalist system seem deceptively close to destruction at this time – though its durability was increasingly evident as the century drew to a close.[13]

This encouraged the growing body of socialists and social reformists to make apocalyptic prophecies of the advent of a new system, thus creating just those conditions of mingled hope and apprehension, of future possibility and present impotence, in which utopian thought tends to thrive. The last twenty years of the Victorian era witnessed an unprecedented growth in the publication of utopian tracts and novels. In particular, the popularity of the American novelist Edward Bellamy's *Looking Backward*, which in 1888 unleashed a flood of imitations, parodies and polemics, consolidated the status of self-consciously fictional utopian speculation as a legitimate political discourse on both sides of the Atlantic. Hitherto, however, and despite the prominence and popularity of women novelists in the nineteenth century, the utopian genre had remained a predominately male domain, in which on the whole anti-feminist authors relegated female characters to familiar domestic roles, either moral or mechanical. Women's entry into the industrial workplace in the latter half of the nineteenth century, as well as the advances made by the mid- to late-century feminists, forced the 'woman question' beyond the periodical press and into utopian fiction. There, as Bellamy's radical revision of his views on female equality in the sequel to *Looking Backward* demonstrate, it functioned as a political litmus test for a writer or reformer's views on the eventual outcome of capitalist civilization – much as the position of women had served as an index of general social development for Fourier and Marx in the earlier part of the century. In this context, the New Woman of the 1880s and 1890s was widely perceived, by both supporters and detractors, as an emissary of Nowhere.

It is in the light of late-nineteenth-century socialists' and feminists' search for what I have called 'evidence' of their ideal future that utopian thought at this time has to be understood. For New Women novelists, the utopian form provided a means of 'seizing the tools to mark the world that marked them as other',[14] and as such it proved a useful heuristic and mythopoeic device in the struggle to create a kind of reverse continuity between the emancipated future they anticipated and the bondage they experienced in the here and now. This was in part because the novel's narrative conventions, long dominated by female writers, licensed the exploration of those interpersonal issues on which their immediate political concerns centred; it was also, of course, because its potential audience was far greater than that of any programmatic political statement. With its populist blend of romantic adventure story and social blueprint, the utopian fiction represents a kind of exotic archaeology of the imaginary society, or romantic history of the future, whose polemical task was to reinforce the progressive teleology seen to be working its way through the present.

In the space that remains, I want to examine a single, representative feminist utopian fiction in some detail. *New Amazonia: A Foretaste of the Future* was written in 1889 by Elizabeth Burgoyne Corbett, about whom little is known except that she contributed to the *Newcastle Daily Chronicle*, and in addition published some fifteen popular novels of mystery, adventure and society (a few of which are explicitly feminist in content despite the narrative conventions within which they operate). Set in the middle of the third millennium, the novel represents a dream-narrative that envisages a state-controlled society of men and women run by highly evolved 'Amazonians,' who, as the descendants of a successful suffragist movement in the nineteenth century, have colonized Ireland and turned it into Utopia. Its plot is easily told. The female narrator, initially encountered in her study, where the preface is set, awakes beside a startled male time-traveller, who is aware only that he has arrived from an opium den, in an Edenic garden. There they are greeted by gigantic yet elegant women who lead them on a tour, first, of the country's history since the Victorian era, and, second, of the utopian state itself, which is replete with the sort of rational institutions typical of contemporary utopian accounts of state socialism. The narrator's assimilation to this society seems assured (and not least because of her romantic interest in one of the island's rather enfeebled male inhabitants), until her compatriot, who throughout the narrative has proved recalcitrantly masculinist and who is consequently judged insane, begins to endanger his very existence. Attempting to protect him, for all that he is an unattractive character, the narrator accidentally sniffs the drug that transported him to Amazonia, and is immediately returned to the cold reality of her late-Victorian study.

From the book's title, as well as from this bare description of its content, it should be clear already that the novel deploys a playful mythopoeic function, one that relies on the nineteenth-century anthropological belief both that a Golden Age of primitive communism or matriarchal social relations once existed, and that 'myths and legends could be used as historical evidence to prove the existence of this era'.[15] A 'utopian epistemology' evidently underlies this novel, then, and it is for this reason, and because it uses the utopian form as a polemical, even propagandist tool within contemporary feminist debates, at the same time reflecting on its own status as a piece of writing, that I have chosen to focus on *New Amazonia*. (Florence Dixie's more famous feminist utopia, *Gloriana; or, the Revolution of*

1900, published a year later, exemplifies many of the same ideological tendencies so typical of feminism at the *fin de siècle*, but it does not foreground the act of writing utopia itself as suggestively as Corbett's work.)

Jean Pfaelzer, in her study of the American utopian novel in the late nineteenth century, has written that 'Utopia is "nowhere" not because it is not real, but because it contains more truth, more information – hence more political possibility – than does everyday reality, in which truth, information, and political possibility are often tucked away, hidden in institutions, personal relations, and cultural traditions.'[16] *New Amazonia* is just such an exercise in accumulating 'information' about the future in order to identify and expand the 'political possibility' of the present. Its narrator and heroine is a professional writer who, while in Amazonia, expresses her desire to return to Victorian England in order to advance what she terms 'the "Onward" portion' of her sex (that is, effectively, those middle-class members of the women's movement who styled themselves as an historical elite at the forefront of future change): 'I hope to win an immense number of recruits when I get home again, and describe all I have seen here.'[17] Corbett's implicit (if somewhat vanguardist) understanding of the relationship between utopian thought and social change, as explored on her imaginary Amazonian island, was effectively summarized by Ernst Bloch, the Marxist philosopher of utopianism, when he discussed Thomas More's *Utopia* with Theodor Adorno in 1975: 'This island does not even exist. But it is not something like nonsense or absolute fancy; rather it is not *yet* in the sense of a possibility; *that* it could be there if only we could only do something for it. Not only if we travel there, but *in that* we travel there the island utopia arises out of the sea of the possible ...'[18] Bloch's statement is the answer to a question that underlies my discussion of Corbett's novel. It is a question that Dixie put to the reviewers of *Gloriana* in anticipation of spiteful criticism of her utopian romance: 'Why is the book written?'[19]

The critics who read *New Amazonia*, taming its political implications, declined to ask this question, let alone answer it. The *Glasgow Herald* described it as 'an excellent shilling's worth of entertainment', the *Literary World* deemed it 'amusing', and the *Public Opinion* remarked with some confusion that '[t]here is much that is curious in the book'.[20] They all down-played the immediate polemical context for the book's publication. This was the appearance of 'An Appeal Against Female Suffrage' in the June 1889 issue of the *Nineteenth Century*, a political event that, over the next few months, sparked a fierce debate conducted in print. The 'Appeal' was the brainchild of Mrs Humphry Ward, who, on hearing that a private members bill on female enfranchisement might gain government approval, had concocted what she called 'a women's manifesto against women's suffrage'.[21] One hundred and four 'ladies,' as Corbett contemptuously classifies them, signed the statement, which argued that women's social influence should remain restricted to a moral role within the domestic sphere. And J. T. Knowles, the editor of the *Nineteenth Century*, appended a patriarchal seal of approval in the form of a postscript which urged female readers of the periodical that 'in order to save the quiet of Home life from total disappearance, they should do violence to their natural reticence, and signify publicly and unmistakably their condemnation of the scheme now threatened.'[22] He was obviously unaware of the painful irony underscoring this 'Appeal', that a movement determined to maintain women's enforced political silence by an ideological insistence on their 'natural reticence' should nonetheless be forced to entreat them to contradict their nature and break that silence. Corbett's literary rejoinder to the article, which loudly denounced it as 'the most despicable piece of treachery ever perpetrated towards women by women', suggests that the irony was not lost on her at least (*NA*, 1). Unlike the American Mary Lane's feminist utopia *Mizora*, which, also published in 1889, portrays its female population as silent and static, and so replicates the ideological pattern of Victorian patriarchy, *New Amazonia* depicts the men and women of the future talking, writing and attending public meetings on equal terms, reproducing instead, idealistically enough, for sure, the structures of communication set up amongst socialists and feminists in the late nineteenth century. Elizabeth Corbett, it is clear enough, was a 'go-to-meetings-woman'.[23]

Corbett's twenty-fifth century utopia actually conceals within it a subtextual, self-reflexive utopian project, which centres on the desire of a professional female writer to reach out to an imaginary community of politically active readers with the capacity to affect the future in fundamental ways. This meta-utopia, to which I will return in further detail, is the source of the sense of political urgency that runs through her novel (an urgency, incidentally, that also recognizably inflects Cherneshevsky's celebrated utopian appeal to an incipient feminist constituency of readers in his 1863 novel *What is to be Done?*, which was translated from Russian into English in the mid-1880s). Corbett's Amazonian society itself is comparatively conventional in political terms, since it transposes many of the ideological inconsistencies of *fin-de-siècle* feminism onto the terrain staked out by *Looking Backward* in the previous year – and not least because of its assumption that all class difference will be dissolved in the culture of what William Morris contemptuously called 'the present "refined" middle-classes'.[24]

Bellamy-like, Corbett's gradualist utopia is based on a centralized social system in which every citizen is a shareholder of the state-run economy. The state itself, nurturing but rigidly rationalistic, is known as 'the Mother': the narrator, recalling Victorian England in conversation with a male denizen of New Amazonia, notes that 'a true and tender interest will never be felt in the units of the nation until our Constitution becomes less that of rulers and ruled, and more like that of mothers and children' (*NA*, 130). This world, as the categorization of individuals as 'units' confirms, is closer to Bellamy's twenty-first century Boston than it is to Charlotte Perkins Gilman's *Herland*. The mechanisms of social control with which so many late-Victorian variants of socialism and feminism toyed, most notably eugenics, are here put into principled practice. Indeed, Corbett's fantasy ultimately bounces up against 'the bourgeois barriers erected for it', to borrow Bloch's expression.[25] This is clearest in her suppression of the sexual problematic. Rejecting the parthenogenetic solution that Gilman was to favour in her all-female utopia of 1915, and relying instead on an unspoken assumption of heterosexual intercourse, Corbett evasively concentrates on societal *re*generation rather than biological generation, inventing a technology of longevity – 'nerve rejuvenation' – that circumvents all allusions to sexuality. The 'widespread revolt against sexual instinct' advocated by George Gissing's Rhoda Nunn thus functions as the repressed structure of the future feminist society.[26] If the New Amazonians are not silent, they are certainly sexless. Reflecting an ideological double bind itself indebted to patriarchal orthodoxy, Corbett, like many of her feminist contemporaries, by simultaneously desexualizing her ideal women and exalting their maternal status, insisted that motherhood was 'the most valuable attribute of femininity – *the* definer of sexual difference, even of women's superiority'. As Lucy Bland has asserted in her account of sexual politics in the 1890s, 'this notion of motherhood formed a crucial part of the "new woman" utopian vision'.[27] For all that Corbett figured an alternative future ostensibly dramatically different from the present, then, she is entrapped within the limits of late-nineteenth-century liberal feminism, which could only 'question ... the traditional status of women from within the ideology that insist[ed] on it'.[28]

In an apparent paradox, it is not what Corbett's dream-narrative imports from the future but what it exports from the present that defines the politics of her feminist 'utopian function'. In other words, it is the role of her narrator-protagonist – subject to the ideological aporias as well as political aspirations typical of late-nineteenth-century bourgeois feminism – and not the social landscape that she maps onto the dystopian contours of Victorian society, which contains the key to her utopia. As I have already hinted, Corbett's narrator, who finally wakes from her dream to find herself in a study filled with 'nineteenth century magazines and newspapers', remains very much the professional woman writer when she is in Nowhere (*NA*, 146). This emphasis must be understood within the context of the growth of both the 'new journalism' and the cheap book trade in the 1880s.[29] Discussing her own century with one utopian interlocutor, she informs him that she writes for a living, excitedly insisting, in a sentence that recalls the proliferation of mass-produced publications in her own time, that 'I could probably find employment on one of your numerous journals.' The subsequent discussion of the New Amazonian book trade, which presents the state as a sort of benevolent vanity publisher, underlines the impression that the novel's utopian subtext centres on a literary and political freedom licensed by a marketplace in which '[n]o grasping publisher [is] allowed to step in and reap the profits of an author's brain toil'. Corbett's social fantasy is thus also a professional one: she dreams of the fulfilment of the promise represented by the new journalism, a promise to bypass the circulating libraries and so secure a literary realm of relative ideological autonomy, beyond which an unmediated relationship with some ideal audience becomes imaginable.

At the same time, her very narrative dreams of displacing the literary hegemony of those reactionary and sensational adventure stories that dominated the popular publishing industry of her own day. Fitz-Musicus, the time-traveller with whom the narrator coincidentally arrives in New Amazonia, is an effete, misogynistic pseudo-aristocrat, whose utopian vision, inspired by hashish rather than political ire, degenerates into a dystopia of increasingly dominant women (much as Terry's experiences in Herland do). Corbett mercilessly satirizes the romantic explorer-hero of adventure fiction here; but she also ridicules the male novelist, so that, when Fitz-Musicus announces that he intends to write a book about his time-travelling, it is implicitly quite clear which generic conventions he will employ. But it is significant that from a short time after her arrival in New Amazonia, the narrator is also keen to write an account of her experiences there. The narrative thus effectively traces her attempt to collect information on the place prior to her return, and in this way the reader is constantly reminded both of the historicity of utopia, its status as a species of 'evidence', and of the political import of the act of writing itself. Penny Boumelha's assessment of the way in which the New Woman novel blurs the boundaries between author and character proves particularly pertinent to *New Amazonia*: 'It is as if at moments there is no mediating narrator; the writing of the fiction becomes for a time its own action, its own plot, enacting as well as articulating the protest of the text.'[30]

Mary Haweis's 1894 injunction to the Women's Writers Dinner – 'In women's hands – women writers' hands – lies the regeneration of the world' – could be described as the utopian conviction that underlies Elizabeth Corbett's romance.[31] It is the product of a period wherein 'women were exhilarated by the prospect of a new age in which female ability would have more scope', and 'wherein writers were the anointed priestesses of their sex, and their creed was Influence'.[32] It dreams of a community of active women readers, the feminist readers of those newspapers and periodicals that surround the narrator when she wakes up in the nineteenth century. In the conclusion to one of her other novels, *Mrs. Grundy's Victims*, an attack on the patriarchal system that sponsors prostitution, Corbett addresses her readers directly as '[m]y sisters'. She goes on to say that she hopes that, at best, her story will have moved people 'to an attempt to remove some of the evils that reign rampant in our midst', and that, at the very least, it will have altered the judgement of its readers.[33] Her utopian fiction encodes analogous expectations of its imagined audience.

If the New Woman fiction, in Kate Flint's words, 'may be said to have created and consolidated a community of woman readers, who could refer to these works as proof of their psychological, social, and ideological difference from men',[34] then *New Amazonia* could be said to be in search of just such a female readership, who might refer to it as heuristic 'evidence' of a possible future precisely *different* from the patriarchal present, 'evidence' to be put to a political purpose in the feminist struggle. All genres, as Fredric Jameson has argued, are 'social contracts between a writer and a specific public, whose function is to specify the proper use of a particular cultural artifact'.[35] The contract inscribed within Corbett's utopia is akin to the contract that emerges so clearly in the last chapter of *News from Nowhere*, where Morris reflects on his socialist fantasy and urges that 'if others have seen it as I have seen it, then it may be called a vision rather than a dream'.[36] Unlike Corbett's utopia, of course, Morris's was written for the organ of the Socialist

League, and so had a deducible and dependable readership of activists when it was first published. Furthermore, *New Amazonia* remains stuck within the idealist and individualist assumptions of contemporary feminism, investing its faith as it does in the moral and educational influence of the progressive female writer. But, like *News from Nowhere*, it nonetheless represents a call to arms, a disciplinary appeal to a fellowship of readers. Both books want to begin building the new society, and both base this imperative on the political bonds forged between writer, reader and a wider audience, on an incipient sense of solidarity that, like Bloch's Not Yet, contains traces of a realizable future.

Notes

1. Rebecca West, 'So Simple,' *The Freewoman*, 12 October 1912, *The Young Rebecca: Writings of Rebecca West 1911–17*, ed. Jane Marcus (London: Macmillan, 1982), 70.
2. Edward and Eleanor Marx Aveling, 'The Woman Question', reprinted in *Marxism Today* 16, 3 (March 1972), 81.
3. J. H. Clapperton, *Margaret Dunmore: or, A Socialist Home* (London, 1888), 22.
4. Barbara Taylor, *Eve and the New Jerusalem: Socialism and Feminism in the Nineteenth Century* (London: Virago, 1983), 241.
5. See Sheila Rowbotham's essay on 'Edward Carpenter: Prophet of the New Life,' in Sheila Rowbotham and Jeffrey Weeks, *Socialism and the New Life: The Personal and Sexual Politics of Edward Carpenter and Havelock Ellis* (London: Pluto, 1977).
6. Edward Carpenter, *Love's Coming of Age, Selected Writings Volume I: Sex* (London: GMP, 1984), 127–8 (italics mine).
7. For this context, see, for example, Barbara Caine, *Victorian Feminists* (Oxford: Oxford University Press, 1992), ch. 7.
8. See Judith R. Walkowitz, 'Science, Feminism and Romance: the Men and Women's Club 1885–1889', *History Workshop Journal* 21 (Spring 1986), 37–59.
9. *Shafts*, no. 6, vol. 6, Sept. 1895, 82.
10. Rita Felski, *The Gender of Modernity* (Cambridge, Mass.: Harvard University Press, 1995), 47.
11. Frederick Engels, *The Origin of the Family, Private Property and the State* (London: Lawrence & Wishart, 1972), 145.
12. In his twelfth 'Thesis on the Philosophy of History' Benjamin talks of the working class being 'nourished by the image of enslaved ancestors rather than that of liberated grandchildren'. See *Illuminations*, trans. Harry Zohn (London: Fontana, 1973), 252.
13. See E. J. Hobsbawm, *The Age of Empire* (London: Cardinal, 1989), ch. 2.
14. Donna Haraway, from whom this suggestive phrase is taken, is here discussing the critical and utopian power of cyborg writing. *Simians, Cyborgs, and Women: the Reinvention of Nature* (London: Free Association, 1991), 175.
15. See Rowbotham on Carpenter's belief in the historicity of this harmonious past, in *Socialism and the New Life*, 102.

16. Jean Pfaelzer, *The Utopian Novel in America 1886–1896: The Politics of Form* (Pittsburgh: Pittsburgh University Press, 1984), 158.
17. Mrs George Corbett, *New Amazonia: a Foretaste of the Future* (London, 1889), 133. Subsequent references to this work, abbreviated as *NA*, will appear in the main text.
18. Ernst Bloch, *Utopian Function of Art and Literature: Selected Essays*, transl. Jack Zipes and Frank Mecklenburg (Cambridge, Mass.: MIT, 1988), 3 (editor's italics).
19. Lady Florence Dixie, *Gloriana; or, The Revolution of 1900* (London, 1890), viii.
20. Advertisements for *New Amazonia*, in Mrs George Corbett, *Mrs. Grundy's Victims* (London, 1893), 254.
21. For a brief account, see John Sutherland, *Mrs. Humphry Ward: Eminent Victorian, Pre-Eminent Edwardian* (Oxford: Oxford University Press, 1991), 198–9.
22. 'An Appeal Against Female Suffrage', *Nineteenth Century* 148 (June 1889), 788.
23. See Sally Alexander, *Becoming a Woman and Other Essays in 19th and 20th Century Feminist History* (London: Virago, 1994), 72.
24. William Morris, 'On Some "Practical" Socialists' (February 18, 1888), in Nicholas Salmon, ed. *Political Writings: Contributions to* Justice *and* Commonweal *1883–1890* (Bristol: Thoemmes, 1994), 338.
25. Ernst Bloch, *The Principle of Hope*, vol. 2, trans. Neville Plaice, Stephen Plaice and Paul Knight (Cambridge, Mass.: MIT, 1986), 585.
26. George Gissing, *The Odd Women* (1893; London: Penguin, 1993), 67.
27. Lucy Bland, 'The Married Woman, the "New Woman" and the Feminist: Sexual Politics of the 1890s,' *Equal or Different: Women's Politics 1800–1914*, ed. Jane Rendall (Oxford: Blackwell, 1987), 153.
28. John Goode, 'Woman and the Literary Text', *The Rights and Wrongs of Women*, eds Juliet Mitchell and Ann Oakley (London: Penguin, 1976), 238.
29. For an account of the New Woman and the new journalism, see ch. 2 of Rita S. Kranidis, *Subversive Discourse: The Cultural Production of Late Victorian Feminist Novels* (New York: St. Martin's Press, 1995).
30. Penny Boumelha, *Thomas Hardy and Women: Sexual ideology and Narrative Form* (Brighton, Harvester, 1982), 66.
31. Quoted in Lucy Bland, *Banishing the Beast: English Feminism and Sexual Morality 1885–1914* (London: Penguin, 1995), 144.
32. Elaine Showalter, *A Literature of Their Own: British Women Novelists from Brontë to Lessing* (London: Virago, 1978), 182–3.
33. Corbett, *Mrs. Grundy's Victims* (London, 1893), 250, 252.
34. Kate Flint, *The Woman Reader 1837-1914* (Oxford: Clarendon, 1993), 205.
35. Fredric Jameson, *The Political Unconscious: Narrative as a Socially Symbolic Act* (London: Routledge, 1981), 106.
36. William Morris, *News from Nowhere*, in *Three Works by William* Morris (1891; London: Lawrence & Wishart, 1986), 401.

13
The Next Generation: Stella Browne, the New Woman as Freewoman

Lesley A. Hall

New Women at the end of the nineteenth century were leading activist and outward-looking lives, openly challenging many of the most cherished conventions of British society. Linked networks of women, not just odd rebellious individuals, were protesting in very various ways both personal and political against the established order. Emma Brooke, author of the prototypical New Woman novel, A *Superfluous Woman* (1894), was a Fabian and the compiler of *Tabulation of the Factory Laws of European Countries*, with special reference to women and children (1898). A former member of the Fellowship of the New Life and participant in the 'Fellowship House' experiment, she was thus an associate of Edith Lees Ellis, whose *Seaweed: A Cornish Idyll* (1898: revised and republished as *Kit's Woman* in 1907), set in rather humbler social circles than most New Woman novels, dealt with the right of a sensual woman married to a loving but paralysed miner-husband to seek sexual satisfaction elsewhere. Liz Stanley has illuminated Ellis's connections with various overlapping networks of activist women from the 1880s to the 1910s.[1]

Socialist, Malthusian, marriage-reformer, suffragist and advocate of cooperative housekeeping, Jane Clapperton, in her 1888 novel, *Margaret Dunmore, or a Socialist Home* presented a wealthy young woman feeling trapped in unproductive idleness establishing a cooperative household somewhat along the lines of Fellowship House.[2] Clapperton, through the Malthusian League, presumably knew Dora Kerr, contributor to *The Adult*, journal of the Legitimation League.[3] A *cause célèbre* taken up by the Legitimation League was that of Edith Lanchester (1895), which reads like a particularly sensational novel. A self-styled 'New Woman', a science graduate of London University, active in the Social Democratic Federation (and one-time secretary to Eleanor Marx), her middle-class family had her incarcerated in a lunatic asylum when she proposed to undertake a free union with James Sullivan, a railway clerk and fellow-socialist.[4]

It sometimes seems that the wide-ranging discontents characteristic of the New Woman had been focused, once the new century was well under way, into a new and purposeful concentration on the fight for suffrage, and their more socially subversive and unrespectable elements dissipated or regarded as something that should be kept under wraps for the good of the struggle. Disillusioned with the increasingly narrow and militant emphasis on the vote, in 1911 Dora Marsden, a former Women's Social and Political Union activist, founded a fortnightly journal named *The Freewoman*. It did not oppose suffrage, but Marsden argued that 'Feminism is the whole issue, political enfranchisement a branch issue'.[5] The WSPU and the Pankhursts in particular were attacked in its columns for their narrowness and autocracy.

In a retrospective account looking back from 1926, one of its leading contributors, Rebecca West, claimed that *The Freewoman*'s greatest service was 'its unblushingness. ... [It] mentioned sex loudly and clearly and repeatedly, and in the worst possible taste.' It provided a forum in which women could vent their dissatisfactions as 'vexed human beings who suffered intensely from the male-adaptation to life',[6] a phrase which could equally describe the protagonists of the New Woman literature of the nineties, and indeed the contributors to such transient periodicals of the 1890s as *Shafts* and *The Adult*.

The very title of the journal possibly alluded to an important feminist tract first published in 1894, Charlotte Carmichael Stopes's *British Freewomen: Their Historical Privilege*. Stopes, one of the first women to study at the University of Edinburgh, though denied her degree, and mother of the notorious advocate of birth control, Dr Marie Stopes, argued that there was substantial historical evidence to indicate that citizenship was not some new whimsical fancy craved by the modern woman, but a traditional right of British women eroded over the centuries.

Among the topics ventilated in the columns of *The Freewoman* were contraception, divorce law reform (and the state of marriage more generally), prostitution, venereal diseases, illegitimacy, and homosexuality. Many contemporaries found *The Freewoman* the manifestation of their darkest fears: it was (not surprisingly) characterized as 'the dark and dangerous side of the "Woman Movement"' by leading anti-suffragist,

Mrs. Humphry Ward. Millicent Garrett Fawcett, leader of the constitutional suffragist organization, the National Union of Women's Suffrage Societies, found the one issue she read 'so objectionable and mischievous' that she tore it up into small pieces. Fawcett had a record of antipathy to anything that smacked of sexual impropriety, having refused to share a platform with male suffrage supporter Edward Carpenter in case association with this advocate of sexual reform (who made little secret of his homosexuality) brought the movement into disrepute.[7] The novelist Olive Schreiner, a New Woman of a former generation, was appalled by its sexual frankness (even though she herself had hoped to produce a book on sex from the woman's angle). She wrote to her old friend the sexologist Havelock Ellis of her distress on reading *The Freewoman*: 'It's got the tone of the most licentious females or prostitutes. It's unclean, and sex is so beautiful' and believed that it should be renamed *The Licentious Male*.[8] (This is particularly curious since *The Freewoman*, radical though it was, scarcely matched Ellis's own voluminous *Studies in the Psychology of Sex* in explicitness and emphasis on women's rights to sexual pleasure.) Evelyn Ansell wrote to Dora Marsden on 14 July 1912 complaining about 'your disgusting publication. I consider it indecent, immoral, and filthy, and I am sending it to the Director of Public Prosecutions'.[9] Nineteen-year-old Cicely Fairfield was forbidden to read it or bring it into the house, and thus adopted the pseudonym of Rebecca West by which she is much better known, in order to sign her contributions to it.

The list of subscribers does not give ages,[10] and it is hard to establish exact generational details, except in the case of well-known individuals such as socialist-feminist Isabella Ford, herself a 'New Woman' novelist (*Miss Blake of Monkshalton*, 1890, *On the Threshold*, 1895).[11] Edith Lees Ellis, although she does not appear on the list of subscribers, certainly gave a very successful lecture to the Discussion Circle on 17 July 1912, on 'Eugenics and Ideals': a 'very full attendance' was reported, and 'lengthy discussion' followed.[12] Her views on *The Freewoman*, as reported by her husband Havelock Ellis to Dora Marsden at the time of its revival as *The New Freewoman*, were that she both strongly liked and disliked it (perhaps finding, as he did, that '*The Freewoman* often displayed her vigour by attacking causes which I had advocated').[13] Because contributors and correspondents frequently employed pseudonyms or used only initials, it is impossible to identify all individuals whose opinions appeared. However, it would seem that it was not merely an organ for a rebellious younger generation.

Stella Browne was one of the most notably shameless and unblush-ing contributors to the correspondence columns of *The Freewoman*. Writing to Dora Marsden about the later incarnation of *The Freewoman* as *The New Freewoman*, Rebecca West commented 'in reference to our desertion of sex problems... . All the Stella Brownes and people are so upset',[14] which suggests that even within *Freewoman* circles, she was registered by her contemporaries and colleagues as being particularly associated with this aspect.

As far as can be ascertained, it was in the correspondence columns in *The Freewoman* that Stella Browne as we now know her, articulate and uncompromising advocate for female sexual freedom and reproductive rights, first emerged. Born in Halifax, Nova Scotia, in 1880, Stella was educated in Germany and then at St Felix School, Southwold, and Somerville College, Oxford. After a brief foray into teaching her health broke down and she spent some time with family in Germany. In 1907 she was appointed Librarian at Morley College, the adult education institution in South London, a post which had been tentatively offered to Virginia Stephen (later Woolf) in the previous year.[15] Stella later claimed that her contacts there with both working women and those of the professional class first gave her insight into the 'unnatural suffer-ings and complications in the lives of women'.[16] Stella seems to have become a supporter of the suffrage movement as early as 1907, joining the Women's Social and Political Union, although she later claimed that it was only in 1911 that she reached the position which defined the rest of her life as a 'Socialist and "extreme" Left-Wing feminist'.[17] Another important event in her life which took place in 1907 was the beginning of her love-affair with a man whom she described as 'my demi-semi-lover from 1907 to 1910, & my – well shall I say technically complete, though very intermittent and occasional – lover from 1910 on'. This relationship was clearly an important influence on Stella's views on the positive benefits of sexual experience, although the iden-tity of the man involved so far remains a mystery.[18]

Stella's contributions to the *Morley Magazine* on library matters hardly provide a basis for predicting the way she would burst upon the world under the soubriquet of 'A New Subscriber' on 22 February 1912 (some months later she wrote to *The Freewoman* revealing her identity and thereafter signing her own name; the reason for this initial anonymity is not clear). She began by admitting that 'there is much in the last issue of your fine paper with which I entirely agree' but wished to take issue with certain statements made by correspondents on the beneficial, or at least not deleterious, effects of sexual abstinence on women's health. While not doubting that the 'cool-blooded woman' might not suffer adverse effects from this self-control, she argued that women of this kind should not 'make their temperamental coldness into a rigid standard for others'. Stella made the point, which underlay all her subsequent arguments about women, their sexuality, and their place in society, that 'there is probably *a far greater range of variation sexually* among women than among men' and that some women were 'capable of intense sexual emotion'. In such cases 'the health, the happiness, the social usefulness and the mental capacity of many women' were 'seriously impaired and sometimes ruined by the unnatural conditions of their lives'. She conceded that 'many woman have been made ill and wretched by the unrestrained indulgence of married life with ignorant or brutal husbands', but should this abuse of 'a natural pleasure' make it 'entirely injurious and to be deprecated'? Sex, she reminded *The Freewoman*'s correspondents, was 'only beginning to be scientifically studied in its various aspects'.

All this was risky enough for 1912. The admission of female sexual desire as something not only potentially good but entitled to satisfaction (without any concession to conventional ideas about the licit place of sex within marriage) must have horrified many readers. The allusion to the new science of sexology, including the citation of the Swiss sexologist Auguste Forel and the doyen of British sexology, Havelock Ellis – was also avant-garde and somewhat daring. But then – citing the authority of Ellis, whose magisterial six-volume *Studies in the Psychology of Sex* had recently been concluded – Stella proceeded to raise the even thornier subject of 'auto-erotism'. Had the proponents of abstinence refrained from all forms of this – 'including psychic and emotional excitation'? Going yet further, in both repudiating 'any "moral" judgement on these various forms of onanism', and claiming that their 'danger to health and sanity has, on the whole, been much overrated', Stella concluded that 'without having recourse to their aid, many women would find abstinence from normal sexual relations impossible'.[19]

The subsequent debate between (predominantly) Stella on the side of sexual liberation and Kathlyn Oliver (chiefly) on the side of abstinence and the innate chastity of women, has been much written about.[20] Stella was not, in fact, recommending that all women should throw off their inhibitions and start having active sex lives. She was, after all, profoundly committed to the idea that women were extremely various.[21] In this first blast of her trumpet she agreed that 'one must

admit that there are many women whose constitution and temperament are what Professor Forel calls "sexually anaesthetic", without
thereby suffering any lack of mental or motor energy, or of capacity for
affection, or even the maternal instinct. Let women so constituted by
all means abstain from what affords them no pleasure.'[22]

As Lucy Bland has pointed out, women (and particularly the correspondents of *The Freewoman*) were trying to find new ways of talking
about sex, and one of the resources they were drawing on was sexology.[23] Rebecca West later characterized these discussions as 'utterly
futile and blundering ... even when conducted by earnest and intelligent people', rather patronizingly suggesting that Freud and Jung had
transformed serious discussion about sex since that time.[24] This may
rather exaggerate the general knowledge and influence of psychoanalytic concepts by the 1920s, when terms such as 'repressions' and 'com-
plexes' were very often being bandied about to give an impression of
modernity without any deep understanding, although West, who
herself underwent analysis, was probably better informed than most. It
does however explain why present-day readers, to whom Freudian concepts have become part of the climate of thought about sexuality,
sometimes have difficulties with the language used in the *Freewoman*
debates. Women had enormous problems with finding ways to express
their feelings about sex and relationships. As Stella Browne put it in her
famous 1917 paper *The Sexual Variety and Variability Among Women*,
'The realities of women's sexual life have been greatly obscured by the
lack of any sexual vocabulary ... the conventionally "decently brought-
up" girl, of the upper and middle classes, has no terms to define many
of her sensations and experiences'.[25] The extent to which women were
picking and choosing from the texts of the perceived authorities of the
new scientific study of sex to find useful tools with which to conduct
their own arguments and explorations, rather than taking on their
messages wholesale, has perhaps been underestimated.[26]

What have also perhaps been underestimated are the continuities
between these 'New' New Women ventilating their concerns in *The
Freewoman*, and those of previous generations. Women of roughly
speaking Stella Browne's generation, or perhaps her somewhat younger
contemporaries who came into their own during the 1920s, have been
seen as a radically new departure in their assertion of women's capacity
for sexual desire and their advocacy of women's rights to sexual experimentation – even without the excuse of the 'intense spiritual and physical experience' of a great love (which Stella herself suggested was 'the
privilege of comparatively few').[27] Stella was not implying 'indulgence

in indiscriminate promiscuity. The passionate woman may be, and often is, as fastidious in her choice of a lover as her placid sister'.[28] But the idea of a woman deliberately and with forethought choosing a lover, possibly lovers plural, was startling and transgressive.

There were earlier groups of women with whom Stella can be compared and to whom her intellectual indebtedness may be posited. Karen Hunt has indicated that 'free love' was debated within the Social Democratic Federation, given socialist critiques of bourgeois marriage, and some SDF couples did choose to live in free unions. However promiscuity was reprehended ('free unions' being seen as equivalent to monogamous marriage but unconsecrated by church or state) and ideas about sexuality were often still inflected by the model of male and female sexuality as active and passive respectively.[29]

Women in the Malthusian League (founded in 1877, the only British organization publicly advocating the use of contraception), as Lucy Bland has pointed out in *Banishing the Beast*, were giving a uniquely female slant to the sometimes rather austere economic arguments of male Malthusians for the employment of 'preventive checks' (contraceptives). Relatively well-known figures such as Annie Besant (prior to her conversion to theosophy), Alice Vickery, Lady Florence Dixie, and Jane Clapperton, and less prominent female members of the League, argued on public platforms and in non-Malthusian publications as well as those of the League that contraception was a vital contribution to women's health and well-being, which should be made more widely available, especially to less fortunate women. Some other women who admitted that contraception might be at least be a legitimate expedient, if only as a 'necessary evil' on the way to the 'better state', such as Emma Brooke and Mona Caird, were only prepared to do so in such private and privileged spaces (and in Brooke's case under the anonymity of a paper read by Karl Pearson) as the Men and Women's Club of the 1880s.[30]

Some of the Malthusian women even advanced a positive vision of the potential pleasures of female sexuality. They were additionally involved in broader questions of marriage reform, and active in opposition to a sexual system based on prostitution and resulting in the widespread prevalence of venereal disease.[31] While an emphasis on sex (freed from the pressures of unplanned procreation) as both good for women's health and a natural pleasure was a long tradition within neo-Malthusianism, from the writings of Place and Carlile in the 1820s through those of George Drysdale in the 1850s,[32] this persistent theme was conceptualized in the context of overtly feminist concerns about women's place in society by female Malthusians of the 1880s and 90s (though the aetiology of their arguments might be traceable back to early nineteenth century Chartist and Owenite circles[33]). There were even some suggestions that contraceptive information might be taught to unmarried women, for example working girls in lodgings who 'might easily get into trouble'.[34] But this seems to have been aimed more at preventing illegitimate pregnancy and protection from the worst consequences of sexual harassment, than at enabling sexual experimentation. Early issues of *The Freewoman* contained articles by Bessie Drysdale and her husband C. V. Drysdale on issues of population and preventive checks, and the subject continued to be a subject of intense debate both in articles and the correspondence columns.

There is no evidence for Stella Browne herself having joined the Malthusian League until after C. V. Drysdale's address to the Freewoman Discussion Circle, reported in *The Malthusian*, 15 September 1912, with a mention of her contribution to the discussion. The *Annual Report* of the League for that year commented that a number of new members had joined as a result of the Freewoman meeting, but it was not until 1914 that Stella was described as one of their 'new speakers', and reviews by her began to appear in *The Malthusian*.[35] However, given Stella's interest in sexual questions, manifested in her seeking out of contemporary sexological literature by no means easy to acquire, it is not unlikely that she had read Malthusian literature and was thus aware of, for example, Jane Clapperton's arguments in her pamphlet *What do women want?* (1900) that society should honour the sexual function, which was (if voluntarily exercised) healthful and pleasurable for women.[36]

Lucy Bland has also drawn attention to continuities between the Legitimation League of the 1890s and the circles around *The Freewoman*. The Legitimation League was initially set up in 1893 to advance a specific programme for the lifting of the penalties and injustices to which the illegitimate were subject, but in 1897 became explicitly connected with promoting free relationships. While it was a mixed organization, women were strongly represented both as members and officers. The ideology of 'free love' seemed consistent with women's desire to be their own persons, not the property of men. 'Free love' also embodied a critique of the existing control of unions between the sexes by church and state. *The Adult*, the League's journal, provided a space for discussion of sexual relationships, and many women associated with this body would doubtless have self-identified as 'New Woman'.[37]

The limitations on the agendas of the Malthusian and Legitimation Leagues should also be registered, and the ways in which Stella Browne and other women of the new century were taking the logic of their positions even further. The official line of the Malthusian League was that the employment of 'preventive checks' within marriage would not only conduce to better health of both wife and husband, and a better standard of living for the family, but, by enabling marriages to take place at an earlier age, would also tend to eradicate prostitution, promiscuity among men, and the ailments due to prolonged celibacy among women. Thus, while generally positive about sexuality and its benefits to health, Malthusians still located licit sexual relations within the monogamous marital relationship. When, at last (1913) they produced their much requested practical leaflet, it was specifically 'for married persons only'. Similarly, the discussions around 'free love' in the 1890s defined it as the monogamous union of two individuals free from intrusive regulation by church or state. However, the practical problems which arose for the woman in the current state of society were recognized. Doubts were also voiced about the capacity of most men to honour this commitment without external sanctions, and (by men) about how far males would surrender ownership rights in women's bodies.

Stella Browne's responses to Kathlyn Oliver (in particular) align her, as can be seen, with this somewhat submerged but nonetheless long-standing tradition of free-thought sexual radicalism. More attention has been given to her letters participating in this heated debate (indeed, the chastity debate tends to be depicted as epitomizing the *Freewoman*'s engagement with questions of sex) than to her other contributions to *The Freewoman*. Yet in these it is possible to discern even more obvious continuities with older feminist traditions, which have perhaps been overlooked when positioning Stella as a startlingly new sex-positive kind of feminist. For example, she harked back to earlier feminist critiques of marriage in her letters 'The Immorality of the Marriage Contract' and 'Divorce and the Marriage Contract'.

In the first she did suggest that there had been some changes in women's status within marriage 'which have somewhat improved her position *ethically*'. Stella differentiated the marriage situation of 'women of the poorer classes' whose lives were 'spent in hard and repulsive manual toil . . .. not to speak of the bearing and rearing of what are generally large families', from that of the 'smaller, articulate educated class' with deferred marriages and smaller, sometimes deliberately limited, families. Stella thought this latter development far from deplorable, being part of desirable structural alterations in the nature of marriage. Nonetheless, she exhorted her readers to support the Divorce Law Reform Union, commenting that 'the thorough investigations it has pursued give it a scientific as well as humanitarian importance'.

Next she turned to what she designated the obverse of the picture – the "seamy side" of civilization on a cash basis' to make an attack on the state regulation of prostitution in terms which would not have sounded strange on the lips of Josephine Butler: 'State regulation subtly but unmistakeably debases the status of *all* women', exposing them to 'the possibility of arrest, detention, and forcible medical examination, as the result of police stupidity or malice'. And even so, it had failed to eradicate the menace of venereal disease. While claiming that the socialized state was the true remedy, Stella also plugged Auguste Forel's work, offering to lend interested readers her own copy of the German edition of his work (presumably *Die Sexuelle Frage eine Naturwissenschaftliche Psychologische Hygienische und Soziologische*, 1905, translated into English as *The Sexual Question: A Scientific, Psychological, Hygienic and Sociological Study*), praised the 'incomparable' Havelock Ellis, and enquired for information about the availability of Iwan Bloch's work.

Within the bounds of the seven paragraphs of this letter – which Stella concluded 'I must apologize for the length of this letter! But I hope you can find space for it intact! – associations were made between longstanding feminist concerns with 'The Marriage Question', prostitution and the iniquity of state regulation, the contemporary anxiety (soon to be loudly voiced in Christabel Pankhurst's *The Great Scourge*) about the prevalence of venereal diseases (which had also figured in New Woman writings such as Emma Brooke's *A Superfluous Woman* and Sarah Grand's *The Heavenly Twins*), and the investigations of contemporary sexologists British and foreign (and the censorship of their writings protested).[38] Stella's perception that the new science of sex tied in with a range of feminist causes of concern, old and new, is thus amply demonstrated.

Stella's deep roots in an enduring feminist critique of male sexual institutions is further revealed in a letter provoked by an article by a Dr Wrench commenting favourably on the Japanese regulated brothel area, the Yoshiwara, which aroused a heated response among readers of *The Freewoman*. Stella reiterated her critique of prostitution, in the form of rhetorical questions to Wrench about the legal position of the Yoshiwara women – did they own the money they earned, or were they leased to entrepreneurs in return for food and lodging, did they have any freedom of movement, could they refuse a client? and also querying the efficacy of the system in controlling venereal diseases. 'Are venereal diseases', she enquired pointedly, decidedly less prevalent in Japan than in Europe generally?' and would Dr Wrench 'recommend that venereal diseases be made notifiable by *men* as well as women?' Would he, she also asked, given the inevitability of prostitution which he assumed, 'advocate the establishment of a minimum wage for these necessary women?', their legal right to sue for debts, and the provision of pensions for their old age? While emphasizing that she was very far from advocating state regulation of prostitution, she suggested that 'if regulation by the State be insisted upon, endowment is the barest justice!'[39] This point looked forward to the argument advanced in her 1917 article 'Women and Birth-Control' in which she suggested that if the state demanded motherhood and the production of children from women, it should at least provide decent conditions under which they could do so (but signally failed).[40] While *The Freewoman* provided a forum for Stella's own views, these were strongly in tune with the overall tendency of the journal, though Stella took ideas and implications found in, for example, Dora Marsden's leading articles, to an extreme limit.

Stella has from time to time been identified as a rampant eugenicist.[41] However, attention has also been drawn to the ways in which the discourse of eugenics enabled women to articulate protests against and critiques of the male-dominated structures controlling marriage and motherhood.[42] Stella's allegiance belonged to this group, though her vision of free motherhood must have shocked some of the more pronatalist celebrants of women's maternal function both actual and spiritual. While numerous writers deployed the sacredness of motherhood to sustain a variety of arguments, from the necessity of women's having the vote to their right to choose their own mates free from conventional social and economic criteria, Stella did not glorify the maternal function. Throughout her career she emphasized both women's right to choose, whether married or not, to bear children, and their absolute right to refuse maternity.

This gave her writings on eugenics a possibly unique inflection. Her critique of the Eugenics Education Society (f. 1907) was advanced in two letters to *The Freewoman* (and similar criticisms were put forward in other writings). In 'A Few Straight Questions to the Eugenics Society' she admitted that she was not a member of the Society, although 'by birth I belong to that professional and administrative class' which it deemed most desirable as breeding stock. At the personal level, however, Stella 'gravely doubt[ed] whether I am a "fit" and "desirable" person ... for various relatives and acquitances have ... emphatically pronounced me incapable of managing my affairs with ordinary prudence'. Thus 'in a spirit of humility, quickened by acute personal fear' she 'crave[d] enlightenment' from 'the wise, who have met to decide ... who is to be born and who is not'. To the demand that '*ladies of England*' should 'bear children "early and often" within the bonds of matrimony', while 'the majority of women of this country ... are assumed to be congenitally "undesirable", if not "unfit"', she opposed to the claims of 'the individuality of the woman ... the importance to the child that it should be *loved* and *wanted*, not merely accepted and put up with'. 'A decent chance in material environment' was necessary for every child, while in the ideal state of society 'the woman who is passionately and pre-eminently maternal shall not be condemned to childlessness through economic pressure and mediaeval conventions'. But, above all, Stella claimed '*our right to refuse maternity* is also an inalienable right. Our wills are ours, our persons are ours; nor shall all the priests and scientists in the world deprive us of the right to say "No".'[43] She returned to the attack in a further letter a fortnight later, in which she not only demonstrated familiarity with contemporary scientific research on 'testicular and ovarian extracts' (what would now be called the sex hormones) but made a plea for eugenicists to meditate on 'the nature and power of love',[44] thus demonstrating the interest in both the physiological and the psychological which informed much of her later writing on female sexuality.

In conclusion, therefore, the common depiction of Stella Browne as an uncritical advocate of an untheorized liberated sexuality, the female mouthpiece of male sexologists with sinister agendas, does her a considerable injustice. She had all the concerns which had agitated earlier New Women about marriage, prostitution, motherhood, female choice and the right relations of the sexes. She was perhaps not so much the rebellious daughter revolting against the older purity feminist generation, but a representative of a new generation pushing yet further at the boundaries they had already established. In fact, it could be said that she, and the *Freewoman* group as a whole, were deliberately looking back, in an era in which attention was focused on the political struggle, to an older feminist tradition of the reform of personal and intimate relations and the interrelation, rather than the separation, of the personal and the political. This may also remind us, given that successive feminist generations are often defined by their differences and even seen as rejecting their predecessors, to look for continuities as well as rebellions.

Notes

1. *The Feminist Companion to Literature in English* (London: Batsford, 1990) gives a brief overview of the lives and writings of these two women. On Ellis, see P. Grosskurth, *Havelock Ellis: A biography* (London: Allen Lane, 1980), and for a more feminist interpretation, Liz Stanley, *Feminism and Friendship: Two Essays on Olive Schreiner*, Studies in Sexual Politics no. 8 (Manchester: Department of Sociology, University of Manchester, 1985), 24–7, and diagrams, 14, 17, 20, 25, 29.
2. Chris Waters, 'New Women and Socialist-Feminist Fiction: the novels of Isabella Ford and Katherine Bruce Glasier', *Rediscovering Forgotten Radicals: British Women Writers 1880–1939*, eds Angela Ingram and Daphne Patai (Chapel Hill: University of North Caroline Press, 1993), 29.
3. Lucy Bland, *Banishing the Beast: English Feminism and Sexual Morality, 1885–1914* (Harmondsworth: Penguin, 1995), 172.
4. Karen Hunt, *Equivocal Feminists: The Social Democratic Federation and the Woman Question, 1884–1911* (Cambridge: Cambridge University Press, 1996), 94–109.
5. *The Freewoman*, 23 November 1911, 3, cited in Les Garner, *Stepping Stones to Women's Liberty: feminist ideas in the women's suffrage movement 1900–1918* (London: Heinemann Education Books, 1984), 63.
6. Rebecca West, 'The Freewoman', *Time and Tide*, 16 July 1926, reprinted in Dale Spender, *Time and Tide Wait for No Man* (London: Pandora Press, 1984), 65–6.
7. Les Garner, *A Brave and Beautiful Spirit: Dora Marsden 1882–1960* (Aldershot: Avebury, 1990), 60.
8. Ruth First and Ann Scott, *Olive Schreiner: a Biography* (London: André Deutsch, 1980), 291–2.
9. Evelyn Ansell to Dora Marsden 14 July 1912: Dora Marsden papers in Princeton University Library, CO283 IIIA Periodicals edited by Marsden, *The Freewoman*, Correspondence A–G, Box 2/25.
10. List of subscribers to *The Freewoman*, undated: Marsden papers, IIIA Periodicals edited by Marsden, *The Freewoman*, Misc Box 3/12.
11. Waters, 'New Women and socialist-feminist fiction'.
12. '"The Freewoman" Discussion Circle', *The Freewoman*, 25 July 1912, 193–4.
13. Havelock Ellis to Dora Marsden, 23 January 1913: Marsden papers, IIA: Correspondence: Literary Contemporaries, Box 1/16.
14. Rebecca West to Dora Marsden 21 February 1913: Marsden papers, IIA Correspondence: Literary Contemporaries, Box 1/26.
15. Virginia Stephen to Violet Dickinson, 16 December 1906, letter no. 323 in Nigel Nicolson, ed., *The Flight of the Mind: the Letters of Virginia Woolf Volume I 1888–1912* (London: Hogarth Press, 1975).
16. Minutes of Evidence at Eighth Meeting of the Interdepartmental Committee on Abortion, Ministry of Health, 17 November 1937: Evidence of Miss F. W. Stella Browne. Ministry of Health records at the Public Record Office: PRO: MH71/23.

17. Stella Browne to Olaf Stapledon, 7 February 1949, Olaf Stapledon papers, Sydney Jones Library, Liverpool University Library, STAP HVIIIB,.

18. Stella Browne to Havelock Ellis, 25 December 1922, Havelock Ellis papers, Department of Manuscripts, British Library, Additional Manuscripts 70539; the 'demi-semi lover' is specifically stated to be a man, but there is considerable evidence that Stella also had female lovers.

19. 'A New Subscriber' [Stella Browne], 'The Chastity of Continence?' *The Freewoman*, 22 February 1912, 270.

20. Sheila Jeffreys, *The Spinster and Her Enemies: Feminism and Sexuality 1880–1930* (London: Pandora Press, 1985); Margaret Jackson, *The Real Facts of Life: Feminism and the Politics of Sexuality c. 1850–1940* (London: Taylor & Francis, 1994); Bland, *Banishing the Beast*.

21. Lesley Hall, '"I have never met the normal woman": Stella Browne and the politics of womanhood', *Women's History Review*, 1997, 6, 157–83.

22. 'The Chastity of Continence?'.

23. Bland, *Banishing the Beast*, Chapter 7, 'Speaking of Sex', 250–93.

24. West, '*The Freewoman*', 66.

25. F. W. Stella Browne, *The Sexual Variety and Variability Among Women, and their Bearing upon Social Reconstruction* (London: British Society for the Study of Sex Psychology, 1917).

26. Lesley A. Hall, 'Suffrage, Sex and Science', *The Women's Suffrage Movement: New feminist perspectives*, eds Maroula Joannou and June Purvis (Manchester: Manchester University Press, 1998), 188–200.

27. 'A New Subscriber', 'Wanted – The Grounds for Differentiation', *The Freewoman*, 18 April 1912, 436–7.

28. 'A New Subscriber', 'Who are the "Normal"?', *The Freewoman*, 7 March 1912, 312–13.

29. Hunt, *Equivocal Feminists*, 86–94.

30. Bland, *Banishing the Beast*, 214–15; Caird was, however, a member of the Malthusian League and had a letter published in *The Malthusian*.

31. Bland, *Banishing the Beast*, 205–17.

32. Lesley A. Hall, 'Malthusian mutations: the Changing Politics and Moral Meanings of Birth Control in Britain', *Malthus, Medicine and Science*, ed. Brian Dolan (forthcoming).

33. Barbara Taylor, *Eve and the New Jerusalem: Socialism and Feminism in the Nineteenth Century* (London: Virago, 1983).

34. Bland, *Banishing the Beast*, 206.

35. *The Malthusian* 15 September 1912; *Annual Report of the Malthusian League for 1912; The Malthusian* 1914, *passim*.

36. Bland, *Banishing the Beast*, 211.

37. Bland, *Banishing the Beast*, 156–9, 172.

38. 'A New Subscriber', 'The Immorality of the Marriage Contract', *The Freewoman*, 4 July 1912, 135–6.

39. F. W. Stella Browne, 'Concerning the Yoshiwara', *The Freewoman*, 18 July 1912, 176.

40. F. W. Stella Browne 'Women and Birth-Control', *Population and Birth-Control: A Symposium*, eds Eden and Cedar Paul (New York: Critic and Guide, 1917), 247–57.

41. Jane Lewis, *Women in England 1870–1950* (Brighton: Wheatsheaf Books, 1984), 105: Greta Jones 'Women and Eugenics in Britain: the Case of Mary Scharlieb, Elizabeth Sloan Chesser, and Stella Browne', *Annals of Science*, 1995, 52, 481–502.

42. Bland, *Banishing the Beast*, chapter 6, 'Eugenics, the Politics of Selective Breeding and Feminist Appropriation', 222–49; George Robb, 'Race Motherhood: Moral Eugenics *vs* Progressive Eugenics, 1880–1920', *Maternal Instincts: Visions of Motherhood and Sexuality in Britain, 1875–1925*, eds Claudia Nelson and Ann Summer Holmes (London: Macmillan, 1997), 58–74.

43. F. W. Stella Browne, 'A Few Straight Questions to the Eugenics Society', *The Freewoman*, 1 August 1912, 217–18.

44. F. W. Stella Browne, 'More Questions', *The Freewoman*, 15 August 1912, 258.

14
Women in British Aestheticism and the Decadence
Regenia Gagnier

At a conference on Oscar Wilde in 1997 at the University of Birmingham the feminist critic Elaine Showalter regretted that Wilde and some of the late Victorian feminists had made so little common cause. This essay is an attempt to think through this lack of solidarity, though its optic is one of difference and tension rather than regret. A new volume on women in British Aestheticism edited by Talia Schaffer and Kathy Psomiades, like an Exhibition on Women Pre-Raphaelite Artists the previous year (Manchester, 1998), shows how critical women could be of male so-called Decadents.[1] Whereas the male Decadents often proposed aesthetic models of consumption, taste, and pleasure, women in the aesthetic movement, especially in the more popular, or applied, forms of aestheticism, such as decorative arts and suburban literatures, were more conscious of their roles as reproducers of daily life and as producers subject to audiences. Essays by Ann Ardis, Annette Federico, and Edward Marx show that the women artists and writers often sided with male 'Counter-Decadents' in negating the Decadent negation of bourgeois life. Their work in country cottages, London suburbs, or the empire itself popularized aestheticism for broader audiences while simultaneously expressing the desires of sub-ordinated groups for ideals beyond production and reproduction. Thus what Ardis calls Anne Page's 'elegantly ageing self' in Netta Syrett's *Anne Page* (1909) rejected the anti-bourgeois stance of Wilde and company but created an aesthetic life in a Warwickshire garden untrammelled by husband or children. Or Marie Corelli negotiated the conflict between the artistic value of autonomous literature and the cash value of literary commodities by a complex narrative 'trade' between aestheticism and popular fiction. In Edward Marx's accounts of Sarojini Naidu and Violet Nicolson ('Laurence Hope'), the popular demand for 'exotic' literature created opportunities for women writers 'who possessed direct knowledge of the empire'; and Marx proposes a history of women's readership, or literary consumption, in our analyses of Decadent exoticism.

As the art historian Alison Matthews has put it, while aestheticism may function as an elite form of consumerism, in which aesthetic rhetoric conceals structural inequalities of class, race, or gender and limited access to luxury goods, in the cases just mentioned consumption is also driving the production of women and other marginal writers. In Talia Schaffer's reading, 'Lucas Malet's' (Mary St. Leger Kingsley Harrison's) *History of Sir Richard Calmady* (1901) provides a highly self-conscious, literary critique of late Victorian commodification and consumption in the character of a crippled, emasculated aristocrat who cannot engage in 'productive' activity himself but who ultimately devotes his life to helping the victims of industrial casualties. It would seem that the women of Aestheticism were consistently sensitive to the manifold politics of aesthetic production and consumption. If they sometimes reinforced gender and heterosexual stereotypes of production and reproduction while countering the excesses of male Decadents, they also confronted their implication in commodity culture more directly than some of the male aesthetes. It is a useful thought experiment to consider how William Morris's socialist, productivist aesthetic looks when its actual *products* are compared with Mary Eliza Haweis's. Both Haweis and Morris dealt in book production, typesetting, fashion, and furniture design; both were deeply influenced by medievalism; and both produced commodities that suburbanites could use to beautify their homes. Is it Morris's work, his status as a socialist activist, or his gender as a craftsman that distinguishes him from Haweis as a home decorator, or does his socialist practice but make his participation in a high-end niche-market all the more ironic? Another way of putting the point is, was the manifestly productivist aesthetic of Ruskin and Morris always implicated in consumer culture, their aestheticism an 'elite form of consumerism' as Matthews has it, but its commodification displaced onto women? Already, at the height of mid-Victorian productivism, Matthew Arnold uneasily acknowledged that his time was an age of criticism, or consumption, rather than creation, or production ('The Function of Criticism at the Present Time' [1865]), to be answered by Wilde in 'The Critic as Artist' (1891) that criticism/consumption was indeed a higher form than creation or production. It is arguable that the commodification so resisted by Morris and Arnold, from their very different but equally elevated platforms (it was 'machinery' in Arnold and 'exploitation' in Morris), was typically displaced onto the products of women or homosexuals, resulting in the ultimate trivialization of their creative labour. Such an analysis builds on Lyn Pykett's describing how women's writing was coded as mass culture in relation to male expressions of individuated artistic genius.[2]

These observations indicate the kinds of tensions within aestheticism as women's productive activity, often relegated to 'applied arts' like 'home decoration', began to challenge the art world in which women themselves were commodified as aesthetic objects. It is precisely such tensions between aesthetics, and within one aesthetic movement alone, that I have come to study within the last few years, and I have come to understand aesthetics not as philosophically monolithic but as a diverse if often overlapping group of claims made for art and culture, each with particular motivations and specific audiences in a web of social relations.[3] In this web, those who were aesthetic objects for the consumption of others, like women, might become aesthetic subjects, agents, or producers; conversely, those who had been aesthetic subjects, like the Aesthete, the Man of Taste, or the Critic, might be objectified, in a society in which commodification applied as easily to people as to goods, with all the accompanying psychological repercussions. At the level of ideology, some aesthetics were concerned with the human as liberal, ethical individual and others with the human as creator fulfilling her role as producer of the world. Some aesthetics were concerned with the object produced or created; and others with the consumers of objects and their modes of apprehension. Another way I have put this is that some were concerned with productive bodies, whose work could be creative or alienated, while others were concerned with pleasured bodies, whose tastes established their identities.

Sally Ledger's book *The New Woman* is helpful in showing the tensions between the New Woman in both her fictional and real forms and other social and cultural movements of the *Fin*: the New Woman in tension with socialism, with Naturalism, with Imperialism, with Decadence, with urbanism, with modernism and mass culture.[4] I shall now turn to the New Woman in relation to the Decadence in light of just two of the aesthetic models mentioned above, those that conceived of people as producers, reproducers, and creators, and as consumers or creatures of taste and pleasure – productivist aesthetics and hedonics.

Consumption or pleasure

Ledger cites Olive Schreiner's essay of 1899 'The Woman Question' for Schreiner's attack on male homosexuals as products of what she called the Female Parasite, despised by Schreiner as the idle woman, the woman who did not labour (except to reproduce 'effete and inactive males'). Schreiner explicitly uses the term 'decay' to describe these men and opposes their consumption of leisure to her socialist ethos of productive labour:

> Only an able and labouring womanhood can permanently produce an able manhood; only an effete and inactive male can ultimately be produced by an effete and inactive womanhood. The curled darling, scented and languid, with his drawl, his delicate apparel, his devotion to the rarity and variety of his viands, whose severest labour is the search after pleasure; ... this male whether found in the late Roman empire, the Turkish harem of today, or in our northern civilizations, is possible only because generations of parasitic women have preceded him. More repulsive than the parasitic female herself, because a yet further product of decay, it is yet only the scent of his mother's boudoir that we smell in his hair.
>
> (cited in Ledger, 76)

Here Schreiner's valuing of labour led to an attack on male *consumers* while it simultaneously attacked the Female Parasite for *producing* them. The Female Parasite or bourgeois woman reproduced pleasure-seekers but, locked into the cycle of reproduction, could not fully devote herself to pleasure.

Elsewhere Ledger refers to the feminist attacks on male pleasure that led to the passing of the Criminal Law Amendment Act that brought Wilde down; but even then the social purity movement left women with little voice to express their own sexuality; and Ledger shows how social purity ultimately forced lesbians like Radclyffe Hall to submit to the discourses of male sexologists. These sexologists had anatomized Wilde as much for his aesthetic *taste* as for his sexual *preference*. Here I am using the terms taste and preference as economists had begun to use them by the end of the century, as consumption patterns, as the choices one makes in the satisfaction of needs and desires. In fact it is notable that the feminist New Women who were so critical of the male consumer or Decadent devoted 'to the rarity and variety of his viands, whose severest labour [was] the search for pleasure' rarely spoke of their own choices at all, but only of their constraints on choice. So that by the time of Radclyffe Hall, sexual choice was also a constraint, biologically determined – something that the male Decadents had tried hard to resist.[5]

Production and reproduction

As Rita Felski and others have argued (see Ledger, 97), the male Decadents also resisted stylistic reproduction, or realism, by an anti-realist decadent style that self-consciously performed its femininity in relation to the more masculine realism of mid-Victorian fiction. This stylistic femininity, in a novel like *The Picture of Dorian Gray* (1890), was also in contrast with the embodied realism of women within the text, like Sybil Vane, whom Dorian loses interest in the minute she steps from her role as an actress into life. It seems clear now that the great age of literary realism was also that of industrial production and Malthusian reproduction. The New Woman novelists still committed to realism and its late Victorian efflorescence in Naturalism – Ella Hepworth Dixon, Mary Cholmondeley, and Margaret Harkness – were those most committed to the production and reproduction of daily life. On the other hand, the life of the consumer, of intense sensation, of what Pater called the 'flood of external objects pressing on us with a sharp and importunate reality' and the 'swarm of impressions' they ignited in the desiring brain, contributed increasingly to the fevers of the Decadence and modernist streams of consciousness.[6] I shall discuss below how it also contributed to the longed-for disembodiment of the male aesthete and Decadent.

A story by Hubert Crackanthorpe illustrates the wishes and struggles ignited as women's activities gained power in the marketplace, especially in relation to aesthetic production and consumption.[7] Entitled 'A Conflict of Egoisms' in Crackanthorpe's *Wreckage* (1893), it is the story of two ambitious but monadic individuals who marry as if to escape their respective solitudes. (See Pater's description of 'the individual in his isolation, each keeping as a solitary prisoner its own dream of a world' [Pater, 60].) The man is a famous writer described thus:

All by himself, in a quiet corner of Chelsea, he lived, at the top of a pile of flats overlooking the river. And each year the love of solitude had grown stronger within him, so that now he regularly spent the greater part of the day alone. Not that he had not a considerable circle of acquaintances; but very few of them had he admitted into his life ungrudgingly. This was not from misanthropy, sound or morbid, but rather the accumulated result of years of voluntary isolation. People sometimes surmised that he must have had some great love trouble in his youth from which he had never recovered. But it was not so. In the interminable day-dreams, which had filled so many hours of his life, no woman's image had ever long occupied place. It was the sex, abstract and generalized, that appealed to him; for he lived as it were too far off to distinguish particular members. In like manner, his whole view of human nature was a generalized, abstract view: he saw no detail, only the broad lights and shades. And, since he started with no preconceived ideas for prejudices concerning the people with whom he came in contact, he accepted them as he found them, absolutely; and this, coupled with the effects of his solitary habits, gave him a supreme tolerance – the tolerance of indifference.[8]

The female protagonist is a sub-editor, eventually the editor, of a ladies' weekly whose success in her work leads in a familiar economy to free time, enhanced taste for personal comforts (new rooms, new clothes), the idle reading of 'sentimental novels', and finally desire for a man. Attempting to acclimatize herself within her rapid progress from necessity to leisure, Letty fluctuates from being a producer of literature to a consumer of romance to a nonproductive literary muse for, or a critic of, her husband's work, a role which also leaves her unsatisfied. After their marriage, he produces more in order to escape from her need for affection, she is driven mad by the frustrated desire to communicate with him, and he finally drops dead on the verge of suiciding on the banks of the Thames.

The son of a well-known feminist, Crackanthorpe himself committed suicide at the age of 26 by throwing himself in the Seine, forestalling a divorce action in which he would have been accused of infecting his literary wife with venereal disease. His stories were highly praised in the 1890s for their psychological and sexual frankness and they attracted the attention of the early British School of Psychoanalysis. The self-styled Counterdecadent Richard Le Gallienne called them 'little documents of Hell'.[9] For our purposes, the story illustrates, with its stages of aesthetic development and hierarchies of taste familiar to the Victorians and Decadents, the complex psychological circuits of production, reproduction, and consumption that were so central to Aestheticism and the Decadence. It also illustrates the gender valences and gender threats that came to bear on the production and consumption of aesthetic commodities and, perhaps most importantly, the isolated, monadic nature of egos in conditions of competition. 'A Conflict of Egoisms' describes both male/female relations in modern society as well as atomistic individuals in modern conditions of work and the pursuit of leisure.

The urban migration

The master narrative of political economy tells us that our labour was alienated when we were torn from the land and propelled to the cities with their divisions of commodified labour, divisions and commodifications that would eventually make obsolete the original division itself – the division of labour in biological reproduction. At the beginning of the nineteenth century, twenty per cent of the British population lived in towns; by the end of the century, twenty per cent lived in the country. Ledger quotes Judith Walkowitz on the way that the women who now flooded the streets of the city confronted the men who were increasingly left behind in their idleness: the 'stare of the prostitute repeatedly challenged the glance of the *flaneur* in the great metropolis of the *Fin*' (Ledger, 153). Although he may in reality have been scrambling to make a living, the Decadent *flaneur* represented himself as outside the circuits of production and reproduction consuming the spectacle of the city, wandering aimlessly amid the New Women striding purposively past him to work, or to work the streets. The stare of the woman working the streets, the stare that said a fair bit of work for a wage, shames and frightens the *flaneur*, whose *glance* – codeword for flirtation – reveals itself as unproductive, aimless, effete, a byproduct of more leisured existences.

In a typology of *flaneurs*, *flaneuses*, and other urban pedestrians, Deborah Parsons has distinguished the Paterian/Jamesian line of collectors and hoarders, the consumers of the sights of the city, from the women who walk to work and their divergent aesthetic standpoints.[10] Parson's study shows not only the more *active* engagement with the city on the part of the women walkers, but also the effects of the urban migration on perspective. The wide philosopher's view of the country that led to universalist and objective aesthetics of the Beautiful, which much of the English countryside epitomizes, is replaced by the subjective perspectives of the city, only seen in angles obstructed by buildings or traffic or the social status of the perceiver, very much a perspective constructed within social relations in which women's perspectives were increasingly prominent.

Both the male Decadents and the New Women participated in the modern perspectivism of the city, but the male Decadents tried harder to hold on to universal conceptions of the Beautiful, the coveted interpretation of which enhanced their status as Aesthetes. Their self-representation then as idle consumers of urban aesthetics was to some extent an image produced in crisis, under the shadow of women's mobility and productivity. One might recall Arthur Symons' unwitting demonstration of this *flaneur* attitude not toward women but toward working people in his impressionistic account of Edgware Road in *London: A Book of Aspects*, privately printed in 1909:

> As I walk to and fro in Edgware Road, I cannot help sometimes wondering why these people exist. Watch their faces, and you will see in them a listlessness, a hard unconcern, a failure to be interested ... . In all these faces you will see no beauty, and you will see no beauty in the clothes they wear, or in their attitudes in rest or movement, or in their voices when they speak. They are human beings to whom nature has given no grace or charm, whom life has made vulgar.[11]

Here the working poor are aestheticized, i.e. consumed by the man of taste for his aesthetic effect, while they are simultaneously excluded from the world of aesthetes, or taste. The effect would be perfected in T. S. Eliot's descriptions of the urban poor in *The Waste Land* (1922).

The division of labour

Victorian feminists from the Mills to Schreiner argued that the alienation or commodification of labour was not all bad for women, slaves, or Jews. Sex and race domination were yet worse, in the progressive terms of the age, than the exploitation of the wage, which could liberate women, slaves, and Jews into contractual social agency. I shall conclude with what Victorian anthropologists called the original division of labour in the sexual act. Although both male Decadents and New Women claimed to be progressive, they differed in key ways. Male Decadents thought that progress lay in the liberation from sexual roles, an end to which so much of their fictive role-playing inclined. If Angelique Richardson is right that a significant strand of the New Woman, most notably in Sarah Grand's formulation, sought to replace both romantic and passionate love with 'eugenic' love, or love for the race, then this love as a form of citizenship is modelled on the more deterministic political economic 'stages of development'. Richardson quotes Grand, 'Love, like passion, may have its stages, but they are always from the lower to the higher. And as it is in the particular so it is in the general; it prefers the good of the community at large to its own immediate advantage.'[12] Eugenics was the biologization of class: saving the bourgeoisie from the degenerate barbarism of the aristocracy and the primitive savagery of the urban working classes. It also saved women from male sexual freedom.

I have written about how the division of labour as understood under political economy – as contingent on technological development – became biologized in the course of the nineteenth century, so that by the end of the century so-called 'noncompeting groups' based on class and to a lesser extent on race were seen to be fixed and inherent.[13] Richardson demonstrates that Grand was not alone among New Women in her advocacy of eugenic love.[14] Women themselves were key contributors to the biologization of the division of labour at the *Fin*. Not only did they often join the Counter-Decadents in countering the Decadents' artifice; whereas only in their greatest trials, like Wilde's, did the male Decadents fail to resist biology. But the New Women eugenicists were also distinctly different in purpose from Grant Allen's sublimation of romantic sexual love in 'The New Hedonism' (1894).[15] There the most visible publicist of the New Woman specifically contrasted the New Hedonism, or the philosophy of pleasure and pain, with the Old Asceticism, which he associated with the work ethic and self-restraint, specifically targeting the productivist tradition represented by Carlyle. 'Self-development,' he proclaimed, 'is greater than self-sacrifice' (382), and the document is specifically an argument in favour of sex. Yet Grand's eugenization of love, as Richardson argues, was not guided by pleasure or sensation but rather (as in the homophobic quotation by Schreiner above) by self-sacrifice in the service of the State. Richardson discusses how Grand's pronatalism extended in her fiction to an emphasis on creative production and to the pathologizing of French literature as 'vain, hollow, cynical, ... *barren*' (Richardson, Eugenization, *vs* 244). This is counter-decadence with a vengeance, at levels of both art and life.

I conclude with this question of the biological dimension of the New Woman, for if it is widespread then it would necessarily oppose her to the Decadents, who resisted biology while devoting themselves to physical sensation. This would mean that New Women had to control their reproduction for the State while Decadents were inclined to avoid reproduction altogether in favour of the life of choice and preference.

Sex and freedom

Right up to our own contemporary sociobiology and evolutionary psychology, biological destiny tends to point to social unfreedom. The question is, was there something profoundly contradictory between the freedom that the Decadents wanted in the aesthetic life of sensations, the consuming life of Paterian aestheticism 'burning with a hard gemlike flame' that had to do with the 'passage and dissolution of impressions, images, sensations' that eventually led to 'that continual vanishing away, that strange, perpetual weaving and unweaving of ourselves' (Pater, 60), and the very embodied self-control of reproductive powers central to New Womanism? The Decadent men wished to unravel and wear away their bodies in the pursuit of pleasure while the New Women shored up theirs as productive vessels. In a now-famous sentence from the second-wave of feminism, Ti-Grace Atkinson said, 'I do not know any feminist worthy of that name who, if forced to choose between freedom and sex, would choose sex. She'd choose freedom every time.'[16] When Grand, Schreiner, and other New Women rejected sex for pleasure in favour of pronatalism, were they choosing biological sex as a higher destiny or a Kantian freedom in perfect service to the state? Were they choosing a kind of Kantian autonomy in the face of the apparent heteronomy, the being buffeted about by desire, of consumer society? Or were they choosing something else altogether?

Notes

1. *Women and British Aestheticism* (Charlottesville: University Press of Virginia, 1999) Talia Schaffer, 'Connoisseurship and Concealment in *Sir Richard Calmady*: Lucas Malet's Strategic Aestheticism', 44–61; Annette R. Fredrico, 'Marie Corelli, Aestheticism in Suburbia', 81–98; Edward Marx, 'Decadent Exoticism and the Woman Poet', 139–57; Alison Victoria Matthews, 'Aestheticism's True Colors: the Politics of Pigment in Victorian Art Criticism and Fashion', 172–91; Ann Ardis, 'Netta Syrett's Aestheticization of Everyday Life: Countering the Counterdiscourse of Aestheticism', 233–50.
2. Lyn Pykett, *Engendering Fictions: the English Novel in the Early Twentieth Century* (London: Edward Arnold, 1995).
3. See Gagnier, 'Productive Bodies, Pleasured Bodies: On Victorian Aesthetics,' in Schaffer and Psomiades, 1999.
4. Sally Ledger, *The New Woman: Fiction and Feminism at the Fin de Siècle* (Manchester: Manchester University Press, 1997).
5. Martha Vicinus has recently argued that Hall's deterministic attitude toward lesbianism could be opposed to the more ludic, 'queer' sexuality repre-

sented by Djuna Barnes. Research Seminar, School of English, University of Exeter, October 1998.

6. Walter Pater, 'Conclusion' to *The Renaissance in Selected Writings* ed. Harold Bloom (New York: Signet, 1974), 59–60.

7. I am grateful to Monica Borg at Birmingham for pointing out how closely Crackanthorpe's story reflects the concerns of my recent work. I refer readers to Borg's own work on Crackanthorpe in ms.

8. Hubert Crackanthorpe, *Wreckage* (London: William Heinemann, 1893), 57–8.

9. *The 1890s: an Encyclopedia of British Literature, Art, and Culture*, ed. G. A. Cevasco (New York: Garland, 1993), 684.

10. Deborah Parsons, *Streetwalking the Metropolis: Women, the City and Modernity* (Oxford: Oxford University Press, 2000).

11. Cited in Karl Beckson, *Arthur Symons: a Life* (Oxford: Clarendon Press, 1987), 242.

12. Angelique Richardson, 'The Eugenization of Love: Darwin, Galton and New Woman Fictions of Heredity and Eugenics' (PhD dissertation, University of London, 1999), 174. See also Richardson, 'The Eugenization of Love: Sarah Grand and the Morality of Genealogy', *Victorian Studies* 42 (Winter 1999/2000), esp. p. 230.

13. Gagnier, *The Insatiability of Human Wants: Economics and Aesthetics in Market Society* (Chicago, University of Chicago Press, 2000), esp. ch. 3, 'Modernity and Progress toward Individualism in Economics and Esthetics'.

14. Richardson 'The Eugenization of Love' (PhD diss.); Oxford: Oxford University Press, forthcoming.

15. *Fortnightly Review* (March 1894): 377–92.

16. Cited in Catharine A. Mackinnon, 'Sexuality', in *Theorizing Feminism: Parallel Trends in the Humanities and Social Sciences*, eds Anne C. Hermann and Abigail J. Stewart (Boulder, Colorado: Westview Press, 1994), 277.

Index

Printed in the United States
206384BV00001B/1-30/P

9 780333 990452